ACUA
Underwater Archaeology
Proceedings
2024

edited by

Bert Ho, Della Scott-Ireton, and Douglas Jones

Sarah E. Holland, Series Editor

AN ADVISORY COUNCIL ON UNDERWATER ARCHAEOLOGY PUBLICATION

2024 © Advisory Council on Underwater Archaeology
ISBN: 978-1-939531-62-9
Made possible in part through the support of the
Society for Historical Archaeology

Cover Image: Ferry slip at Oakland Pier (Southern Pacific Railroad) as seen from a departing ferry, ca. 1910. (Cover image kindly provided by the San Francisco Maritime National Historical Park. Mercedes Pearce Collection. B11.8,0151p [SAFR 21374].)

Foreword iii

In Memoriam: Bradley Alan Rodgers 1

In Memoriam: Nicholas Rule 3

In Memoriam: Gregg Stanton 5

In Memoriam: David VanZandt 7

Contributing Authors

A Comparative Approach to Iberian Shipbuilding Design: Preliminary Results 9
    Raúl O. Palomino Berrocal

Investigations of the Punta Espada Shipwreck, a Mid-16th-Century Iberian Transatlantic
Merchant Vessel in the Dombican Republic 17
    Sarah M. Muckerheide, Charles D. Beeker

The Architectural Influence of Ships Sailing the Red Sea Under the Ottoman Empire,
the Contribution of Underwater Archaeology: A PhD Project 25
    Iness Bernier

Archaeological Analysis (Forecast) of Japanese Cognition of Western Vessels from 1790 to 1853 31
    Dante Petersen Stanley

Fully Loaded: The Contents of an 18th-Century Cannon Assemblage 39
    Karen Martindale

Arnold's Bay Project: Material Culture and Connections from a Colonial Battlefield in
Lake Champlain 45
    Cherilyn Gilligan

Wrecks and Williwaws: Archival Identification of Shipwrecks in Shemya and the Semichi Islands,
Alaska 53
    Kendra Kennedy

World War II Survey in Green Cove Springs, Florida 63
    Dorothy Rowland

Shells and Shifting Shorelines: Paleoenvironmental Reconstruction in the Western Gulf
of Mexico Outer Continental Shelf 69
    Emma Graumlich, Hope Bridgeman, Kaitlin Decker, Ramie Gougeon,
    Amanda Evans, August Costa

Abandoned, But Not Forgotten: The Systemic and Archaeological Context of *Hildegarde* 79
    Paul Willard Gates

Tides of Time: Climate Change and its Impact on the Maritime Archaeological Sites of
Fort Mose and Tolomato Bar Anchorage, St. Augustine, Florida 89
    Airielle R. Cathers, Bryce A. Peacher

Revisiting the Little Talbot Island Shipwreck (8DU3157), a 19th-Century Beached
Shipwreck in Duval County, Northeast Florida 97
    Chuck Meide

Effective Management of Recreational Diving on Archaeological and Historical
Shipwreck Sites in the Red Sea: Sadana Island 109
    Alicia Johnson

Public Engagement within Icelandic Maritime Archaeology: Addressing Challenges in
the Management of Submerged Sites 123
    Alexandra Tyas

2024 ACUA Award Winners 131

2024 ACUA Photo Contest Winners 133

Foreword

Portals to the Past, Gateways to the Future

Like several conferences, the Conference on Historical and Underwater Archaeology has been cautiously optimistic on attendance post-pandemic. We know that not all our friends and colleagues are able to join us each January, and the number of papers submitted this year for the 57th annual conference in Oakland reflected our expectations. However, we underestimated attendance, to our pleasant surprise, and the SHA membership, new and longstanding, turned out in great numbers, exceeding attendance of the last West Coast conference. Perhaps it was just a yearning to see old friends or to escape a colder region that resulted in the higher final registration count. We prefer to think that, like the city of Oakland's oak tree symbol, SHA has incredibly strong roots that support the growth of branches in all directions. Our membership came to Oakland reflecting that strength, while supporting our newest members as they begin to extend SHA's branches through their research.

Oakland also served as a 50th anniversary celebration of the Advisory Council for Underwater Archaeology (ACUA), and an opportunity to reflect on our organization's past, while looking to its future. ACUA's Graduate Student Associate (GSA) members led a panel with a mix of emeritus, current board, and past GSAs to discuss issues we see in the discipline and how ACUA might be more effective in the next 50 years. We would like to thank our GSAs for organizing the panel and extend our appreciation to all the panelists, particularly our emeritus members, who are ACUA's own portals to the past. A summary of the panel can be found in the Deep Thoughts Blog on ACUA's website (acuaonline.org).

This year's conference theme, *Portals to the Past, Gateways to the Future*, is reflected throughout the papers selected for the annual ACUA *Underwater Archaeology Proceedings*. Of the 144 underwater program papers, 14 are included in these proceedings representing research in Asia, Europe, the Mediterranean, the Middle East, the Caribbean, and North America. We begin with two papers that connect us to our recent past at SHA 2023 in Lisbon, Portugal: a discussion on Iberian shipbuilding in the 16th and 17th centuries (Berrocal) and an investigation of an Iberian-built shipwreck in the Dominican Republic (Muckerheide and Beeker). Bernier, residing in France and serving as our first French ACUA GSA member, then takes us through Ottoman naval architecture as she presents the research questions that her dissertation will seek to answer. The next paper takes a different approach towards naval architecture by examining through contemporary visual representations how 19th-century Japanese shipwrights understood western vessel construction (Stanley).

After circling the globe just in the first four papers, our next four focus on some of the most significant global events of the 18th–20th centuries: wars. Though both Martindale's and Gilligan's papers discuss artifacts from the American Revolutionary War, they represent dramatically different battlefronts from the Savannah River to Lake Champlain. We see a similarly diverse geographic range again in the next two papers on World War II with the archival analysis of a shipwreck in the Aleutian Islands (Kennedy), and the discovery of multiple sites and artifacts on the United States home front in Green Cove Springs, Florida (Rowland).

The *Proceedings* continue with multiple papers discussing site formation processes, dynamic changes to historic sites, and the increasing impacts from climate change. Gates correlates the commercial use-life of *Hildegarde* with both turbulent economic periods and rapidly advancing technology as he documents the site within a ship graveyard. Graumlich et al. takes us far back in time to examine submerged paleolandscapes in the Gulf of Mexico through the analysis of bivalve (*Rangia cuneata*) shell material. The Lighthouse Archaeological Maritime Program (LAMP) continues their archaeological resource assessments at multiple sites in northwest Florida, documenting rapid changes from the effects of climate change (Cathers and Peacher), and from the increasing frequency of major storm events (Meide).

The final two papers remind us how involving the public and recreational divers are crucial to the preservation and protection of underwater cultural heritage. Johnson, also a current ACUA GSA member and the first residing in Egypt, elaborates on some of the management strategies applied to a Red Sea shipwreck. We conclude with Tyas' examination of the state of underwater archaeology in Iceland, with possible solutions for management and monitoring through community engagement with the diving community and public archaeology training for university students.

As with all conference proceedings, the work of the many authors makes it a success by contributing their research to the larger archaeological community. The editors would like to thank all authors for their time and dedication in writing their manuscripts, meeting all deadlines, and responding to all requests from the editorial team. Many thanks also to Marc-André Bernier and Roberto Junco for their assistance in translating the paper abstracts. We would also like to thank series editor, Sarah E. Holland, for her patience and guidance throughout the process. Last, but certainly not least, we would like to thank Annalies Corbin and the team at the PAST Foundation for their gracious support in producing the 2024 ACUA *Underwater Archaeology Proceedings*.

See you all in New Orleans for SHA 2025! *Laissez les bon temps rouler!*

Bert Ho
Della Scott-Ireton
Douglas Jones

In Memoriam:
Bradley Alan Rodgers
(22 January 1955 to 24 October 2024)

Bradley Alan Rodgers, known as Dr. Rodgers to his students and Brad to his friends, passed away unexpectedly and peacefully at age 69 in his home in Greenville, North Carolina, on October 24, 2024. Brad was born on January 22, 1955, in Des Moines, Iowa, and grew up in Green Bay, Wisconsin.

Brad spent his earliest years rescuing bugs and studying ants. When he was only four, while secretly watching the TV series Sea Hunt after bedtime with his older brother, Brad was captivated by the scuba diving adventures (9" TV, rabbit ear antenna, snowy picture, likely a prelude to Brad's career diving on wrecks with very low visibility). In grade school, he was always playing outside with the hundred kids on the block in his Green Bay Biemeret Street neighborhood. As a teenager, he spent his summers on Wisconsin's Two Sisters Lake driving boats, carrying out practical jokes, and water skiing with his lake gang; at Green Bay's Southwest High School, he developed a group of lifelong friends.

Brad earned a Bachelor of Arts degree (Anthropology/Archaeology) from the University of Minnesota, Minneapolis in 1979. Combining his love of archeology and water, he pursued a Master of Arts in Maritime Studies from East Carolina University in 1985, and completed his doctorate in Maritime Studies from the Union Institute in 1993. Along the way, Brad became an experienced scuba diver and licensed captain, and embarked on a life on and under the sea.

Dr. Rodgers became a widely published and respected author in the fields of maritime history, underwater archaeology, and artifact conservation. He was one of the earliest graduates of the Program in Maritime Studies at East Carolina University and would go on to hold almost every position in the program, including staff archaeologist (1986–1993) and all ranks of professor (1991–2018), while concurrently serving as program director (2012–2018). Dr. Rodgers was awarded the status of Emeritus Professor in the Department of History upon his retirement. From the late 1980s, in addition to writing dozens of articles, chapters, reports, and reviews (sole- and co-authored), he obtained many grants and contracts, and published three major monographs, *Guardian of the Great Lakes: The U.S. Paddle Frigate Michigan* (Ann Arbor, University of Michigan Press, 1996, winner of the Cleveland State Great Lakes History Prize Award); *The Archaeologist's Manual for Conservation: A Guide to Non-Toxic, Minimal Intervention Artifact Stabilization* (Kluwer Academic, New York, 2004, translated into a number of languages); and co-authoring *The Steamboat Montana and the Opening of the West: History, Excavation, and Architecture* (University Press of Florida, 2008).

Brad's research projects in rivers, lakes, and oceans brought him and his students to many far-flung places around the world, from the Great Lakes, to the Caribbean, Bermuda, Hawaii, and Midway Island in the Pacific. Brad was especially known for his passionate interest and expertise in the maritime history and archaeology of the Great Lakes, and he was an innovator in the development of techniques for recording underwater cultural heritage sites in difficult environmental conditions, especially in restricted visibility settings. One of Brad's final book projects was to be *Ice Water Mansions*, an account of Great Lakes ship construction told through his groundbreaking shipwreck research.

Over his many decades as an educator, Professor Rodgers taught a wide variety of courses within East Carolina University's history and maritime studies curriculum, and directed a large number of successful field projects. His interests and specialties were American maritime history after 1815, ship construction (antiquity to the present), archaeological conservation, material culture analysis, and wreck site surveys with detailed analysis. He was known as a gifted archaeological illustrator, ship model builder, and archaeological conservator. Today's Maritime Studies Program proudly houses the "Professor Bradley A. Rodgers Ship Model Collection," comprised of archaeological ship models constructed by him and his students.

Brad was a mentor to many students, young scholars, and faculty, including being the advisor for over forty graduate theses and serving on at least eighty others. He was rightly proud of the work and the careers of his students—having set so many on trajectories of success as archaeologists, historians, and museum professionals. Many of his past students went on to become his colleagues, collaborators, and friends. The legacy of Dr. Rodgers' willingness to share his knowledge and talents is seen in the work of many present-day underwater archaeologists, who have built upon a foundation shaped by his great enthusiasm, intellect, and physical energy.

Perhaps the only area of life in which Brad excelled more than as a scholar was as a partner and a friend. He and the love of his life, Vera, had amazing experiences together, including running countless races; owning and restoring a home in Algoma, Wisconsin; hosting notorious Halloween parties and "bad movie nights"; installing a pond at their home in Greenville, North Carolina, and turning it into a garden oasis; and co-owning a lake home with his sister. Brad's tales of (mis)adventure inspired Vera's son Alex and Brad's students to strike out in pursuit of their own adventures. Brad taught Alex not to be afraid to live. Brad's telling of his experience on Midway Island was so captivating, that Alex took a volunteer job there when he had the opportunity, which started him on a path that may shape the rest of his career. Brad was a great storyteller, with a wonderful sense of humor and an infectious laugh. His friends were often amused to meet mutual friends and hear his outrageous stories retold and confirmed by them.

When he passed, Brad was working on another book about his crazy exploits, *The Cowboys of Science*, intended to inspire the general public to love science as much as he did. Brad's interests were many and varied. He was a lover and protector of all animals, especially cats. He also loved music, science fiction, the Green Bay Packers, and good food and wine. He was a true "Renaissance Man"—a chemist, a carpenter, a builder, a mechanic, a baker, a gardener, and a guru. He was the best of company and a role model for so many.

Brad was a genuinely good man with a kind soul—honest and humble, witty and wise, dependable and smart. He was quick to offer help to those in need, including the many stray animals he took in through the years. There are many stories about Brad that follow a pattern: the person who was about to fall, and Brad caught them; the loved one going through a rough time, and Brad calling to let them know he was there. His friends and family all agree that they are better people for having known him. Perhaps most of all, those lucky enough to have had Brad in their lives will always remember his outrageous stories and the uproarious laughter they created. The photo included above, showing Brad working on the steamboat *Montana*, perfectly embodies his spirit to his many friends.

In Memoriam:
Nicholas Rule
(27 October 1958 to 17 November 2023)

Nicholas Rule, son of the British archaeologist Margaret Rule, passed away in November 2023 after a couragous and sadly brief battle with cancer. He once told friends that one of his earliest memories was being in a baby walker/push chair, while his mother was excavating the Fishbourne Roman villa site in Chichester, England.

As a former diver and member of the *Mary Rose* Trust, Nick developed the direct survey method (DSM) during the excavations of the *Mary Rose,* the excavation and raising of the wreck marking one of the pinnacle moments of his mother's career. The excavation, raising, and preservation of the ship over the course of the subsequent 44 years of Nick's life remained a focus of his passions, including his unending support to mark the celebrations of the 40th anniversary of the raising of the ship and the creation of the Dive the *Mary Rose* 4D experience.

Through his DSM program, Nick was involved with, and helped many, archaeological groups to use his survey program on their own sites, taking him around the UK, Malta, Sweden, the Baltic, and the Scottish Islands. Colleagues say he was often seen sitting in his dry suit between dives processing DSM data on his laptop (as evidenced in the photo shown above). Recent experiments in reprocessing *Mary Rose* artifact locations proved that most locations were within the 10-centimeter tolerance that Margaret Rule found acceptable given the challenging dive conditions in Portsmouth Harbour, and many were within millimeters of correct/verified locations, proving the efficacy of the system that Nick dedicated his work to on numerous archaeological sites. Nick was also a regular visiting lecturer at the University of Southampton, England, working closely with the Master's students completing their coursework at the Centre for Maritime Archaeology, including practical work in applying DSM in real-world contexts.

Over the course of his life, Nick's hobbies and passions ran the gamut from archaeology, computer programming, apple-tree grafting and countless other interests. He is remembered by his family for his kind-hearted disposition, his ability to always look for the best in people, and to always show a genuine interest in everyone he met.

He is greatly missed by his children and family, and the countless friends and colleagues that he worked with, whether having adventures above or underwater, over the course of his lifetime.

In Memoriam:
David VanZandt
(25 December 1953 to 01 June 2024)

It is with a heavy heart that we share the passing of David VanZandt, RPA. Dave was a fixture in the northeast Ohio SCUBA-diving community for many years, and the organization he founded, Cleveland Underwater Explorers (CLUE), has discovered and identified numerous shipwrecks since its founding 23 years ago.

Dave earned a degree in Nuclear Engineering, with a minor in Rocket Propulsion at Purdue University. After graduation, he embarked on a trajectory of technical innovation at NASA Marshall Space Flight Center, where he contributed significantly to the Advanced Propulsion Branch. Notably, he assumed the helm of the High Energy Laser Propulsion Laboratory, overseeing groundbreaking advancements in laser propulsion technologies. Transitioning to Phillips Electric Energy Resources, Inc. (PEER), David's expertise found new avenues of expression in projects of national and international significance.

David's journey continued at ZIN Technologies, Inc., where he rose to the esteemed position of Senior Principal Engineer. Over three decades, his pioneering work in space flight hardware design and operation garnered widespread recognition. His contributions spanned diverse platforms, from sounding rockets to the International Space Station, earning him numerous accolades, such as NASA's prestigious Silver Snoopy award for exceptional performance in flight safety. Most recently, Dave was named Distinguished Engineer at Holt/Murphy Advisors, Ltd., leading to groundbreaking advancements in technical arenas, from electric motor design for Dupont to offshore wind farm development.

Dave was always fascinated by maritime investigation of historic shipwrecks, and it was in furtherance of this pursuit that in 2009 he earned his Master of Arts degree in Maritime Archaeology from Flinders University. Some of the shipwrecks discovered and identified by Dave and CLUE include the *Anthony Wayne, Argo, Cortland, Craftsman, Dundee, Ivanhoe, Sarah Sheldon, Sultan,* and *Plymouth.* He was also involved in the effort to gain National Register of Historic Places recognition for several Lake Erie shipwrecks. In 2016, CLUE was recognized along with the

Maritime Archaeological Survey Team with a State Historic Preservation Award for the *Sultan* Shipwreck Mooring Buoy and ArchaeoProject in Lake Erie.

Dave was a member of the Ohio Archaeological Council, the Association of Great Lakes Maritime History, the Great Lakes Historical Society, and the Society for Historical Archaeology. He was also a fellow of The Explorers Club (FN '08). Dave is survived by his wife and two daughters and will be dearly missed by them, as well as well his many friends and associates.

In Memoriam

Gregg Ramsey Stanton

(29 August 1947 to 11 July 2024)

Gregg Stanton was the first and longest-tenured Diving Safety Officer for Florida State University (FSU), and the founder of FSU's Academic Diving Program (ADP) and its first director from 1975 to 2000. He subsequently founded FSU's Panama City Campus Advanced Scientific Diving Program and served as the first director of its Underwater Crime Scene Investigation Program until his retirement from the university in 2004. In his retirement, Gregg kept busy as the owner and manager of the Wakulla Diving Center, where he specialized in teaching technical, cave, and rebreather diving, until he moved back to Hawaii in 2019, and founded a new technical diving training facility. Health problems prevented his development of this institution as he had done successfully with previous ones, and he passed away peacefully after a battle with cancer in July 2024.

Gregg was born on 29 August 1947 in Needham, Massachusetts. As the son of an Air Force officer, Gregg grew up in a variety of places across the world, including Greenland, Spain, Ohio, Thailand, and Hawaii. In the early 1970s, he and his wife Ann moved from Hawaii and settled in Florida, where Gregg worked for Aquatic Sciences in Boca Raton and the Harbor Branch Foundation in Ft. Pierce. In 1974, he participated in the Scientist-in-the-Sea (SITS) program, a collaborative program with the United States Navy that taught advanced diving skills, including saturation diving, to new scientists. The following year he became the Diving Coordinator for FSU, a position which would turn into the Research Diving Officer and Diving Safety Officer for the university, and the first Director of the ADP. At FSU he would organize and run additional SITS programs in 1976 and 2000, as he developed the ADP into one of the most advanced and respected scientific diving programs in the country. In his 29 years at FSU, he taught basic scuba and advanced specialties, scientific diving, marine biology, and underwater archaeology to thousands of students.

Although Gregg was a marine biologist, he was a proponent of an interdisciplinary approach to diving for science, and he had an enormous impact on how underwater archaeology was taught to FSU students and carried out by FSU researchers. He was a strong supporter of the ANT 4131: Techniques of Underwater Site Research course, a field methods class sponsored by the Department of Anthropology, and also of the Department's underwater archaeological field school. Under Gregg's stewardship, the biology class BSC 5936: Applications of Diving to

Research also included a strong underwater archaeology component, and this suite of classes provided a broad body of scientific diving and hands-on logistical and archaeology experience for decades of FSU underwater archaeology students.

Gregg also participated in many of the underwater archaeology projects carried out by FSU researchers. Perhaps most notable was his role in the documentation and excavation of the 1748 wreck HMS *Fowey* off Miami, where he generated the site photomosaic in July 1980, discovered the fourth cannon and iron ballast concentration in September 1980, and helped oversee diving safety for the 23-day excavation in May–June 1983, which saw a total of 372 dives and 500 hours of bottom time. He famously rode the raised cannon all the way back to the dock in full scuba gear, just in case it worked loose from its rigging while under tow. For the *Fowey* investigation, along with many others in National Park Service (NPS) waters, he worked very closely with his colleague, George R. Fischer, NPS underwater archaeologist and FSU professor (Skowronek and Fischer 2009:57, 65, 68, 102). He participated in FSU research at submerged prehistoric sites, most notably at Warm Mineral Springs. Gregg also codirected the 1988 FSU underwater archaeological field school which, in conjunction with Indiana University and the State of Florida, documented a number of Spanish shipwrecks from the 1733 flota in the Florida Keys. In 1995, he discovered a 19th-century shipwreck in the Dry Tortugas, while conducting a marine biology study from his sailboat. Naming it the "FSU Wreck," he participated in its archaeological assessment the following year.

Gregg was known throughout the scientific diving community for his outside-the-box thinking regarding the development of new technologies to further diving for science, and was honored with the Conrad Limbaugh Award for Scientific Diving Leadership in 2014 by the American Academy for Underwater Sciences (AAUS). He played a prominent role in many important advanced diving projects and the adaptation of many new technologies, including an Antarctic under-ice surface-supplied diving expedition, manned undersea habitat projects, the development of using 100% oxygen during surface intervals to reduce decompression stress, open-circuit mixed gas when many were still opposed to even the use of nitrox, cave diving, the early use of rebreathers, and the use of argon as a cooling inflator gas for drysuit diving in an environmentally hazardous tropical lake in Palau. Many of his ideas had a positive impact on archaeological research; for example, his early adoption of nitrox and his concept of the "dive locker in a box" meant that when a group of FSU graduate students and Institute of Maritime History archaeologists traveled to St. Vincent and the Grenadines in 1997 to document a late 18th-century warship later identified as the French frigate *Junon* (1780), they could send ahead a shipping container filled with diving gear, compressors, equipment, and 40 K-bottles of oxygen so that the team could mix their own nitrox for safer and longer diving at great depths in a remote locale (Johnson and Meide 1998:81).

Gregg's vision for the ADP, as a centralized program serving all of the marine science departments along with diving education and even student recreational diving, resulted in a world-renowned institution that could serve more than a hundred divers at any given time. When he was at FSU, students found robust support for hundreds of diving projects in Florida and across the world. His energy and dedication harnessed the enthusiasm of these students and volunteers to further safety while seeking data from the underwater world, and his impact on generations of scientists and students in underwater archaeology and other disciplines was profound.

References
Skowronek, Russell K. and George R. Fischer
    2009   HMS Fowey *Lost and Found: Being the Discovery, Excavation, and Identification of a British Man-of-War Lost off the Cape of Florida in 1748*. University Press of Florida, Gainesville.

Johnson, David A. and Chuck Meide
    1998   In Soufrerie's Shadow: An Introduction to an Historic Shipwreck in Kingstown Harbour, St. Vincent and the Grenadines. In *Underwater Archaeology*, edited by Lawrence E. Babits, Catherine Fach and Ryan Harris, pp. 79–87. Society for Historical Archaeology, Atlanta, Georgia.

A Comparative Approach in Iberian Shipbuilding Design: Preliminary Results

Raúl O. Palomino Berrocal

During the 16th and 17th centuries, the classic Iberian ship concept was characterized by the nao *(carrack) and galleon. These types of vessels eventually became popular throughout Europe since they were essential for the tranatlantic journeys related to the exploration, commerce, and conquest of the New World. After decades of recovering evidence from various archaeologically excavated shipwrecks, our knowledge of structural features has allowed us to identify characteristics from the Iberian tradition. However, the actual design of the ship has been more difficult to define due to similarity with other traditions and the variability among Iberian shipwrights. The present ongoing research seeks to determine the relationship between structure and agency in the Iberian design through statistical and nautical engineering approaches to define the parameters in which an Iberian ship was conceptualized.*

Durante los siglos XVI y XVII el concepto clásico de barco ibérico se caracterizó por la nao *(carraca) y el galeón. Este tipo de embarcaciones eventualmente se hicieron populares en toda Europa ya que eran esenciales para los viajes transatlánticos debido a la exploración, el comercio y la conquista del Nuevo Mundo. Tras décadas de recuperación de evidencias de diversos pecios excavados arqueológicamente, nuestro conocimiento de las características estructurales nos ha permitido identificar características propias de la tradición ibérica. Sin embargo, el diseño real del barco ha sido más difícil de definir debido a la similitud con otras tradiciones y a la variabilidad entre los armadores ibéricos. La presente investigación en curso busca determinar la relación entre estructura e influencia en el diseño ibérico a través de enfoques estadísticos y de ingeniería náutica para definir los parámetros en los que se conceptualizó un buque ibérico.*

Au cours des XVIe et XVIIe siècles, le concept classique de navire ibérique a été caractérisé par le nao *(carrack) et le galion. Ces types de navires sont finalement devenus populaires dans toute l'Europe car ils étaient essentiels pour les voyages transatlantiques en raison de l'exploration, du commerce et de la conquête du Nouveau Monde. Après des décennies de récupération de preuves de diverses épaves archéologiquement fouillées, notre connaissance des caractéristiques structurelles nous a permis d'identifier les caractéristiques de la tradition ibérique. Cependant, la conception réelle du navire a été plus difficile à définir en raison de la similitude avec d'autres traditions et de la variabilité parmi les architectes navals ibériques. La présente recherche en cours cherche à déterminer la relation entre la structure et influence dans la conception ibérique par le biais d'approches statistiques et d'ingénieurs nautiques pour définir les paramètres dans lesquels un navire ibérique a été conceptualisé.*

Introduction

The 16th and 17th centuries were a period of expansion and development for the Iberian Peninsula. Both Spain and Portugal started colonization processes in the Asian, African, and newly found American continents that allowed them to become maritime powers despite their humble origins as small and poor nations. Naturally, to permit such expansion a maritime infrastructure is required; that means shipyards, naval routes, shipwrights, and vessels (Scammell 1981). Due to the relevance of maritime transport in this context, the Iberian shipbuilding industry in particular experienced growth both in scale and innovation that characterized Iberian power. For several decades the nautical archaeology discipline has been researching and refining different means to characterize and define Iberian ship design of this period with positive results. Thus, this article will present the preliminary results of a doctoral dissertation that aims to define, determine, and compare the Iberian design through hydrostatic data and statistical analysis to improve and complement previous investigations.

Historical Background

The end of the 15th century, with the contact between Old and New Worlds, marked the beginning of European expansion into the Americas, but also into Africa and Asia. Eager for commercial exploitation, the Spanish Crown invested heavily on the exploration and colonization of various regions in the American continent. Early settling of the Caribbean was soon followed by Spanish expansion on the mainland in Mesoamerica and then North and South America. After the discovery of the Pacific Ocean by Vasco Nuñez de Balboa, which he called "the southern sea," exploration of the south Pacific started (Agudo Rey 2013). Therefore, by the 16th century, Spain controlled territories from modern Mexico to Chile. Moreover, Spanish expansion also took place in parts of Asia, specifically the Philippines, named after Spanish King Philip II (Parker 2014:3).

After witnessing the success of the Spanish campaign, Portugal decided to follow with political expansion in a different direction. Due to the journey of Vasco de Gama in 1498 that traced the route to India through Africa, Portugal started the colonization of the coasts of Africa and part of southern Asia. Economic control over the Indian subcontinent was of major advantage since it guaranteed Portugal the spices and textiles of the region as well as from surrounding areas such as the Middle East and Asia. In the New World, Portugal focused on colonizing the eastern coast of South America, in present-day Brazil (Scammell 1981:225–259).

The actual expansion into and control of the diverse territories around the world by both Iberian nations was regulated by the Treaties of Tordesillas (1494) and Zaragoza (1529) as an attempt to keep balance between the two powers. However, by 1580, after the death of Henry I left Portugal without an heir, Portugal and its properties were added to the Spanish Empire, making it the largest power in the world (Flanagan 1988:8).

In order to sustain imperial expansion, the maritime infrastructure played a key role during these centuries. Early naval treaties can be traced back to the 15th century in the Mediterranean Sea (Chapin 1934:25), but those of Iberian origin started to popularize in the 16th century due to the growing interest of the shipbuilding industry (Castro 2008:80–81). Moreover, the first nationally funded armadas were deployed precisely for the transatlantic journey. The Tierra Firme and Nueva España fleets were funded by the Spanish Crown as an effort to protect their economic resources. Similarly, the Armada del Mar del Sur followed the same goal by guarding the resources traveling through the southern Pacific (Mira Caballos 2019).

Shipbuilding practice itself experienced a major development due to demand for commercial exploitation. In the early beginnings of the exploration era of the American continent, the preferred vessel was the caravel due to its shallow draft, which was ideal for uncharted waters (Schwarz 2008). However, for the export of resources back to Europe, different vessels were required, like the *nao* or carrack. This watercraft was characterized by a rounded shape and a larger cargo capacity. Furthermore, during the 16th century a new type of ship was created and became a staple for this period of Spanish power: the popularly known galleon, designed based on similar characteristics to the carrack but better prepared for combat. The "Iberian design" was defined in this context of commercial exploitation.

Main Features of the Iberian Ship

In order to explain the purpose and scope of the research for this article, it is necessary to understand some previously studied concepts and characteristics related to the Iberian ship. Because of the privileged position of the Iberian Peninsula facing both the Mediterranean Sea and northern Europe, the naval industry could adopt techniques and features from the two different traditions. The classic rounded shape and distinct rigging configuration were characteristics of the Iberian vessel and were later implemented in the ships from different European nations. This rounded shape was obtained from using a Mediterranean stem that was approximately a quarter of a circumference. However, instead of using a curved stern like Mediterranean watercraft, this section was based on the ships of medieval northern Europe: a flat stern with a prominent sternpost that holds the central rudder through gudgeons. The rigging was a combination of both square and lateen sails; the fore and main masts carried a northern European square sail, but the mizzenmast (and sometimes the bonaventure mast) had a Mediterranean-style lateen sail (Humble 1978:44–51).

Some of these characteristics already were in use by the 13th century with the popularization of the caravel. This vessel type was originally a small coastal fishing vessel apparently of Muslim origin, but eventually evolved into larger sizes with more complex designs such as a caravela redonda (rounded caravel) that was better suited for longer travel with more cargo. It was characterized by square rigging and, as the name suggests, more rounded hulls to increase the capacity of the hold (Schwarz 2008:25–30). This early ship was similar to the vessel later employed for transatlantic commerce, the carrack.

One of the vessels of interest for this research is the *nao* or carrack. The early references to this ship date back to the 14th century and it is one of the better-known examples of Iberian seafaring for the study period. It presents all the characteristics mentioned before, but it is also worth mentioning that, unlike caravels, carracks had more prominent upper structures: both castles present multiple decks, and the forecastle is characterized by extending far beyond the stem. The rigging was similar to that stated previously: three masts plus a spritsail at the bowsprit (Castro 2008:72–73; Hormaechea et al. 2012b:24–25). The proportions of the carrack followed the classic as-dos-tres rule of the period, meaning 1:2:3, where the keel is twice as long as the maximum breadth, and the overall length is three times that same basic dimension. Naturally, this rule of proportionality was not followed strictly by the shipwrights, and it always had a degree of variance, but in general terms, it was an approximation for the ideal proportions of a carrack (Garcia de Palacio 1587 in Laanela 2008).

The second ship of interest for the present research is the galleon. This watercraft was a product of the 16th century to fulfill the demands for an ideal warship to protect cargo in transport from the New World. For this reason, the galleon had many of the same characteristics as the carrack, but the main difference was the slightly longer overall length; instead of following the 1:2:3 rule, the galleon was 1:2:3.5 (Phillips 1994:101). This longer shape allowed the galleon to be faster, a feature especially required for combat (Dhoop et al. 2020:52). Moreover, the forecastle was considerably shorter than the carrack's and it did not extend beyond the stem. This was due to the fact that the sterncastle was taller, giving the hull a crescent shape in order to be used as a defensive tactic in case of boarding by enemies (Konstam 1988). Additionally, due to the longer extension of the galleon, it sometimes included the bonaventure mast that held a lateen sail as mentioned before. Finally, the galleon was characterized by having stronger internal bracing in comparison to the carrack to make it sturdier against enemy fire (Meide 2002:4).

Regarding the midship frame, Iberian shipwrights commonly designed it based on the tracing of a single arc to provide the rounded shape. Although sometimes a multiple-arc design could have been used, this was more common to the Basque region due to their proximity to the English. The location of the center of the arc depended on the purpose of the ship: higher centers allowed better stability for the carracks and their cargo, while lower centers provided wider gun deck space for the galleons (Hormaechea et al. 2012a:167–176).

These general characteristics are considered classic features of the Iberian vessels, but they can also be found to some degree in European ships of other nations. For this reason, Thomas Oertling (2001, 2004) proposed a set of structural characteristics that can be used as identifiers of the transatlantic Iberian shipbuilding tradition. These 11 traits consist of (1) dovetail scarves and transverse treenails and nails to join floors and futtocks; (2) carvel planking fastened with treenails and nails through the centerline; (3) a natural-grown knee scarfed at the stern to connect with the sternpost; (4) a single-piece heel knee; (5) stern Y-shaped frames tabbed into the heel knee; (6) keelson notched over the floor timbers; (7) a maststep created from an expanded portion of the keelson, which is (8) supported by buttresses and bilge stringers; (9) ceiling planking extending from the keelson to above the floor ends; (10) teardrop-shaped iron strop for deadeyes; and (11) the flat transom with a proud sternpost (Oertling 2004). Although some of these traits can also be found in different traditions, the amount and combinations of them can serve as a cultural marker.

Methodology

The present research proposes a new comparative approach based on hydrostatic data to complement previous research and literature. In order to do so, the coefficients of form were calculated from digital hull reconstructions of selected shipwrecks and the results were compared statistically to determine the parameters in which the Iberian ship was conceived as well as to calculate the degree of agency of the shipwrights while designing the vessels. Preliminary results are presented here.

The study cases selected for this research project were those with the best-preserved physical evidence as well as enough published data for reconstruction. The study cases are *Nossa Senhora dos Mártires* (1606), *San Juán de Pasajes* (1565), Western Ledge Reef Wreck (late-16th century), *San Martín* (1618), *Nossa Senhora da Consolacao* (1608), Studland Bay Wreck (16th century), Angra D (late 16th century to early 17th century), Emanuel Point I Wreck (1559), *Nuestra Señora del Rosario* (1590), and *San Diego* (1600). Because research is still in process, results presented here are from *Nossa Senhora dos Mártires*, also known as the Pepper Wreck; *San Juán de Pasajes*, also known as the Red Bay Wreck; Western Ledge Reef Wreck, and *San Diego*.

The first step of the project is to recreate the general shape of the hull based on the published evidence. For *San Juán de Pasajes* (Grenier et al. 2007:146) and *San Diego* (Desroches et al. 1997:150–151) reconstructions were proposed by the original researchers and are available. In those cases, the two-dimensional designs were imported into DELTship® (2007) to recreate a three-dimensional version of their lines plans. Regarding *Nossa Senhora dos Mártires*, the original set of lines proposed by Filipe Castro (2003:21) was employed, but modifications were made, especially in the lower stern section of the ship, since the software indicated that the original reconstruction did not present fully fair curves. Finally, the Western Ledge Reef Wreck was completely reconstructed by the author based on field information and measurements recorded by Piotr Bojakowski (Bojakowski and Palomino Berrocal 2023). For this task, the reconstruction was started in AutoCAD® (Autodesk 2010) to design the original outline of the ship, and later finished in DELFTship to build the vessel in three dimensions. Figure 1 shows the tridimensional reconstruction of the four study cases currently analyzed in the present research.

Once the models were ready for analysis, the next phase of the research was to calculate the hydrostatic data needed. This data corresponds to the form coefficients, a common tool in naval engineering to determine the shape of the hull in a quantitative way as well as to determine the performance of the ship at sea during the designing phase. The main coefficients used for the project were the Midship Coefficient (CM), Waterplane Coefficient (CW), Block Coefficient (CB), and Prismatic Coefficient (CP). The CM is based on the relation between the submerged portion of the midship section and an area of similar height and length; this value is helpful to determine the cargo capacity of the vessel, larger values are associated with hulls better fit for cargo transport (Tupper 2004:37 in Dhoop et al. 2020:56). The CW follows the same concept, but uses the plane of the hull at the waterline; the larger the value of this coefficient, the more stable the ship (Parsons 2003:11–14 in Dhoop et al. 2020:56). The CB measures the ratio between the submerged hull and cuboid of the same length, width, and depth. This value is also used to calculate the cargo capacity of the ship like the CM (Tupper 2004:37 in Dhoop et al. 2020:56). Finally, the CP is similar to the CB, but instead of using a cuboid it uses a prism with the shape of the midship section. This ratio is useful to calculate how the ship narrows towards the stern and the bow and, therefore, how prone to speed the ship is (Tupper 2004:37 in Dhoop et al. 2020:56).

The results from the coefficients by themselves might be just isolated data, but it is relevant when analyzed as a group and to determine the relationship between them. For this reason, the research project aimed to use statistics to compare the coefficients in order to obtain the model value and standard deviation of each coefficient to understand the level of agency among Iberian shipwrights. Also, the data were used to determine a linear model of the parameters in which the Iberian hull design was conceived. By definition, the model value is the "average" value or measurement from a population of samples; it can be calculated from the median, but most commonly it is obtained from the mean. On the other hand, the standard deviation is the degree of variance of a variable; it indicates how much each specific case of that variable can deviate from the model value (Kaplan 2009:47–51). The linear model is used in statistics as formulas to describe the outcome of a response variable based on the function of one or more predictor variables and has become a standard approach for data prediction (Kaplan 2009:68–70).

As seen in Table 1, the Midship Coefficient ranges from 0.8970 to 0.9499; the Waterplane Coefficient from 0.7035 to 0.9225, being the widest range; the Block Coefficient from 0.4862 to 0.6657; and, finally, the Prismatic Coefficient from 0.5326 to 0.7009. The information was uploaded into the R software for the statistics calculations and the results obtained for the model value and standard deviation are as follows in Table 2.

Ship	CM	CW	CB	CP
"Pepper Wreck"	0.9117	0.8476	0.5843	0.6409
"Western Ledge"	0.9499	0.9225	0.6657	0.7009
"Red Bay"	0.897	0.7719	0.5556	0.6194
San Diego	0.9129	0.7035	0.4862	0.5326

TABLE 1. Coefficient results for each ship.

	CM	CW	CB	CP
Model Value	0.91788	0.81138	0.57295	0.62345
Standard Deviation	0.02254	0.09462	0.07429	0.0697

TABLE 2. Model value and standard deviation for each coefficient.

As indicated in Table 2, the model value for the Midship Coefficient is 0.917845; for the Waterplane Coefficient, 0.811375; for the Block Coefficient, 0.57295; and for the Prismatic Coefficient, 0.62345. Similarly, it is relevant to notice that the standard deviation for each case can be interpreted in percentages and shows a very low degree of variance: 2% for the Midship Coefficient, 9% for the Waterplane Coefficient, and 7% for both the Block and Prismatic Coefficients.

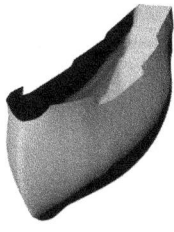
San Juan de Pasajes

Nossa Senhora dos Martires

Western Ledge Reef Wreck

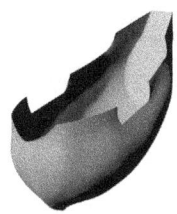
San Diego

FIGURE 1. Tridimensional reconstruction of the hulls. (Figure by the author, 2022.)

The next goal of the research was to calculate a linear model to determine the parameters in which the Iberian design was conceived. Since the master frame is the central piece for the construction of the hull, the Midship Coefficient was selected as the response variable, while the other coefficients serve as predictors. After the software calculated the results of the four study cases, the formula obtained was as follows:

$$CM = 0.91355 + (0.03454 \times CW) + (1.44302 \times CB) - (1.36415 \times CP)$$

When the linear model obtained from the dataset was tested, the R2 calculation resulted in 1, which indicates that the model works in 100% of the cases (Kaplan 2009:127–128). The adjusted R2, however, did not present results because the number of samples and data were considerably fewer. The preliminary data show positive outcomes towards the goals of the project, but analysis is still necessary on the remaining cases to improve the accuracy of the linear model.

Conclusions

Based on the preliminary results, some observations can be made. First, the low percentage of the standard deviation of the four coefficients indicate that, despite the fact Iberian shipwrights had empirical training, the concept and shape of the hull was so standardized and homogeneous that little space was left for individual innovation or agency. Second, the linear model can serve as a formula to identify the cultural affiliation of Iberian shipwrecks discovered in the future.

However, the research needs to be completed with the remaining cases to improve both the results of the model value and the standard deviation, as well as the linear model. Additionally, more features are already undergoing analysis, such as the ratio between the resistance and the displacement of the vessel to determine the average performance of the Iberian hull. Finally, once the complete dataset produces the final version of the linear model, it will be used to compare with non-Iberian vessels of the period, such as the Swedish *Vasa* and the English *Mary Rose*; this will allow determination of similarities or differences in European ship design traditions.

References

Agudo Rey, Cristina
2013   La defensa del virreinato del Perú: El lago español y la Armada del Mar del Sur. In *El mar en la Historia y en la Cultura*, Alberto Gullón A., Arturo Morgado G. and José J. Rodríguez M., editors, pp. 309–324. Servicio de Publicaciones de la Universidad de Cádiz, Cádiz, Spain.

Autodesk
2010   *AutoCAD User's Guide*. Autodesk Inc., San Francisco, CA.

Bojakowski, Piotr T., and Raul Palomino Berrocal
2023   Post-excavation Recording and 3D Modeling in Ship Reconstruction: A Case Study of the Western Ledge Reef Wreck. *Digital Applications in Archaeology and Cultural Heritage* 31. <DOI: 10.1016/j.daach.2023.e00297>. Accessed 22 May 2024.

Castro, Filipe
2003   The Pepper Wreck, an Early 17th-century Portuguese Indiaman at the Mouth of the Tagus River, Portugal. *International Journal of Nautical Archaeology* 32(1):6–23. <https://doi.org/10.1006/ijna.2003.1067>. Accessed 22 May 2024.

2008   In Search of Unique Iberian Ship Design Concepts. *Historical Archaeology* 42(2):63–87. <http://www.jstor.org/stable/25617496>. Accessed 22 May 2024.

Chapin, Frederic
1934   Venetian Naval Architecture about 1550. *The Mariner's Mirror* 20(1):24–49. <https://doi.org/10.1080/00253359.1934.10655733>. Accessed 22 May 2024.

DELFTship
2007   *DELFTship User Manual*. DELFTship, Alblasserdam, The Netherlands.

Desroches, Jean-Paul, Gabriel Casal, and Franck Goddio
1997   *Treasures of the San Diego*. Association Francaise d'Action, Paris, France.

Dhoop, Thomas, Sarah Stark, Juan-Pablo Olaberria, and Julian Whitewright
2020   Quantifying Ship Shape in Archaeology: Evaluating 3D Geometric Morphometrics. *International Journal of Nautical Archaeology* 49(1):49–64. <https://doi.org/10.1111/1095-9270.12413>. Accessed 22 May 2024.

Flanagan, Laurence
1988   *Ireland's Armada Legacy*. Sutton Publishing, Stroud, Gloucestershire, UK.

Garcia de Palacio, Diego
1587   *Instrucción Náutica, para el buen uso y regimiento de las naos, su traca, y su gobierno conforme a la altura de México*. México.

Grenier, Robert, Marc-André Bernier, and Willis Stevens
2007   *The Underwater Archaeology of Red Bay: Basque Shipbuilding and Whaling in the 16th Century*. Volume III. Parks Canada, Ottawa, Canada.

Hormaechea, Cayetano, Isidro Rivera, and Manuel Derqui
2012a   *Los Galeones Españoles del Siglo XVII, Tome 1*. Associació d'Amics del Museu Marítim de Barcelona, Barcelona, Spain.

2012b   *Los Galeones Españoles del Siglo XVII, Tome 2*. Associació d'Amics del Museu Marítim de Barcelona, Barcelona, Spain.

Humble, Richard
1978   *The Explorers*. Time-Life Books, Chicago, IL.

Kaplan, Daniel T.
2009   *Statistical Modeling: A Fresh Approach*. Project Mosaic Books, mosaic-web.org.

Konstam, Angus
1988   16th Century Naval Tactics and Gunnery. *International Journal of Nautical Archaeology* 17(1):17–23. <https://doi.org/10.1111/j.1095-9270.1988.tb00619.x>. Accessed 22 May 2024.

Laanela, Erika
2008   *Instrucción Náutica (1587) By Diego García de Palacio: An Early Nautical Handbook from Mexico*. Master's thesis, Department of Anthropology, Texas A&M University, College Station.

Meide, Chuck
2002   *A Plague of Ships: Spanish Ships and Shipbuilding in the Atlantic Colonies, Sixteenth and Seventeenth Centuries*. Manuscript on file, Department of History, College of William and Mary, Williamsburg, VA.

Mira Caballos, Esteban
2019   La Carrera de Indias: Beneficios y Perjuicios del Monopolio Comercial. *Magallánica: Revista de Historia Moderna* 11(6):62–93.

Oertling, Thomas J.
2001   The Concept of the Atlantic Vessel. In *Proceedings: International Symposium on Archaeology of Medieval and Modern Ships of Iberian-Atlantic Tradition: Hull Remains, Manuscripts and Ethnographic Sources, a Comparative Approach*, Francisco J. S. Alves, editor, pp. 213–228. Instituto Portugues de Arqueologia, Lisbon, Portugal.

2004 Characteristics of Fifteenth- and Sixteenth-Century Iberian Ships. In *The Philosophy of Shipbuilding*, Fred M. Hocker and Cheryl A. Ward, editors, pp. 129–136. Texas A&M University Press, College Station.

PARKER, GEOFFREY
2014 *Imprudent King: A New Life of Philip II*. Yale University Press, New Haven, CT.

PARSONS, MICHAEL G.
2003 Parametric Design. In *Ship Design and Construction*, I. Thomas Lamb, editor, pp. 1–50. Society of Naval Architects and Marine Engineers, New York, NY.

PHILLIPS, CARLA RAHN
1994 The Caravel and the Galleon. In *Cogs, Caravels and Galleons: The Sailing Ship 1000–1650*, Robert Gardiner and Richard W. Unger, editors, pp. 91–114. Naval Institute Press, Annapolis, MD.

SCAMMELL, GEOFFREY V.
1981 *The World Encompassed: The First European Maritime Empires c. 800–1650.* University of California Press, Berkeley.

SCHWARZ, GEORGE R.
2008 The Iberian Caravel: Tracing the Development of a Ship of Discovery. In *Edge of Empire: Proceedings of the Symposium "Edge of Empire"*, Filipe Vieira de Castro and Katie Custer, editors, pp. 43–62. Caleidoscópio, Casal de Cambra, Portugal.

TUPPER, ERIC C.
2004 *Introduction to Naval Architecture*. Fourth edition. Elsevier, Burlington, MA.

· · · · · · · · · · · · · · · ·

Raúl Oswaldo Palomino Berrocal
340 Spence Street
College Station, Texas
77843

Investigations of the Punta Espada Shipwreck, a Mid-16th-Century Iberian Transatlantic Merchant Vessel in the Dominican Republic

Sarah M. Muckerheide, Charles D. Beeker

Indiana University is conducting underwater archaeological investigations on a mid-16th-century Iberian transatlantic merchant ship in collaboration with the Dominican Republic Ministry of Culture. The site was impacted by commercial salvage from 2011 to 2013. However, current investigations indicate significant site integrity, including evidence of ship hull construction, artillery, anchors, and cargo. Analysis of this cargo determined that the shipwreck represents international commerce and the early colonization of the Americas in the 1500s. This international trade is exemplified by goods from Spain, England, Germany, and Flanders. The ultimate goal following academic investigations is to protect this site's unique underwater cultural heritage and associated biology as a "Living Museum in the Sea" within the newly established Southeast Reefs Marine Sanctuary.

La Universidad de Indiana está realizando investigaciones arqueológicas subacuáticas en el pecio de Punta Espada, un buque mercante transatlántico ibérico de mediados del siglo XVI, en colaboración con el Ministerio de Cultura de República Dominicana. El sitio se vio afectado por salvamentos comerciales entre 2011 y 2013. Sin embargo, las investigaciones actuales indican una integridad significativa del sitio, incluida evidencia de construcción de cascos de barcos, artillería, anclas y carga. El análisis de este cargamento determinó que el naufragio representa el comercio internacional y la colonización temprana de América en el siglo XVI. Este comercio internacional está ejemplificado por los bienes de España, Inglaterra, Alemania y Flandes. El objetivo final después de las investigaciones académicas es proteger el patrimonio cultural subacuático único de este sitio y la biología asociada como un "Museo Vivo del Mar" dentro del recientemente establecido Santuario Marino de los Arrecifes del Sureste.

L'Université de l'Indiana mène des recherches archéologiques sous-marines sur l'épave de Punta Espada, un navire marchand transatlantique ibérique du milieu du XVIe siècle, en collaboration avec le ministère de la Culture de la République dominicaine. Le site a été touché par un sauvetage commercial de 2011 à 2013. Cependant, les investigations actuelles indiquent une intégrité importante du site, y compris des traces de la construction de la coque du navire, de l'artillerie, des ancres et de la cargaison. L'analyse de cette cargaison a déterminé que l'épave représente le commerce international et le début de la colonisation des Amériques dans les années 1500. Ce commerce international est illustré par des marchandises en provenance d'Espagne, d'Angleterre, d'Allemagne et de Flandre. L'objectif ultime à la suite des enquêtes universitaires est de protéger le patrimoine culturel subaquatique unique de ce site et sa biologie associée en tant que « musée vivant de la mer » au sein du nouveau sanctuaire marin des Récifs du Sud-Est.

Historical Background

During the mid-16th century, two rulers controlled Spain's geopolitical situation within Europe and its intensifying colonial efforts: Charles V and his son, Philip II, prominent members of the Habsburg line. Charles V was the Holy Roman Emperor and King of Spain from 1519 until his abdication in 1556. During this time, the Holy Roman Empire consisted of modern-day Germany, Belgium, the Netherlands, Austria, Switzerland, the Czech Republic, and parts of eastern France and northern Italy, so Charles V had a far reach throughout the continent. He was the grandson of Ferdinand and Isabella, the Catholic monarchs who sponsored Christopher Columbus's voyages. Charles V's son, Philip II, was king of Spain from 1556 until his death in 1598. Before ascending to the throne, Philip II toured Europe with an entourage of 500 people from 1548 to 1551, traveling throughout the Holy Roman Empire from Spain to northern Italy to Germany to the Low Countries and back again, learning about the cultures and garnering royal support within the empire. In 1554, Philip II married Queen Mary I, the daughter of King Henry VIII, strengthening Spanish Habsburg ties to England (Parker 2014:34–40).

Punta Espada Shipwreck Site

The Punta Espada Shipwreck represents a mid-16th-century Iberian merchant ship that was traveling from

Spain to a destination in the Americas loaded with a cargo of international trade goods for colonization. Based on an examination of the material culture and makers' marks (below), the shipwreck dates to the 1550s. The site was impacted by commercial salvage from 2011 to 2013 and referred to as the "Pewter Wreck" based on the large amount of recovered sadware. Punta Espada (Sword Point) was chosen as a geographical indicator name for the site until the shipwreck can be confidently identified. Geographically, Punta Espada is located on the exposed eastern point of Hispaniola, where the Atlantic Ocean meets the Caribbean Sea. The name Punta Espada can be found on historic maps dating to the early 1700s, where it is located just to the northeast of where naos are documented as passing through (and grounding in) the shallow channel between Saona Island and the mainland (Library of Congress, Geography and Map Division 1700). The intended final destination of this vessel is unknown; additional archival research is necessary in order to determine a destination of Santo Domingo, New Spain, or Tierra Firme.

The Punta Espada Shipwreck is located in shallow water (ranging from 3 to 8 meters [m]) just 100 m from a small beach surrounded by rocky coastline. Throughout the site are a large variety of in situ wrought iron artifacts. Four anchors have been examined: two deployed into the seabed and two in the hold of the vessel. This vessel was traveling heavily armed with artillery, evidenced by at least three bombards, seven breech blocks, and five versos. One breech block on the site still has a lifting ring attached that would have been used to place it into the bombard before firing. Three barrels full of nails (possibly for shoeing horses) are also present on the site. During excavation, a small section of wooden hull (roughly 1.5 × 1 m) was uncovered, consisting of three frames with strakes and multiple treenail fasteners. This indicates significant site integrity despite previous disturbance by salvage and the shallow saltwater environment.

During underwater archaeological fieldwork in 2023, an orthomosaic was created from a photogrammetric model. Photogrammetric modeling has been in use on the site since 2016 to monitor site integrity and changes over time (Hawley et al. 2018). Utilizing the most recent 2023 orthomosaic consisting of over 6,400 photos, a highly accurate site plan was created, mapping the visible in situ artifacts on the site including anchors, artillery, barrels, bar iron, the hull section, ballast scatter, and reef structure (Figure 1).

FIGURE 1. Punta Espada Shipwreck site plan created from a highly accurate orthomosaic model. (Image courtesy Indiana University, 2023.)

Artifacts Illustrating International Commerce

The assemblage of artifacts recovered from the Punta Espada Shipwreck site provides important context for the early colonization of the Americas. The contents of this ship and its multinational cargo were selected deliberately to facilitate Spanish colonization of the the Americas, and the diversity of cargo on this ship illustrates international trade during the 16th century. Artifacts recovered from the site such as pewterware, nested weights, straight pins, customs seals, and beads are important trade items that demonstrate the transport of objects internationally throughout Europe for colonial use in the Americas.

Pewter Dinnerware

Hundreds of pieces of pewter dinnerware, primarily sadware and porringers, including unique octagonal plates, were previously recovered from the site. Starting in 1503, legislation was enacted commanding pewterers in London to mark their pewterware. The pewterware from the Punta Espada Shipwreck are stamped with a large variety of makers' marks, but of particular interest is a crowned Tudor Rose mark flanked by "TC" (Figure 2). The same TC mark was found on an officer's pewter plates recovered from the 1545 shipwreck of *Mary Rose,* King Henry VIII's flagship. The TC mark could represent Thomas Chamberlyn or Thomas Curtis, who were both London pewterers during the early to mid-16th century. Researchers from the *Mary Rose* Trust have suggested that their TC mark was likely from pewterer Thomas Chamberlyn, who was master of the Pewterers Company in 1532 (Gardiner and Allen 2005:490). However, he stopped producing pewter in 1538 (Roberts 2013:38). Roberts (2013:43) identifies the TC mark as belonging to Sir Thomas Curtis, a master pewterer who was part of the Worshipful Company of Pewterers of London and produced pewter from 1520 to 1557. According to Roberts (2013), he was commissioned to produce pewter for Henry VIII and exported his wares to Flanders, Germany, and the Aegean region. A different crowned rose maker's mark on a nine-lobed porringer, currently undergoing laboratory conservation at Indiana University (Figure 2), matches the mark on two nine-lobed porringers recovered from the 1554 Padre Island Shipwrecks (Arnold and Weddle 1978:287, 289). Pewter exported from England during this period often bore the Tudor Rose with a crown over it, marking the piece as highly refined and of high quality (Gardiner and Allen 2005).

FIGURE 2. Top, pewter plate with crowned Tudor Rose TC mark matching examples recovered from *Mary Rose*; bottom, porringer with crowned Tudor Rose mark matching examples recovered from the Padre Islands Shipwrecks. (Image courtesy Indiana University, 2023.)

Nested Weights

Nearly 100 nested weights were collected from the cargo of the vessel. These items were used for measuring goods (such as precious metals, food, pharmaceuticals, and other raw materials) against standardized weights on a balance scale. A nested weight set consists of a hinged case with a carrying handle containing seven weights that stack neatly together inside the case. The nested weights from the Punta Espada Shipwreck were produced in Nuremberg, Germany, determined based on an analysis of makers' marks (Figure 3) (Lockner 1981).

During the 16th century, Nuremberg had a monopoly on not only nested weight production and export, but on brass production or "red smithing" in general (Lockner 1981:10). This involved a system of import-export, as Nuremberg did not have copper or zinc mines (the main components of brass) and exported "highly refined products" all throughout Europe, including Spain, Portugal, Prussia, Amsterdam, England, Italy, Nordic countries, Greece, and Turkey (Lockner 1981:10–16). Nuremberg brass products, particularly nested weights, were desired by colonial powers due to their high-quality production and standardization. Illustrating this precision, the weights of the case and the cups are set in a precise ratio. The case weighs the same as the total weight of the seven cups; the biggest cup thus weighs half the weight of the case. The second largest cup weighs half the weight of the largest, and so on until the last two weights. The last two weights consist of a cup with a solid disk that fits inside it, which are of equal weight. Spanish adjuster's marks on the interior of the cup weights and case, along with file marks on the undersides of the weights, indicate a system in which local Spanish masters ensured the standardization of the nested weights, and thus commerce, within the colonial empire (Kitsch 1965:126, 168). These nested weights were themselves commercial items traveling on a merchant vessel to support Spanish colonial mining production and other activities in the Americas.

One maker's mark, a bird, stamped on the lid of a nested weight from the shipwreck, has been matched to Nuremberg coppersmith (Rotschmiede) Albrecht Weinmann, who produced nested weights from 1541 to 1558 (Figure 3) (Lockner 1981:40). Other makers' marks examined on nested weights from the Punta Espada Shipwreck's cargo date to Nuremberg coppersmiths who were manufacturing weights in the 1540s and 1550s, such as Hans Diebler, who became a master in 1548, and Hans Feihl, who became a master in 1557 (Figure 3) (Lockner 1981:43, 47). Dozens of nested

FIGURE 3. Top, set of nested weights; bottom, selection of Nuremberg coppersmith makers' marks dating to the 1550s: (a) Albrecht Weinmann, who became a master in 1541 and died in 1558; (b) Hans Diebler, who became a master in 1548 and died in 1581; (c) Hans Feihl, who became a master in 1557 and died in 1569 (Lockner 1981). (Image courtesy Indiana University, 2023.)

weight sets from the shipwreck are yet to be conserved, so much information on Nuremberg coppersmiths and the production of nested weights in the 16th century is forthcoming.

Ivory Sundials

Two horizontal writing tablet sundials, possibly produced in Nuremberg, are being examined from the Punta Espada Shipwreck (Figure 4). The hollow inset on the top of the sundial would have held a small magnetic compass with a rotating protective lid covering it; both the compass and lid are missing. The gnomon, the piece of the sundial that casts the shadow, is also missing. The back of the sundial has a recessed space (covered mostly by a concreted ivory lice comb in this example) with a piece of slate for the writing tablet (Figure 4). Schewe and Davis (2019:214) speculate that this style of tablet sundial with only one panel may represent a predecessor to the ivory diptych sundial, a two-paneled sundial associated with production in Nuremberg from the 16th through 18th centuries. Only four other examples of hand-held horizontal tablet sundials are previously reported from the archaeological record and museum collections (Schewe and Davis 2019).

Nueva Cadiz Trade Beads

Numerous Nueva Cadiz-style trade beads have been recovered from the shipwreck. These beads most closely match Smith and Good's Class II Series C Type 2 Variety A (#50), described as a "long tubular bead" with "turquoise blue/thin white/navy blue" layers forming a square cross section, with turquoise as the outermost layer and navy blue as the innermost layer (Smith and Good 1982:29). Beads such as these are noted throughout Spanish colonial sites as trade goods between the Spanish and Indigenous peoples beginning with Christopher Columbus's first voyage and continuing throughout Hernán Cortéz's conquest of Mexico, with "blue glass beads" gifted to Montezuma. These beads were likely of the Nueva Cadiz variety (Smith and Good 1982:3–8). Smith and Good (1982:11) determined that Nueva Cadiz-style beads were losing their popularity by 1560, as they are scarce in the Spanish colonial archaeological record by the late 16th century. Deagan (1987:163) agrees, specifying that Nueva Cadiz beads have only been recovered from sites predating 1550.

Location of manufacture and method of manufacture for the Nueva Cadiz beads have been debated by a variety of scholars. Smith and Good (1982:12–15) describe speculation that Nueva Cadiz beads were manufactured in Spain, though direct evidence is lacking. They do not discredit a Venetian manufacture of Nueva Cadiz-style beads, though, as "Venice was the undisputed master of bead making during the sixteenth century (Smith and Good 1982:14)." Blair et al. (2009:67) argue for Venetian production based on the fact that Nueva Cadiz beads are found in archaeological sites throughout North America, which were unassociated with, or in direct conflict with, the Spanish. Deagan (1987:158–159) also argues for a Venetian manufacture, as Venice produced and supplied glass beads throughout Europe beginning in the 11th century and continuing into the 16th century. The French and Dutch bead industries did not reach large-scale production until around 1600, effectively ruling them out as the origin for beads in a mid-16th-century shipwreck assemblage (Deagan 1987:158–159).

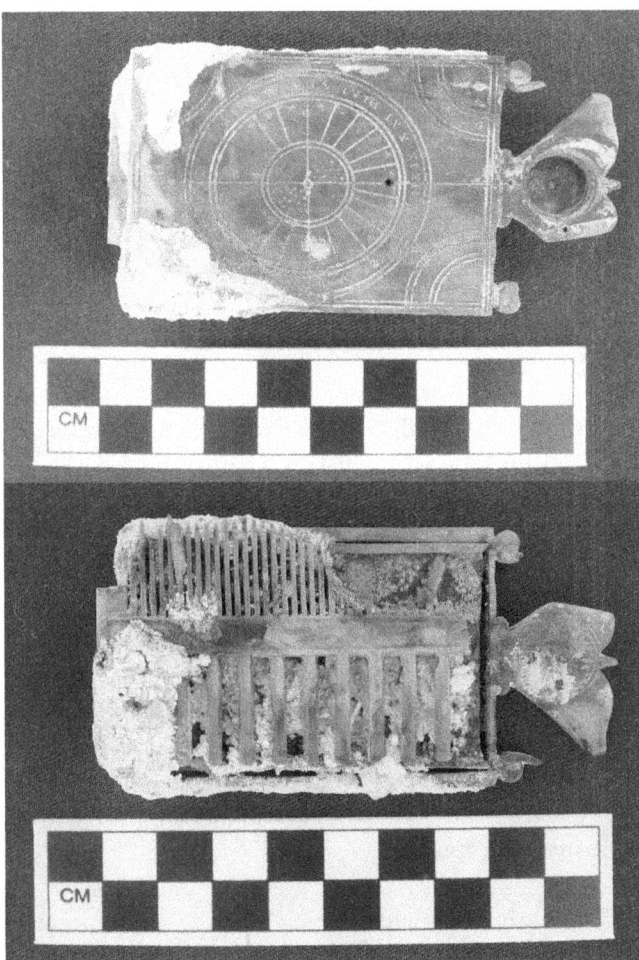

FIGURE 4. Top, ivory horizontal tablet sundial; bottom, ivory lice comb concreted over slate tablet on reverse of dial. (Image courtesy Indiana University, 2023.)

Straight Pins

Thousands of copper-alloy straight pins were in the cargo of the Punta Espada Shipwreck. In Europe in the 16th century, pins were used by both the higher and lower classes. For the upper class, pins were fashionable, as they were used to fasten veils, headdresses, and dresses. Some outfits of women royalty called for thousands of pins to hold elaborate dresses together. The ruffles and pleats of men's outfits were also held in place by pins. For the lower class, pins were cheaper than buttons and were used to fasten clothes together. Pins were also used to swaddle and diaper babies (Beaudry 2007:13–14,22).

Straight pins were an important trade item in the 16th century, as indicated by a record from April 1440, which describes 83,000 pins being transported by seven Venetian merchants on two galleys from Flanders to Southampton, England (Beaudry 2007:12–13). Additional research into the trade of pins throughout Europe in the 16th century and analysis of the copper alloy may identify the precise origin of the pins on the Punta Espada Shipwreck. The production of straight pins was an expensive, labor-intensive process. During the 16th century, pins were produced from two separate pieces of copper-alloy wire. The wire was hand drawn, then cut to the correct length and sharpened. Then, a separate piece of drawn wire was coiled and wrapped two to three times around the shank to form the pinhead, secured by flattening the end of the shank (Beaudry 2007:16).

Lead Cloth Seals and Silk Fragments

A variety of lead cloth seals were examined from the Punta Espada Shipwreck. Lead cloth seals were used in the textile trade throughout Europe. They consist of two lead disks connected in the middle with a lead strap, which was attached to bolts of cloth fabric. Certain markings indicate specifications for the cloth that they marked, details of manufacturing processes, and the individuals or companies that produced the textiles or transported them (Egan 1990:87). During laboratory conservation, silk fabric fragments were noted where the seal would have been attached to the fabric, indicating the transport of luxury European goods. Upon the first transport of silk to the Americas, the fabric was used by the Spanish as a status marker. In the first decades of the 16th century, silk was regulated, with only the Spanish governing elites permitted to wear it. When Nicolás de Ovando arrived in Santo Domingo in 1502 as the new governor of the Indies, Charles V provided legal permission for him to wear silk clothing due to his status (Marsh 2020:51–52). One cloth seal recovered from the Punta Espada Shipwreck has "VALENCIA" stamped onto it, indicating Spanish fabric origins. An examination of the markings on additional cloth seals from the 16th century will track the transport of textiles through Europe prior to their arrival as cargo on the Punta Espada Shipwreck.

Hazelnuts

As the wooden hull remains of the Punta Espada Shipwreck were uncovered, hazelnuts (*Corylus sp.*) (shell, husk, and nut) were collected, signifying remarkable preservation in the shallow, saltwater, nearshore environment. Hazelnuts have been recovered from other 16th century shipwrecks, including the Emanuel Point Shipwrecks (part of the 1559 Tristán de Luna fleet) (Bratten 2018:181) and the Padre Island Shipwrecks (Arnold and Weddle 1978:434). Hazelnuts were not part of official rations carried on Spanish ships (Super 1984), so these foods likely were being eaten by sailors to improve their diet at sea or potentially being transported to be sold in Spanish colonial markets for food or planting. Additional research into 16th-century Spanish colonial diet will function to trace early modern food chains throughout Europe and across the Atlantic.

Long-Term Management

Access to the Punta Espada Shipwreck is currently restricted to research endeavors, but in the future Indiana University proposes to establish the site as a Living Museum in the Sea after academic investigations are concluded and portable artifacts have been documented and recovered. The site is located nearshore in less than 10 m of water, and is readily accessible to recreational divers. The site consists of many large, visible artifacts such as anchors, bombards, breech blocks, and barrels, which will remain in situ so that future diving or snorkeling visitors can personally appreciate the intrinsic value of this mid-16th-century Spanish merchant vessel. Recognizing the site's historical significance and accessibility, Indiana University plans to designate the site as a *Living Museum in the Sea*. Indiana University's *Living Museums in the Sea* model aims to conserve underwater cultural heritage in situ through the creation of marine protected areas. These Living Museums protect submerged cultural and associated biological resources while promoting sustainable local economic benefits as tourism destinations (Beeker 2010). The shipwreck site lies within the Santuario Marino Arrecifes del Sureste, a recently established marine sanctuary that covers the southeastern coastal area of the Dominican Republic. Indiana University is currently performing coral monitoring and restoration on *Acropora palmata* (elkhorn coral, a critically endangered species) colonies on the site in collaboration with local conservation organizations. The opportunity for the public and the community to visit the marine sanctuary and view such an early, significant shipwreck situated within a dynamic period of Spanish colonization should not be overlooked.

Site Significance

Available records to date indicate that fewer than 20 16th-century European shipwreck sites discovered in the Americas have been academically studied; none of these assemblages contain such a rich cargo of imported goods as documented on the Punta Espada Shipwreck (Arnold and Weddle 1978; Bass 1988; Watts 1993; Castro and Fitzgerald 2006; Grenier et al. 2007; Smith 2018; Borrero 2023a, 2023b). A detailed examination of the Punta Espada Shipwreck's cargo is proving to elucidate mechanisms and systems of international commerce and globalization in the early modern period. Additionally, these trade items can provide insights into the furnishings of colonization, in objects desired for colonial households and deemed necessary for resource extraction and commercial activities. The pewter sadware, nested weights, straight pins, glass beads, and cloth seals from the Punta Espada Shipwreck are important indicators of trade within Europe in the 16th century and reveal that the highest quality of manufactured goods were acquired from throughout Europe and gathered in Seville for transatlantic transport, where the items would be sold to colonists in the Americas craving European products. The cargo from this vessel includes manufactured goods from London, Nuremberg, Venice, Valencia, Flanders, and likely additional locations, representing the sourcing of the highest caliber of products that could be obtained throughout Europe and brought to Spanish America.

Acknowledgments

The authors would like to thank the Dirección Nacional de Patrimonio Subacuático and the Ministerio de Cultura for research permits and facilitating access to artifacts for conservation and research. In addition, the authors thank the Museo de las Atarazanas Reales in Santo Domingo for allowing access to their exhibited collection for research. We give our special thanks to

Fundación Cap Cana for logistical support in the form of marina dock space and accommodations, and their ongoing coral monitoring and restoration work on the site. Indiana University thanks ScubaFun for providing boat transport and necessary equipment from Bayahíbe, enabling our underwater archaeological investigations on this and other significant sites. Laboratory conservation and research were conducted within the Indiana University Museum of Archaeology and Anthropology.

References

Arnold, Barto J. III, and Robert Weddle
1978 *The Nautical Archaeology of Padre Island: The Spanish Shipwrecks of 1554*. Academic Press, New York, NY.

Bass, George F. (editor)
1988 *Ships and Shipwrecks of the Americas*. Thames and Hudson, New York, NY.

Beaudry, Mary C.
2007 *Findings: The Material Culture of Needlework and Sewing*. Yale University Press, New Haven, CT.

Beeker, Charles D.
2010 "Living Museums in the Sea: Shipwrecks and Marine Protected Areas." *The Undersea Journal* 3:43–49.

Blair, Elliot H., Lorann S. A. Pendleton, and Peter Francis, Jr.
2009 *The Beads of St. Catherines Island. Anthropological papers of the American Museum of Natural History, No. 89*. American Museum of Natural History, New York, NY.

Borrero, Ricardo
2023a *Bahia Mujeres Wreck, c. 1525*. Nautical Archaeology Digital Library, Texas A&M University, College Station, TX. <https://shiplib.org/index.php/shipwrecks/iberian-shipwrecks/spanish-and-the-new-world/bahia-mujeres-c-1525/>. Accessed 22 May 2024.

2023b *Cayo Nuevo Shipwreck, c. 1550*. Nautical Archaeology Digital Library, Texas A&M University, College Station, TX. <https://shiplib.org/index.php/shipwrecks/iberian-shipwrecks/spanish-and-the-new-world/cayo-nuevo-shipwreck-c-1550/>. Accessed 22 May 2024.

Bratten, John R.
2018 What They Left Behind: The Artifact Assemblage. In *Florida's Lost Galleon: The Emanuel Point Shipwreck*, Roger C. Smith, editor, pp. 122–206. University Press of Florida, Gainesville.

Castro, Filipe, and Carlos Fitzgerald
2006 The Playa Damas Shipwreck, an Early 16th-Century Shipwreck in Panama. In *Underwater Cultural Heritage at Risk: Managing Natural and Human Impacts, Heritage at Risk – Special Edition*, Robert Grenier, David Nutley, and Ian Cochran, editors, pp. 38-41. International Council on Monuments and Sites, Paris, France.

Egan, Geoff
1990 Leaden Seals: Evidence for EIC Trade in Textiles. *International Journal of Nautical Archaeology and Underwater Exploration* 19(1):87–89.

Deagan, Kathleen
1987 *Artifacts of the Spanish Colonies of Florida and the Caribbean, 1500-1800, Vol. 1, Ceramics, Glassware, and Beads*. Smithsonian Institution Press, Washington, DC.

Gardiner, Julie, and Michael J. Allen
2005 *Before the Mast: Life and Death Aboard the Mary Rose. Archaeology of the* Mary Rose: *Volume 4*. The Mary Rose Trust, Portsmouth, UK.

Grenier, Robert, Marc-André Bernier, and Willis Stevens (editors)
2007 *The Underwater Archaeology of Red Bay: Basque Shipbuilding and Whaling in the 16th century, Vol. II, Material Culture*. Parks Canada, Ottawa, Ontario, Canada.

Hawley, Kirsten M., Matthew M. Maus, Charles D. Beeker, and Samuel I. Haskell
2018 Computer Vision Photogrammetry as a Tool for Three-Dimensional Archaeological Recording of a Sixteenth Century Spanish Shipwreck in the Dominican Republic. In *ACUA Underwater Archaeology Proceedings*, Matthew Keith and Amanda Evans, editors, pp. 117–122.

Kitsch, Bruno
1965 *Scales and Weights: A Historical Outline*. Yale University Press, New Haven, CT.

Library of Congress Geography and Maps Division
1700 *Map showing Hispaniola, eastern portions of Cuba and Jamaica, western portion of Puerto Rico, and other adjacent islands*. Library of Congress, Washington, DC. <https://www.loc.gov/resource/g4930.lh000477/>. Accessed 22 May 2024.

Lockner, H. P.
1981 *Die Merkzeichen der Nürnberger Rotschmiede*. Deutscher Kunstverlag, Munich, Germany.

Marsh, Ben
2020 *Unravelled Dreams: Silk and the Atlantic World 1500-1840*. Cambridge University Press, Cambridge, UK.

Parker, Geoffrey
2014 *Imprudent King: A New Life of Philip II.* Yale University Press, New Haven, CT.

Roberts, Martin
2013 *The Punta Cana Pewter Wreck - Pewter: Origin, Styles, Makers, & Commerce.* Pewterbank.co.uk. <https://pewterbank.co.uk/wp-content/uploads/2020/07/The-Punta-Cana-Pewter-Wreck.pdf>. Accessed 22 May 2024.

Schewe, Roland, and John Davis
2019 Time on a Tablet: Early Ivory Sundials Incorporating Wax Writing Tablets. *Early Science and Medicine* 24:213–247.

Smith, Marvin T., and Mary Elizabeth Good
1982 *Early Sixteenth Century Glass Beads in the Spanish Colonial Trade.* Cottonlandia Museum Publications, Greenwood, MS.

Smith, Roger C. (editor)
2018 *Florida's Lost Galleon: The Emanuel Point Shipwreck.* University Press of Florida, Gainesville.

Super, John C.
1984 Spanish Diet in the Atlantic Crossing, the 1570s. *Terrae Incognitae* 16(1):57–70.

Watts, Gordon P., Jr.
1993 The Western Ledge Reef Wreck: A Preliminary Report on Investigation of the Remains of a 16th-century Shipwreck in Bermuda. *The International Journal of Nautical Archaeology* 22(2):103–124.

· · · · · · · · · · · · · · · · ·

Sarah M. Muckerheide
Indiana University Center for Underwater Science
416 N. Indiana Avenue
Bloomington, Indiana 47408-3742

Charles D. Beeker
Indiana University Center for Underwater Science
1025 E 7th St, Room 058
Bloomington, Indiana 47405

The Architectural Influence of Ships Sailing the Red Sea Under the Ottoman Empire, the Contribution of Underwater Archaeology: A PhD Project

Iness Bernier

The Ottoman Empire endured for six centuries, showcasing remarkable complexity and influence. Their naval prowess was central to their dominance, with sophisticated infrastructure including strategic shipyards. Today, maritime archaeology sheds light on Ottoman maritime strength, yet questions linger about their naval architecture's evolution and role. The University of Southampton's project aims to explore Ottoman naval architecture from the 16th to 18th centuries, a period of expansion. By analyzing historical records, archaeology, and plans, the study seeks to compare Ottoman designs with European counterparts, revealing influences and exchanges. Despite challenges like language barriers, interdisciplinary collaboration and technology offer hope for deeper insights. Ultimately, this research aims to enrich our understanding of Ottoman maritime heritage and its lasting impact.

El Imperio Otomano que duró seis siglos, mostró una complejidad e influencia notables. Su capacidad naval fue fundamental para mantener su dominio, con una infraestructura estratégica y sofisticada que incluía astilleros. Hoy en día, la arqueología arroja luz sobre la fuerza marítima otomana, pero persisten dudas sobre la evolución y el papel de su arquitectura naval. Este proyecto de la Universidad de Southampton tiene como objetivo explorar la arquitectura naval otomana de los siglos XVI al XVIII, un período de expansión. Al analizar registros históricos, arqueología y planos, el estudio busca comparar los diseños otomanos con sus homólogos europeos, revelando influencias e intercambios. A pesar de desafíos como las barreras del idioma, la colaboración interdisciplinaria y la tecnología ofrecen la posibilidad de lograr conocimientos más profundos. En última instancia, esta investigación tiene como objetivo enriquecer nuestra comprensión del patrimonio marítimo otomano y su impacto duradero.

L'Empire ottoman a duré pendant six siècles, mettant en valeur une complexité et une influence remarquables. Leurs prouesses navales étaient au cœur de leur domination, avec des infrastructures sophistiquées, y compris des chantiers navals stratégiques. Aujourd'hui, l'archéologie maritime met en lumière la force maritime ottomane, mais des questions persistent sur l'évolution et le rôle de leur architecture navale. Le projet de l'Université de Southampton vise à explorer l'architecture navale ottomane du 16ème au 18ème siècle, une période d'expansion. En analysant les documents historiques, l'archéologie et les plans, l'étude cherche à comparer les conceptions ottomanes avec leurs homologues européens, révélant des influences et des échanges. Malgré des défis tels que les barrières linguistiques, la collaboration interdisciplinaire et la technologie offrent l'espoir d'obtenir des informations plus approfondies. En fin de compte, cette recherche vise à enrichir notre compréhension du patrimoine maritime ottoman et de son impact durable.

Introduction

The Ottoman Empire is a testament to the endurance and complexity of historical civilizations. Spanning more than six centuries, from the 13th to the 20th, this multinational, multicultural entity left an indelible mark on the annals of history. At the height of their power, the Ottomans ruled over vast territories, dominating the Mediterranean and exerting influence far beyond their borders. At the heart of their maritime dominance was their naval capability, supported and reinforced by a sophisticated network of infrastructure including numerous shipyards strategically located throughout their domain.

At the dawn of the 21st century, the field of maritime archaeology offers a unique perspective from which to examine the Ottoman Empire's maritime prowess. Yet, despite the wealth of historical evidence and archaeological remains, many questions remain as to the nature and evolution of Ottoman naval architecture. What can we learn from the remains of Ottoman ships? How did Ottoman shipbuilders adapt and innovate over the centuries to maintain their maritime supremacy? These are some of the central questions driving contemporary research in the field of maritime archaeology.

In this context, a new research project is about to be launched at the University of Southampton. This PhD project aims to delve into the heart of Ottoman naval architecture, focusing in particular on the period between the 16th and 18th centuries. The Ottoman Empire reached its apogee during this period, expanding its naval reach and engaging in extensive maritime activities throughout the Mediterranean and beyond. The primary aim of this research project is to carry out a comparative analysis of Ottoman naval architecture during this pivotal period in the empire's history. By meticulously examining historical documents, archaeological findings, and architectural plans, the study aims to elucidate the distinctive features and technological advances of Ottoman vessels. Furthermore, by juxtaposing Ottoman naval designs with those of their contemporary European counterparts, researchers endeavor to shed light on the interconnection and exchanges that took place in the maritime world in the early modern period. By undertaking a comparative study from the 16th to the 18th century, the author aspires to contribute to a better understanding of the Ottoman Empire's maritime heritage and its enduring legacy in the annals of maritime history.

The Ottoman Empire as a Maritime Puissance

Founded in the late 13th century by Osman I, the Ottoman Empire established itself as a formidable force in the geopolitical landscape of the eastern Mediterranean. Under the dynamic leadership of Mehmed II, better known as Mehmed the Conqueror, the Ottomans reached a milestone with the conquest of Constantinople in 1453, marking the end of the Byzantine Empire (Çelik 1986; Goodwin 1998; Günsel and Gülru 2000). Subsequent sultans extended the territories of the empire, which reached its territorial apogee in the 17th century under the reign of Suleyman the Magnificent. Encompassing vast regions such as Anatolia, the Middle East, the Balkans, North Africa, and parts of Eastern Europe, the Ottoman Empire was a sprawling imperial entity, exerting influence on both land and sea. It is against this backdrop of expansive growth and consolidation that the proposed study of Ottoman naval architecture from the 16th to 18th centuries takes on its full meaning (Anderson 1952).

The Ottoman Empire's maritime ambitions were an integral part of its overall imperial strategy. Control of vital maritime trade routes, particularly in the Mediterranean Sea, was paramount to the empire's economic prosperity and geopolitical dominance. The Ottoman navy was therefore an essential instrument for securing sea routes, safeguarding commercial interests, and extending territorial control. The conquest of key maritime bastions such as Cyprus and Rhodes illustrates the empire's strategic objectives to consolidate its maritime power.

Additionally, the Ottoman Empire's naval prowess extended beyond the Mediterranean, encompassing rivers as vital transportation arteries and supply lines. Fortresses and shipyards along the Tigris and Euphrates Rivers transformed these waterways into communication routes for the empire's military and logistical operations. Shipbuilding sites such as Estergon on the Danube bear witness to the empire's capacity for maritime infrastructure and naval mobilization (Çelik 1986).

Throughout its history, the Ottoman Empire engaged in maritime conflicts with rival maritime powers, notably the Italian navy. The Ottoman navy reached its apogee between the 16th and 17th centuries, culminating in decisive victories such as the naval battle of Preveza in 1538. However, geopolitical changes and technological advances challenged Ottoman maritime dominance, leading to its decline. The Battle of Lepanto in 1571 marked a major setback, symbolizing the Ottoman navy's weakening influence on the European stage (Shaw 1976).

Thus, the Ottoman Empire's maritime activities form a rich tapestry of imperial ambition, economic pragmatism, and strategic maneuvering. By exploring Ottoman naval architecture from the 16th to the 18th century, this study aims to highlight the complexities and nuances of the Ottoman maritime heritage, offering a glimpse of the empire's enduring legacy in the annals of maritime history.

Bridging the Gap: Advancing the Study of Ottoman Naval Architecture through Interdisciplinary Exploration

Despite the rich historical tapestry woven by the Ottoman Empire, the study of Ottoman naval architecture has often been hampered by a general lack of accessible information. This problem is compounded by language barriers, with research mainly published in the researchers' native language—Turkish, Arabic, and French, among others—limiting the dissemination of knowledge across linguistic boundaries. The keywords for this research are internationality and interdisciplinarity, reflecting the Ottoman Empire's ethos of cultural and intellectual exchange.

One of the main aims of this research project is to fill this gap by consolidating existing data through translation and contextualization. However, the task is not without obstacles, as much of the information remains inaccessible or restricted. Research on *Umm Lajj*, an 18th-century shipwreck in the Red Sea, is a case in point: despite collaborative efforts between institutions such as the Università L'Orientale di Napoli and the Saudi Arabian Heritage Commission, the protected status of the site prevents access to crucial data.

Maritime archaeology focusing on the Ottoman Empire has attracted international attention, with researchers such as Haldene (Ward) (1996), Zazzaro (et. al. 2017), and Öniz and Gültekin (2024) making significant contributions to the field. This PhD project aims to expand on their work by focusing on naval architecture, with the ultimate goal of providing a comprehensive typology of Ottoman vessels based on a comparative analysis of existing shipwrecks. By untangling the complex web of the transmission of architectural knowledge across the empire, the research also promises to provide insight into the evolution of Ottoman shipyards.

Moreover, beyond the confines of maritime archaeology, this study has wider implications for understanding the historical dynamics between Western powers and transnational Muslim societies in the Indian Ocean. Through the prism of naval architecture and shipbuilding, it offers a nuanced perspective on the interconnection of cultures and economies, highlighting the complexities of maritime trade routes and diplomatic relations in the early modern era. By synthesizing disparate strands of research and opening up new avenues of inquiry, this PhD project aims to contribute to a more comprehensive understanding of Ottoman naval architecture and its wider historical significance.

Unveiling Ottoman Shipwrecks: Insights from Mediterranean Shipwrecks

The Mediterranean Sea boasts many examples of Ottoman shipwrecks, providing valuable insights into the maritime activities of the Ottoman naval empire. Discovered in the construction sites of Istanbul's Yenikapı district, the wrecks of Yenikapı are maritime witnesses to the Byzantine, Ottoman, and early modern eras (Kocabaş 2015). Similar to the Yenikapı wrecks, the Akko Tower wreck off the Israeli coast, likely a small coaster wrecked in the late 18th or early 19th century, was excavated by the Recanati Institute of Maritime Studies at the University of Haifa, enabling the discovery of a well-preserved hull and cargo (Cvikel 2022).

Off the coast of Tektaş Burnu, near Bodrum in Turkey, lies the TK06-AD wreck, dating from the 16th century. This medium-sized merchant ship plied the waters of the Mediterranean. The excavations were carried out by the Institute of Nautical Archaeology (INA) in collaboration with Dokuz Eylül University and revealed a well-preserved wooden hull, offering an insight into Ottoman maritime trade and shipbuilding techniques (Royal 2008; Royal and McManamon 2010).

The Mediterranean Sea is a rich repository of Ottoman maritime history, evident by the diversity of Ottoman shipwrecks discovered in its depths. Whether archaeological treasures unearthed at the Yenikapı shipyards in Istanbul, spanning the Byzantine, Ottoman, and early modern eras, or the well-preserved remains of vessels such as the Akko Tower wreck off the Israeli coast, which shed light on the maritime activities of the late 18th and early 19th centuries, each wreck offers an invaluable insight into the maritime legacy of the Ottoman Empire (Cvikel 2022).

Discoveries in the Red Sea

The Red Sea, whose significance to the Ottoman Empire is just as marked as that of the Mediterranean, has revealed other Ottoman ships, albeit in a less preserved state. Located off the coast of Saudi Arabia, the mid-18th-century Umm Lajj wreck was discovered in 1997 during a survey conducted by the Saudi Arabian Heritage Commission. Excavations uncovered a well-preserved wooden hull and a diverse cargo, providing valuable insights into maritime trade and shipbuilding during this period in the Red Sea region (Zazzaro et al. 2017).

In 1969, Israeli archaeologists excavated the remains of a large ship that had sunk at anchor in the port of Sharm el Sheikh, discovering over 1,000 earthenware water vessels, pipes, and broken porcelain dating to the early 18th century. Following this, various sites in the Sinai Peninsula were investigated, revealing artifacts such as a mercury-carrier from the late medieval period and scattered wrecks with anchors.

Since 1994, the Institute of Nautical Archaeology-Egypt (INA-Egypt), in collaboration with the Supreme Council of Antiquities for Egypt (SCA), has conducted surveys and excavations in the Red Sea and the Mediterranean, documenting shipwreck sites and excavating an Ottoman-period vessel. The Red Sea surveys have identified few remains predating the 14th century.

The Sadana Island Shipwreck, discovered by Egyptian sport divers, represents a significant find dating to the late 17th to early 18th century. Excavations revealed a diverse collection of artifacts, including porcelain, ceramics, copper objects, and organic remains. The hull's construction features a combination of familiar and unfamiliar elements, indicating a unique shipbuilding tradition. The excavation of the Sadana Island Shipwreck offers insights into trade routes, maritime commerce, and shipbuilding techniques of the Ottoman period in the northern Red Sea. The ongoing research aims to provide a comprehensive understanding of Egypt's nautical heritage while preserving valuable archaeological resources (Haldene [Ward] 1996).

Exploring the Depths of the Black Sea

The Black Sea Maritime Archaeology Project (Black Sea MAP), directed by Rodrigo Pacheco-Ruiz, has unearthed numerous Ottoman shipwrecks. These wrecks, lying at a depth of several hundred meters, are well-preserved due to the anoxic conditions of the Black Sea, offering researchers invaluable information on the maritime history of the region, particularly that of the Ottoman period. Further study of these wrecks is still required to examine construction techniques and gain valuable insights into the economic, technological, and social dynamics of maritime activities in the Ottoman Empire (Ballard et al. 2001).

As we continue to explore the depths of the Black Sea, technologies including remotely operated vehicles (ROVs), multi-beam sonar, and side-scan sonar are playing an increasingly vital role in underwater archaeology. These tools enable us to conduct high-resolution surveys and excavations, enhancing our ability to study and document Ottoman shipwrecks with unprecedented precision and detail.

As we reflect on the discoveries made so far and anticipate the future of maritime archaeology, one thing remains clear: through continued exploration, collaboration, and technological innovation, we will soon unveil the enduring legacy of Ottoman maritime history in the Black Sea region.

Conclusion: Sailing the Seas of Ottoman Maritime Heritage

From the shores of the Mediterranean to the depths of the Black Sea and the mysteries of the Red Sea, the legacy of Ottoman maritime domination bears witness to the enduring spirit of historic civilizations. The Ottomans fashioned a multinational, multicultural empire that left an indelible mark on the annals of history. At the heart of Ottoman maritime supremacy was a formidable naval capability, supported by a sophisticated network of infrastructures and shipyards strategically positioned in their fields. The empire's maritime ambitions were an integral part of its wider imperial strategy, securing vital trade routes, safeguarding commercial interests, and extending territorial control.

The study of Ottoman naval architecture offers a unique window on this maritime heritage, highlighting the evolution of shipbuilding techniques, navigation practices, and cultural exchanges that shaped the empire's maritime identity. Through a meticulous examination of historical documents, iconography, and archaeological discoveries, researchers seek to elucidate the distinctive features and technological advances of Ottoman ships. As we embark on a new PhD project focusing on Ottoman naval architecture from the 16th to the 18th century, we are ready to discover fresh perspectives on this fascinating chapter of maritime history. Through the analysis of Ottoman naval architecture, our goal is to shed light on the interconnections and exchanges that influenced the maritime world in the early modern period.

Interdisciplinary collaboration and the integration of cutting-edge technologies will be key to this research. Using multibeam bathymetry, photogrammetry, and ROVs, we aim to extend the boundaries of exploration and innovation in underwater archaeology and thus shed light on the enduring legacy of Ottoman maritime history. This is the introduction to a long doctoral journey into Ottoman naval architecture, inviting academics, researchers, and enthusiasts to join us in this study of the Ottoman Empire's maritime legacy.

References

ANDERSON, R. C.
1952   *Naval Wars in the Levant, 1559–1853*. Princeton University Press, Princeton, NJ.

Ballard, Robert D., Fredrik T. Hiebert, Dwight F. Coleman, Cheryl Ward, Jennifer S. Smith, Kathryn Willis, Brendan Foley, Katherine Croff, Candace Major, and Francesco Torre
2001   Deepwater Archaeology of the Black Sea: The 2000 Season at Sinop, Turkey. *American Journal of Archaeology* 105(4):607–622.

Çelik, Zeynep
1986   *The Remaking of Istanbul: Portrait of an Ottoman City in the Nineteenth Century.* University of California Press, Berkeley.

Cvikel, Deborah
2022   The 19th-Century Akko Tower Shipwreck, Israel: Final Report. *International Journal of Nautical Archaeology* 51(1):3–20.

Goodwin, Jason
1998   *Lords of the Horizons: A History of the Ottoman Empire.* Henry Holt and Company, New York, NY.

Günsel, Renda, and Necipoğlu Gülru
2000   *The Sultan's Portrait: Picturing the House of Osman.* A Turizm Yayınları, Istanbul, Türkiye.

Haldane [Ward], Cheryl
1996   Archaeology in the Red Sea. *Topoi* 6(2):853–868. <DOI:https://doi.org/10.3406/topoi.1996.1699>. Accessed 17 May 2024.

Kocabaş, Ufuk
2015   The Yenikapı Byzantine-Era Shipwrecks, Istanbul, Turkey: A Preliminary Report and Inventory of the 27 Wrecks Studied by Istanbul University. *International Journal of Nautical Archaeology* 44(1):3–58.

Öniz, H., & Gültekin, H.
2024   Deterioration of Wooden Shipwrecks Along the Mediterranean Coast of Türkiye. International Journal of Nautical Archaeology, 1-13. https://doi.org/10.1080/10572414.2024.2317821

Royal, Jeffrey G.
2008   Description and Analysis of the Finds from the 2006 Turkish Coastal Survey: Marmaris and Bodrum. *International Journal of Nautical Archaeology* 37(1):88-97.

Royal, Jeffrey G., and John M. McManamon
2010   At the Transition from Late Medieval to Early Modern: The Archaeology of Three Wrecks from Turkey. *International Journal of Nautical Archaeology* 39(2):327-344.

Shaw, Stanford J.
1976   *History of the Ottoman Empire and Modern Turkey: Volume 1, Empire of the Gazis: The Rise and Decline of the Ottoman Empire 1280-1808.* Cambridge University Press, Cambridge, UK.

Zazzaro, Chiara, Romolo Loreto, and Chiara Visconti
2017   An Eighteenth-Century Merchantman off the Red Sea Coast of Saudi Arabia. *Proceedings of the Seminar for Arabian Studies* 47:253–268.

. . . .

Iness Bernier
Chem. de la Censive du Tertre
44312 Nantes
France

Archaeological Analysis (Forecast) of Japanese Cognition of Western Vessels from 1790 to 1853

Dante Petersen Stanley

This article is an investigation into Japanese understanding of Western vessels from 1790 to 1853. From 1640 to 1853, Japan held an isolationist outlook on foreign diplomacy, slowly moving to a paradigm of limiting trade and external relations to a few locus points, with the Dutch existing as the sole accepted European presence. At the turn of the 19th century, this world order started to crumble, with a noted increase in American, British, and Russian vessels off the coast of Japan. This increase was in spurts with four discrete periods, the fourth leading to the "opening" of Japan in 1853–1854 by Commodore Perry of the United States Navy. By fully elucidating Japanese knowledge of these vessels through contemporary prints, drawings, and imported line plans, a rounded conception emerges of the foreign vessels and people, Japanese construction elements, and Japanese attempts at building Western-style vessels.

Este artículo es una investigación sobre la comprensión japonesa de los buques occidentales desde 1790 hasta 1853. De 1640 a 1853, Japón mantuvo una perspectiva aislacionista sobre la diplomacia exterior, avanzando lentamente hacia un paradigma de limitar el comercio y las relaciones exteriores a unos pocos puntos, con los holandeses existiendo como única presencia europea aceptada. A principios del siglo XIX, este orden mundial comenzó a desmoronarse, con un notable aumento de embarcaciones estadounidenses, británicas y rusas frente a las costas de Japón. Este aumento se produjo a borbotones, con cuatro períodos discretos, y el cuarto condujo a la "apertura" de Japón en 1853–1854 por el comodoro Perry de la Marina de los Estados Unidos. Al dilucidar plenamente el conocimiento japonés de estas embarcaciones a través de grabados, dibujos y líneas contemporáneas importadas surge una concepción completa de la embarcación, los pueblos extranjeros, los elementos de construcción japonesa y los intentos de construir embarcaciones de estilo occidental.

Cet article est une enquête sur la compréhension japonaise des navires occidentaux de 1790 à 1853. De 1640 à 1853, le Japon a adopté une vision isolationniste de la diplomatie étrangère, passant lentement à un paradigme de limitation du commerce et des relations extérieures à quelques points de repère, les Hollandais étant la seule présence européenne acceptée. Au tournant du XIXe siècle, cet ordre mondial a commencé à s'effondrer, avec une augmentation notable des navires américains, britanniques et russes au large des côtes du Japon. Cette augmentation s'est faite par à-coups, avec quatre périodes distinctes, la quatrième menant à l'ouverture du Japon en 1853–1854 par le commodore Perry de la marine américaine. En élucidant pleinement les connaissances japonaises sur ces navires à travers des estampes et des dessins contemporains ainsi que des plans des formes importés, il émerge une bonne conception des navires étrangers, des éléments de construction japonais et des tentatives japonaises de construction de navires de style occidental.

Introduction

The lack of a robust maritime archaeological record in Japan and Asia has led to a silent revolution in methodology. While the record is more present than some outside of the field might believe, common types of Japanese vernacular watercraft, such as the Bezaisen, are still absent. A dilemma is ever present: wait until a vessel type is found either through active or passive means, or at the same time pursue studies to better understand future sites without a current extant site. This started to occur in the late 2000s with Master's theses from Dr. Michelle Damian (2010) and Dr. Kotaro Yamafune (2012), who both focused on Japanese images to foster a given understanding of contemporary vessels. This dilemma is linked to an understanding of the historical paradigms responsible for the unique divide between knowledge of construction and actual construction.

In 1853, in response to Commodore Matthew Perry delivering an ultimatum to open Japanese ports to foreign trade, commerce, and whalers, the Japanese repealed a ban on the construction of large vessels over 90 tons (Adachi 1995). A spate of "Western-style" vessels were built in response to the Western threat (Adachi 1995), colliding with a unique environment of restrictive sociological and political paradigms that had completely separated knowledge from construction for at least the prior 60 years. A constant yet undulating stream of Western contact off the shores of Japan from 1790 pockmarks the historiography, existing alongside the steady endorsed trickle of the Dutch in Nagasaki (Sakamaki 1939:174–190). Concurrently, desultory attempts to import and transliterate lines and other ship plans occur throughout the 60-year period (Adachi 13 年 [Year] 11 月 [Month]). The visual evidence of the vessels and the lines forms a data set of Japanese cognition of Western vessels. This is unique because generational cognition of Western vessels was wholly removed from the actual process of their construction, leading to a process of elucidating 60 years of visual knowledge to better understand Japanese construction attempts in 1853–1863, and the potential archaeological record of at least two of these vessels.

A clear delineated sequence exists; cognition of Western vessels over 60 years completely separate from construction; construction attempts in the 1850s based on that cognition; and potential underwater cultural heritage (UCH) related to that construction. The historiography of 19th-century Japan has mentioned and discussed these vessels (Adachi 1995), but there is no follow through to identify potential UCH. By attempting to identify given cognitive nodes (aspects) with the potential to be present in future sites or related sites, we may begin to reconstruct the site without the site. Without the site, it is simply a future model, but if a shipwreck from one of the periods in question is discovered and the model is supported by the site, then the model is further strengthened. If some miscalculations occurred, retooling of the model is possible.

History

Background

In the first half of the 17th century, after the end of the Sengoku period, the Tokugawa Shogunate implemented a series of edicts restricting Christianity, expelling the Spanish and Portuguese, prohibiting foreign travel by Japanese subjects during the 1630s, banning the construction of large vessels, and establishing the Dutch in Nagasaki after 1840 as the sole European trading partner. These edicts formed what is now known as "closed country" (Sakamaki 1939:1); however, Japan was still active in trade and diplomacy in East Asia, albeit in a highly regulated form (Toby 1991).

Russian and British Aggression, 1790s–1808

This paradigm largely held until the late 18th century, with the first departure traced to the Russians in Hokkaido and Sakhalin in the 1780–1790s. Japan's refusal to trade in 1804 led to armed skirmishes with the Russians between 1806 and 1813 (Shmagin 2022). This is coupled with the HMS *Phaeton* Incident in 1808, which was an armed incursion into Nagasaki Harbor by the British Royal Navy, seeking to seize Dutch merchant vessels (Wilson 2010). American merchants also sailed under the Dutch flag in the 1790s and early 1800s between Batavia and Nagasaki, capitalizing on the opportunity afforded by the Napoleonic wars (Sakamaki 1939:179–183).

Western Whaling, 1810s–1825

Western whaling increased in the 1810s and 1820s, with at least seven known vessels operating off the coast of Mito (northern Japan) for several years and trading with local fishermen (Howell 2014:302). These interactions were not known by officials until 1824–1825, but were coupled with known stops of British whalers in Uraga (located in present Tokyo Bay) in 1818 (*Brothers*) and 1822 (*Saracen*) (Howell 2014:302). A series of events between Japanese officials and unruly whalers led to discovery of the interactions between whalers and local fishermen. This, and a fear of continued Russian aggression, led to the Expulsion Edict of 1825, which authorized shelling and repelling any non-Dutch Western vessels seen off the Japanese coast (Howell 2014:323).

Contact during the Expulsion Edict, 1825–1842

A few notable contacts occurred during the Expulsion Edict between 1825 and 1842, bucking trends seen before and after. In 1830, *Cyprus* was taken over by English mutineers, sailed to Japan, and sunk off the coast of China. The surviving mutineers stated that Japanese cannon fire sunk the vessel, but this story was spun by officials as a tall-tale (Robertson 2017). The mutineers' story was validated by Japanese images of *Cyprus* and the incident (Robertson 2017). In 1837, *Morrison* was hired by an American missionary in Canton to repatriate Japanese castaways but was repelled by cannon fire (Howell 2014:320).

Parabolic Rise of Western Whalers, 1840s

Repeal of the Expulsion Edict occurred in 1842 in response to the First Opium War when the Edict was countermanded with orders to supply provisions and send the vessels on their way (Sakamaki 1939:184).

This coincided with the recorded parabolic rise of Western whalers off the northern Pacific coast, especially Hokkaido and the Tsugaru Strait (Sakamaki 1939:185–189). Several Western whalers repatriated Japanese castaway fishers back to Japan, most notably *Manhattan* in 1845, and the United States government started to send envoys to "open" up Japan for trade and repatriation of American whalers, starting in 1846 with Commodore Biddle but ending in failure. Commander Glynn in 1849 successfully negotiated the repatriation of deserters from *Lagoda* (Sakamaki 1939:185–189). This led to Commodore Perry's expedition to open Japan in 1853–1854. This event saw repeal of the 17th-century Ka'ei edicts and allowed for the building of warships larger than 90 tons, leading to a boom in construction attempts (Adachi 1995).

Dataset - Introduction

The dataset is a collection of contemporary prints and drawings totaling over 40 images of 11 distinct vessels, and 5 sets of imported transcribed lines plans from 1790 to 1853 illustrating the numerous points of contact between Japan and the West during this period, specifically with Western-style vessels. This dataset of images (excluding lines) creates a visual record (VR) because evidence from the archaeological record has not been discovered. Furthermore, each image in the VR can be definitively linked to the historical record, with each vessel in the dataset a named Western vessel. The VR includes 37 images of at least 11 American and British vessels overlapping four distinct periods of time, segmenting into three distinct themes: fulsome (a full conception or attempt to understand the whole dynamic of a given Western vessel); abstracting (modification of known Western construction elements, best seen in multiple prints of the same vessel, going from fairly accurate depictions of specific elements to either those elements being conflated with other elements, or entirely absent); and façade (the depiction of the hull is more focused on external elements such as davits and canon with construction elements absent). Dutch and Russian vessels were excluded from the VR due to the current lack of available Russian and Dutch information pertaining to the larger dataset time periods, yet Dutch and Russian depictions are part of the larger dataset with a keen focus on future research. Each image is a visual node directly linked to the historical record and a possible node indicating cognition of construction, potentially forecasting to the currently undocumented archaeological record.

The VR is supplemented with an analysis of imported lines plans from 1808 to 1853 with a much firmer impact to construction, but crafting a parallel story. They are used interchangeably with the VR but not included in the VR, because of the VR's tangible historical connection to Japanese-Western contact while lines fall into Dutch studies. Distillation of data occurred in two general ways, qualitative and quantitative. Qualitative data from the VR involved a general analysis of the print, and a recognition of whether certain features, i.e., a stem, were present or not. Quantitative data are the ratio of given elements seen in the prints. The recognition of features seen through the data set is defined as nodes of cognition and, when knowledge drifts from its original meaning, it results in cognitive drift.

Fulsome, 1790s–1808, 8 images, 5 vessels: **Lady Washington, Eliza, Nagasaki Maru, Emperor of Japan, HMS Phaeton**

Keels, garboard strakes, and bitts are depicted in an attempt to understand the vessel in its entirety. One of the best examples of this fulsome depiction is a set of three prints in the Kobe City Museum illustrating the sinking of *Eliza* in 1797 and its eventual refloating by the Japanese (文化遺産オンライン [Cultural Heritage Online[1797). One of the prints depicts the refloating and has multiple perspectives of the vessel being refloated (文化遺産オンライン [Cultural Heritage Online[1797). This is coupled with Japanese attempts to build a Western-style vessel in the 1780s, culminating in the Japanese acquiring a lichter model (a type of Dutch barge) and building a vessel called *Sankoku Maru*, the three-country ship, in 1787, based on Chinese, Japanese, and Dutch methods. Japanese shipwrights also worked on repairing Dutch vessels throughout the 1790s. Discussions of further attempts at Western construction faltered and any serious attempt ended after 1793 because of continued political pressure (Blusse 2019:240–243).

Abstracting, 1810s–1830s, 9 Images, 3 Vessels: **Brothers, Saracen, Cyprus**

The form of Western whaling vessels (notably *Brothers* and *Saracen*) depicted is generally known but parts of their construction are slowly abstracted and lose their place. Japanese vernacular ship construction starts to seep in and possibly affect cognition, but it is not obvious enough to be declarative. This coincides with the rise in whaling off the Japanese coast, most notably the northeast Pacific coast (Mito Domain and Hokkaido), and the political response to Western whaling best seen in the Expulsion Edict of 1825 (Howell 2014). The edict itself has a depiction of a Western vessel, but it is a clear transformative artistic interpretation of a Dutch East Indiaman.

Façade, 1840s, 20 Images, 3 Vessels: Manhattan, USS Columbus, USS Vincennes

As Western interactions and overtures increased, construction elements largely disappear, and the hull almost transforms into a façade. Clear depictions of the vernacular emerge and are seen in depictions of *Manhattan* and USS *Columbus*. Even though multiple depictions of the vessels exist, they visually undercut the previous 60 years of interaction by their seemingly simplistic depictions. The limited depiction of construction during the 10 years before Perry highlights potential vectors of understanding.

Lines

No direct evidence that the VR directly impacted construction exists, as if a Japanese carpenter studied an image of a Western vessel to build a Western-style vessel. However, the trends seen in the VR are supported by matching other sets of evidence, mainly imported lines. While a Dutch half-model was in Japan during the 1780s (Blusse 2019), the model no longer exists, and the earliest plan is Gunkan Zukai, roughly translated as Warship Plans, which was imported and transcribed from Europe to Japan by 1808 in response to Russian aggression in the far north. It is a compilation of late 17th- to early 18th-century French, British, and Dutch plates, with a mixture of Atlantic and Mediterranean traditions (The Schoenberg Institute for Manuscript Studies 2014), and an 1822 Dutch ship manual's (Rijk 1822) six plates transcribed and transliterated (Adachi 13 年 [Year] 11 月 ([Month]). The manual is a synthesis of early 19th-century advances in maritime architecture and engineering. While the original copy is in Japan, Japanese copies spread throughout the country and do not match the original. The copies lack details and, critically, shift meaning of certain features, notably in the sheer plan, bow, and transom. The sheer plan lost all detail, and possibly conflated with a depiction of copper plating on Western vessels (Adachi 13 年 [Year] 11 月 [Month]). The bow is moved forward, with only external elements present. The transom has a hole, a possible Japanese vernacular construction element. Japanese captain's manuals that included the plates also show these shifts, and where those specific shifts originated—whether in the original or the copy—is not clear. These shifts highlight how knowledge transformed in transition, and these transitions likely impacted future construction.

Cognitive Drift

Coupled with the trend towards abstract depictions is cognitive drift in construction elements. Three areas of drift have been explicitly defined, with two connected to each other, the first likely leading to the second. The first is the divide between the bow and the rest of the vessel. The second is the movement, conflation, and creation of elements related to the bow; specifically, the stem, knightshead, and external elements such as cutwater or knee of the head. The third is the shift in the construction of the stern and transom, shifting from a Euro-Western construction to vernacular depictions of transoms in Western vessels. These three transitions are not the only transitions but are the ones identified so far. Sites discovered in the future will offer more evidence of construction elements prone to cognitive drift.

Divide of the Bow

Depictions of the divide exist from the first image of an American vessel (*Lady Washington*) off the Japanese coast in 1791 and exist until the Expulsion Edict of 1825 (Sakamaki 1939:1). An architectural trend seen in some images of the VR depicts the stem substituted with a divide between midships and the bow, and the stem is moved forward, conflating external elements such as the knee of the head with a singular large stem. This depiction shifts where the bow ends and starts, altering both shape and construction. While the trend ends approximately 20 years before Perry, it is due to the pictorial and façade-like depictions of vessels after 1840, not a reversal of the depiction.

Shifting of the Bow

The movement, abstraction, and conflation of the stem and related elements are a continuation of the trend seen earlier. The stem, knighthead, and the knee of the head change locations, merging and conflating meaning. This trend can be tracked because of the four images of *Brothers* and the four images of *Saracen*. Both vessels are identifiable in each of their given images, yet depictions of their specific construction elements change dramatically from image to image. The disappearance and conflation are tracked, highlighting the direction of cognitive drift. First, the depiction of the elements shows the knee of the head, the stem, and knightheads connected to each other, similar to Euro-Western construction. Elements such as knightheads and their placement allow for tracking of cognition, given that the placement of the knighthead has an extremely specific connotation, connecting to the stem and bowsprit. The stem and the knee of the head are external and internal elements, and the knighthead is directly linked to the stem. The stem either becomes a lesser divide not reaching the waterline or disappears entirely. The knightheads either disappear completely or are placed randomly in the bow, not connected to the stem. The knee of the head is conflated into the stem, and the apparent stem is also larger. The apparent size increase might be related to vernacular construction, but not enough evidence exists to make a conclusive argument (Figure 1).

Transom Construction

The third example of cognitive drift is a shift in the visualization of stern construction. Earlier depictions of the transom are in line with Euro-Western constructions, but by the 1820s vernacular-influenced Western depictions of the transom start to emerge. They are variations in construction, not Euro-Western but not yet full-formed vernacular construction. By the 1840s, depictions of vernacular stern construction, called a chiri, are present in images of the whaling ship *Manhattan* and USS *Columbus*. A chiri is an open transom, allowing for the up-and-down movement of the rudder. Other transitions are either conflations or misunderstandings of Western-style construction, but the cognitive drift in depictions of the transom is an example of a drift from Euro-Western construction to vernacular (Figure 2).

Handleiding tot de kennis in den scheepsbouw (Guide to knowledge in shipbuilding)

The copies of *Handleiding tot de kennis in den scheepsbouw (Guide to knowledge in shipbuilding)* also show these transitions (Rijk 1822). Drift occurs in the copying of the sheer plan, cartoon of the bow, and transom. These transitions then dovetail with likely construction elements in Western-style vessels constructed post-1853. The bow simplifies with a focus on external elements; the sheer plan is transformed to a bare outline combined with possible depictions of copper plating; and the transom transformation includes a hole. Cognitive nodes are an exceptional indicator drift occurred, when it occurred, and what drifted; they are not a good indicator for why it drifted. The depictions line up with patterns seen in the visual record, potentially explained by the political crackdown in the 1820s (Howell 2014) (Figure 3).

Construction of Vessels after 1853

The ban of large vessels was repealed by the Shogunate in 1853, and a torrent of Western-style vessel constructions were contracted and built with five of note: *Shohei Maru, Hoo Maru, Asahi Maru, Hayatori Maru,* and *Jingo Maru*. *Shohei, Hoo,* and *Asahi Maru* were either ordered and built after 1853 by the Shogunate or ordered by daimyos but with heavy Shogunate influence (Adachi 13 年 [Year] 11 月 [Month]) (Damian 2010:160). *Hayatori* and *Jingo Maru* were ordered and built by Himeji Domain without direct S--hogun influence between 1856–1863 (播磨町 "Harima Town" 2021). The

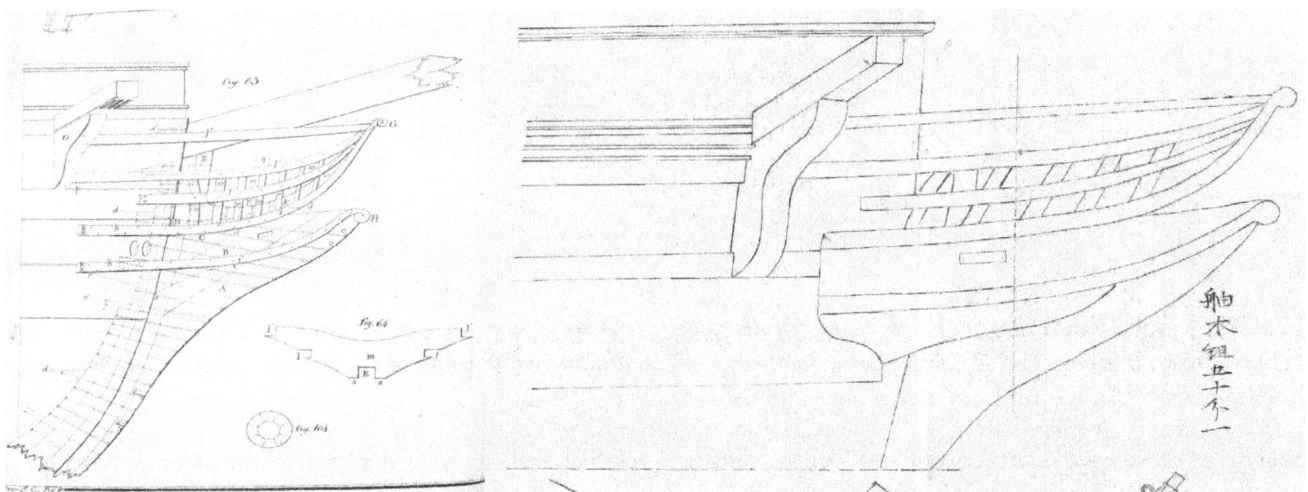

FIGURE 1. Left: *Handleiding tot de kennis in den scheepsbouw (Guide to knowledge in shipbuilding)*, courtesy of New York Public Library; Right: 船散図 (Ship Scatter Plan) copy of *Handleiding tot de kennis in den scheepsbouw (Guide to knowledge in shipbuilding)*. (Courtesy of University of Tokyo Komaba Library.)

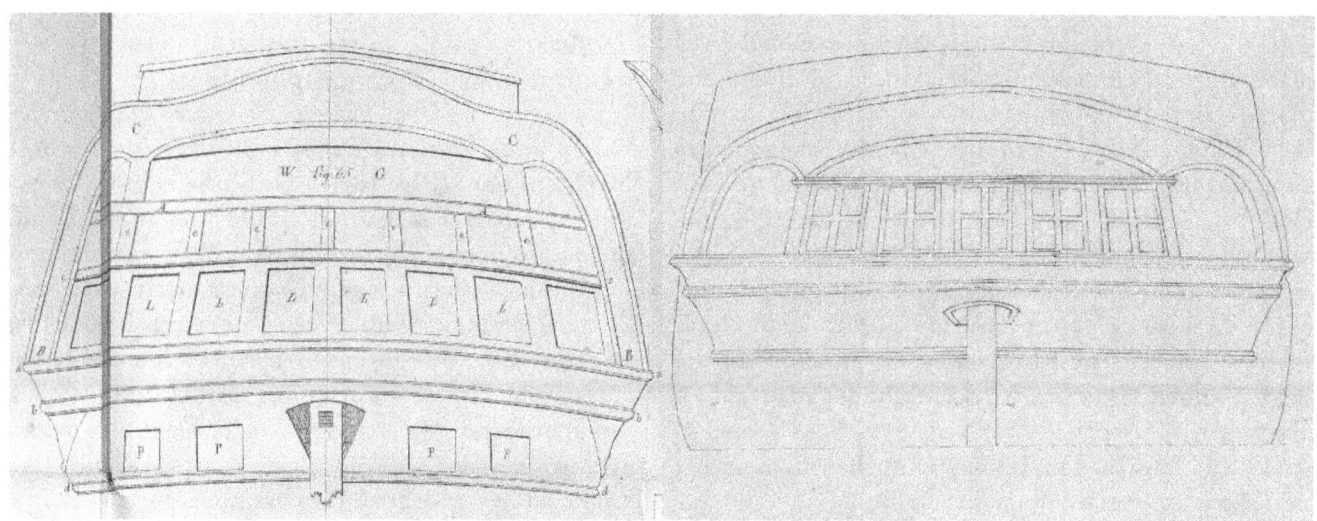

FIGURE 2. Left: *Handleiding tot de kennis in den scheepsbouw* (*Guide to knowledge in shipbuilding*), courtesy of The New York Public Library; Right: 船散図 (Ship Scatter Plan) copy of *Handleiding tot de kennis in den scheepsbouw* (*Guide to knowledge in shipbuilding*). (Courtesy of University of Tokyo Komaba Library.)

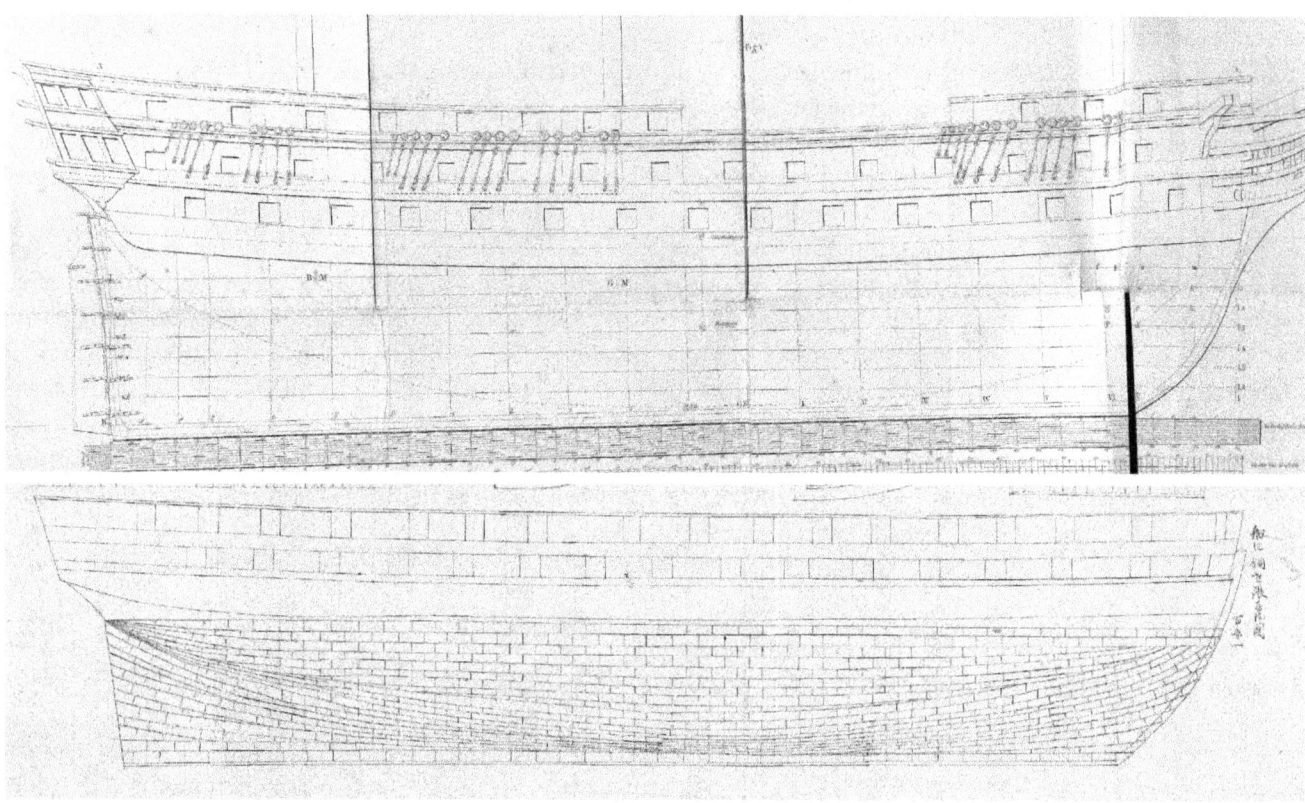

FIGURE 3. Top: *Handleiding tot de kennis in den scheepsbouw* (*Guide to knowledge in shipbuilding*), courtesy of New York Public Library; Bottom: 船散図 (Ship Scatter Plan) copy of *Handleiding tot de kennis in den scheepsbouw* (*Guide to knowledge in shipbuilding*) (Courtesy of University of Tokyo Komaba Library.)

analysis of these vessels rests on visual evidence available and is not the total sum of Western-style vessels constructed (播磨町 [Harima Town] 2021).

Asahi Maru's bow links to visual nodes seen in the VR elements, such as the stem/divide and the forward stem. Unlike earlier visual depictions, the stem is not represented by a line, with the divide likely representing the start of the bow, evidenced by cannon immediately next to the divide. The knee of the head is likely conflated with the stem, now the most forward element. A fusion chiri is likely present, with a sternpost emerging from the keel, but a smaller hole is present to horizontally access the rudder from a deck above the waterline.

Hoo Maru has an extant lines plan, possibly influenced by an imported lines plan of a cutter. The shape somewhat lines up with contemporaneous Japanese castaway depictions of whaling vessels yet has a pronounced stem. It has a very blunt bow but then the stem juts out, almost like a two-liter bottle. Evidence that the stem and bow moved forward lies on the headrails being solely decorative and the lines plan showing the stem as the forward-most element. If built-up from a lines plan of a cutter, that would also explain the stem being the most forward element. A Western-style chiri (a sternpost being merged with Japanese vernacular construction) might be present but only visible in the plans.

Shohei Maru has a stem and an external element, but the knee of the head emerges above the waterline and defeats the purpose of a cutwater/knee of the head. In the stern, a very tiny Western-style chiri is likely present above the sternpost. In *Hayatori Maru*, the stem follows the trend of moving the bow forward, conflating the stem and external elements. The stem is also exceptionally large. However, there is no chiri. In *Jingo Maru*, a large external element is present, almost identical to *Hayatori*, however, the bow curvature suggests an internal stem. Post-1853 knowledge of Western construction exists, but contemporary gaps exist for vernacular transformations to form. These likely vernacular elements disappear in later Western-style constructions.

Conclusion

Western and Japanese vernacular forms of construction merged and clashed as a result of cognitive drift as evident through the Visual Record. When approached with a continued threat of Western incursion into the maritime space, cognition and construction merge in interesting ways not caught in the historiography. Certain construction elements quickly became obsolete while others likely continued. This is a very rare case where overall cognition came years if not decades before construction, but also impacted construction in interesting ways. In some ways, it reflects this study in that it predicates the focus. The focus of this study is on a not yet found record, an analysis toward the record. Of the five vessels discussed, two wrecked and one, *Shohei Maru*, is the subject of an ongoing survey mainly due to the efforts of Randy Sasaki. The site is essential to confirm whether or not the lines of thinking are correct. The site is fundamental, but this type of analysis might be able to forecast potential gaps.

References

ADACHI, HIROYUKI
1995 Iyō no fune: Yōshikisen dōnyū to sakoku taisei, 異様の船: 洋式船導入と鎖国体制. (*Strange ships: The introduction of Western-style ships and the national isolation system.*) Shohan edition. Heibonsha, Tōkyō, Japan.

ADACHI, HIROYUKI
平成 (Heisei) 13年 (Year) 11月 (Month) 近代造船の曙 一 昇平丸・旭日丸・鳳凰丸. Kindai Zōsen No Akebono: Shohei Maru, Asahi Maru, Houou Maru. (*Modern shipbuilding: Akebono's Shohei Maru, Asahi Maru, and Houou Maru.*) Techno Marine)(第864号). 日本造船学 会誌:665–672.

BLUSSE, LEONARD
2019 Towards a Hybrid Seagoing Ship: The Transfer and Exchange of Maritime Know-How and Shipbuilding Technology Between Holland and Japan Before the Opening of Japan (1853). In *Early Global Interconnectivity across the Indian Ocean World, Volume II: Exchange of Ideas, Religions, and Technologies*, Angela Schottenhammer, editor, pp.__. Palgrave Macmillan, London, UK:221–248

文化遺産オンライン (CULTURAL HERITAGE ONLINE)
1797 長崎蘭船挽揚図解・防州喜右衛門工夫ヲ以挽揚方仕掛大略 下. (*Illustrated illustration of how to salvage the Nagasaki orchid ship - Outline of how to salvage the ship from Hoshu Kiemon's invention Part 2.*) 文化遺産オンライン. 文化遺産オンライン. (Cultural Heritage Online) <https://bunka.nii.ac.jp/heritages/detail/401388>. Accessed 4 June 2024.

DAMIAN, MICHELLE M.
2010 *Archaeology through Art: Japanese Vernacular Craft in Late Edo-Period Woodblock Prints*. Master's thesis, Department of History, East Carolina University, Greenville, NC. <https://thescholarship.ecu.edu/handle/10342/2738>. Accessed 4 June 2024.

大日本海志編纂資 (DAINIHONKAISHI COMPILATION FUNDS)
1823–1853 船散図 (Ship Scatter Plans)・東京大学学術資産等アーカイブズ共用サーバ. 大日本海志編纂資料. (*Dainihonkaishi compilation funds*) <https://iiif.dl.itc.u-tokyo.ac.jp/repo/s/kaishi/document/5c569079-8924-9b69-3dd4-265b63f9167b#?c>. Accessed 4 June 2024.

播磨町 "Harima Town"
2021   西洋型帆船の父. 播磨町. "*Father of Western-style sailing ships. Harima Town.*" <http://www.town.harima.lg.jp/kyodoshiryokan/seiyougatahannsennnotiti.html>. Accessed 4 June 2024.

Howell, David L.
2014   Foreign Encounters and Informal Diplomacy in Early Modern Japan. *The Journal of Japanese Studies* 40(2):295–327.

Rijk, Julius Constatijn
1822   *Handleiding Tot de Kennis in Den Scheepsbouw: Ten Dienste de Jonge Officieren En Adelborsten, van de Koninklijke Nederlandsche Marine.* Arbon en Krap, Rotterdam, Netherlands. <https://catalog.hathitrust.org/Record/008600743>. Accessed 4 June 2024.

Robertson, Joshua
2017   *Australian Convict Pirates in Japan: Evidence of 1830 Voyage Unearthed.* The Guardian 27 May. <https://www.theguardian.com/australia-news/2017/may/28/australian-convict-pirates-in-japan-evidence-of-1830-voyage-unearthed>. Accessed 4 June 2024.

Sakamaki, Shunzo
1939   *Japan and the United States, 1790–1853.* Scholarly Resources, Wilmington, DE.

Shmagin, Viktor
2022   The Imperial Peace of 1813: The Golovnin Incident and Tokugawa Authority in Ezo. *The Journal of Japanese Studies* 48(1):63–92.

The Schoenberg Institute for Manuscript Studies
2014   LJS 454 - Seiyō Senpaku Zukai. The Schoenberg Institute for Manuscript Studies, University of Pennsylvania, Philadelphia. <https://schoenberginstitute.org/2014/11/13/ljs-454-seiyo-senpaku-zukai/>. Accessed 4 June 2024.

Toby, Ronald P.
1991   *State and Diplomacy in Early Modern Japan: Asia in the Development of the Tokugawa Bakufu.* 1st edition. Stanford University Press, Stanford, Calif, December 1.

Yamafune, Kotaro
2012   Portuguese Ships on Japanese Namban Screens. Master's thesis, Department of Anthropology, Texas A&M University. October 19. <https://oaktrust.library.tamu.edu/handle/1969.1/ETD-TAMU-2012-08-11735>. Accessed 4 June 2024.

Wilson, Noell
2010   Tokugawa Defense Redux: Organizational Failure in the "Phaeton" Incident of 1808. *The Journal of Japanese Studies* 36(1). Society for Japanese Studies:1–32.

• • • • • • • • • • • • • •

Dante Petersen Stanley
2000 South Michigan Avenue
Apt 307
Chicago, Illinois 60616

Fully Loaded: The Contents of an 18th-Century Cannon Assemblage

Karen Martindale

In early 2023, the Conservation Research Laboratory began work on 17, 18th-century iron cannons and associated artifacts recovered during the Savannah Harbor Expansion Project. Many of these cannons had wood tampions concreted in place, protecting the contents in the bores. The contents, including rope junk wads, solid iron shot, and paper gunpowder cartridges, are currently undergoing conservation and analysis.

A principios de 2023, el Laboratorio de Investigación en Conservación, comenzó a trabajar 17 cañones de hierro del siglo XVIII y artefactos asociados recuperados durante el Proyecto de Ampliación del Puerto de Savannah. Muchos de estos cañones tenían tapones de madera concrecionados, protegiendo el contenido dentro del cañon que incluye trozos de cuerda, perdigones de hierro macizo y cartuchos de papel con pólvora que se encuentran actualmente en proceso de conservación y análisis.

Au début de 2023, le Conservation Research Laboratory a commencé à travailler sur 17 canons en fer du XVIIIe siècle et les artefacts associés récupérés lors du projet d'expansion du port de Savannah. Beaucoup de ces canons avaient des tapes en bois bétonnés en place, protégeant le contenu de leurs âmes. Le contenu, qui comprenait des bourres de corde, des boulets de fer et des cartouches de poudre à canon en papier, est actuellement en cours de conservation et d'analyse.

Project Background

In 2021, during dredging operations for the Savannah Harbor Expansion Project, the U.S. Army Corps of Engineers (USACE) discovered three cannons in the Savannah River near an area called Five Fathom Hole. Commonwealth Heritage Group, Inc., was contracted to perform additional surveys in the area and to recover archaeological resources. By the end of this process, 17 intact iron cannons, 2 damaged cannons, and 2 cannon fragments, as well as 17 associated artifacts—ammunition, anchors, and a bell fragment—were recovered (James et al. 2022:72–75).

All of the artifacts were covered in a layer of concretion, i.e., sediment that collects and hardens around marine artifacts as iron corrodes. While concretion is a byproduct of the iron corrosion process that often hinders investigation in the field, it can also help to preserve materials by protecting them from outside elements. Since the concretion made distinguishing most features difficult, the cannons were generally divided into two categories in the field: "long guns" (nos. CT 01-CT 03, which are approximately 70 in. long) and "short guns" (nos. CT 04-CT 17, which are approximately 60 in. long). Some general characteristics visible under the concretion--for example, distance between reinforcement rings, placement of the tampions, muzzle swell, and shape of the cascabel—led to the initial determination that these cannons were likely from the Revolutionary War period. This was supported by the fact that five ships were scuttled and sunk near Five Fathom Hole during the war, including HMS *Savannah* and transport *Venus*, which were sunk with their armaments (James et al. 2022:21–22). Current investigations of the cannons' diagnostic features following removal of the concretion, however, indicate the cannons may have been founded closer to 1800, and do not match any known patterns. The cannons' features and their possible origins were discussed by Carpenter (2024), and will be detailed further in future publications.

Ultimately, USACE, the Savannah History Museum, and the Coastal Heritage Society determined that 17 cannons and the associated artifacts would be sent to the Conservation Research Laboratory (CRL) at Texas A&M University for conservation. When conservation is complete, all artifacts will be curated by the Savannah History Museum.

Removal of Concretion and Contents

Upon arrival at CRL, all artifacts were stored in tanks, where they will remain submerged in water or treatment solutions until conservation is complete. All cannons were measured, weighed, and photographed; these forms of documentation are repeated throughout the treatment process to track changes. Additionally, once all concretion and contents are removed, CRL conservators document the cannons using a FaroArm to create

3D image files that can be used to generate accurate measurements, and to share with researchers and the public.

Bulbous concretion at the muzzle of some of the cannons indicated a tampion may be present; once the cannons were cleaned of concretion (Figure 1), nine of them were confirmed to have tampions in place. During their use life, these wood plugs with rope pulls in the center served to keep the cannon bores and their contents dry between naval battles. As archaeological artifacts, they are a clear indication that the cannons are loaded, and that conservators should proceed with caution; while a waterlogged cannon is highly unlikely to fire, even degraded black powder can spark in the right conditions.

FIGURE 1. Conservators use air scribes to remove concretion from a cannon. (Photo by CRL, 2023.)

To fully conserve the cannons any contents from the bores must be removed, even if those contents are fragmentary or the bore is full of sediment or concretion. When the tampions were removed, conservators found that these plugs, and the concretion that acted as an additional barrier, had preserved the contents of the cannons from pests and other agents of deterioration far better than anyone expected. Additionally, the tampions prevented sediment from entering the bores so little concretion could develop, which meant that conservators were able to unload many of the cannons with relative ease.

All cannons were loaded in the order presented in the headings of Table 1. Cannon CT 03 is notable as the exception, as it contained only the tampion, one junk wad, and the powder cartridge; this was likely a blank, or signal shot. Cannon CT 02 had no tampion and cannon CT 14 contained only fragments of a tampion. Both cannon bores were empty but fuze fragments were found in the vents, indicating they possibly were loaded when they sank into the river but that the contents came out. Cannons CT 09, CT 10, and CT 17 were missing their tampions and first junk wads, but some contents remained; that fragmentary junk wads and cartridges are in place behind the two balls supports the hypothesis that the presence of a tampion protected the contents of the other cannons even after deposition. Conservators are still working to remove concretion from the bore of cannon CT 15. In addition to the contents of the bores, more than half of the cannons also contained rope fragments in their touch holes, likely the remains of fuzes.

As each bore was unloaded, the contents were stored in water, photographed, and then organized by material and expected treatments: iron ammunition would be conserved using electrolytic reduction, the wood tampions and rope junk wads would primarily be conserved with polyethylene glycol (PEG) and freeze dried; and the cartridges would be rinsed of black powder then further assessed to determine the best treatment.

Art. No.	Tampion	Junk wad	Ball	Ball	Junk wad	Cartridge	Fuze
CT 01							
CT 02							
CT 03	F	F				F	
CT 04	F				F	F	F
CT 05							
CT 06							
CT 07							
CT 08							
CT 09					F	F	
CT 10					F	F	
CT 11							
CT 12							
CT 13							
CT 14	F						
CT 15							
CT 16							
CT 17					F	F	

TABLE 1. Contents of the 17 cannons. Gray squares indicate the item was present. The letter "F" indicates that the item is fragmentary, representing less than half of a complete example.

Ammunition

All of the cannons in the assemblage, long and short, are 6-pounders (bore diameters measure approximately 3.5 in., the diameter of a 6-pound solid shot). In addition to the 25 cannon balls removed from the bores by CRL conservators, an additional 12 pieces of ammunition were recovered from the site, all of which measure approximately 3.5-in. diameter. The associated ammunition is composed of eight barshot (four with hemispherical ends, three with cylindrical ends, and one with spherical ends), two expanding barshot with hemispherical ends, and two cannon balls. One ball has a relatively flat section with depressions that may indicate a marking, but is too worn to be certain. No other markings or diagnostic features have been identified on any of the ammunition. Like the cannons, the associated ammunition was covered in a layer of concretion. Before conservation, conservators took X-rays of the ammunition and found that most of the metal appeared to be in good condition; the wrought iron bars on the barshot and expanding barshot had begun to corrode slightly, but not enough to require additional treatments or support during conservation. The concretion was removed by conservators with pen-sized pneumatic chisels called air scribes. All ammunition is in the process of being conserved using electrolytic reduction, and will be coated in tannic acid and microcrystalline wax to protect them from the environment once conservation is complete.

Tampions, Junk Wads, and Fuzes

After photographs were taken the organic materials, like the rope junk wad and wood tampion shown in Figure 2, were transferred to individual mesh bags to allow them to be easily rinsed without excessive handling; any organics inside the bores require thorough rinsing due to the amount of black powder residue they have absorbed, which turns the first several rinse baths black within minutes. Once reasonably clean of black powder and debris, conservators removed samples from each artifact to store in a refrigerator for any future analysis that could be affected by the conservation treatments. All rope samples--junk wads, fuzes, and rope pulls from tampions--were examined under 10-25x magnification. Though many samples remain clogged with black powder, making identification difficult, all rope seems to be made of jute or hemp. Twisted fibers that may be cotton were also present, but very few. To aid in determining the age of the cannons, five rope samples were selected for radiocarbon dating; at the time of writing, CRL has not yet received the results.

Due to decades of exposure to iron, all organics have absorbed high levels of iron residue, which must be reduced before treatment can continue to prevent the iron and PEG from reacting with each other during and after conservation. At the time of writing, the organics are undergoing chelation in baths of 5% ammonium citrate dibasic in water. Once the iron levels are below 10 ppm, they will be cleaned thoroughly in water, then begin pretreatment in PEG before being freeze dried.

The exceptions to this treatment are the fuzes and other very fragile or fragmentary rope artifacts. The largest fuze fragment is only 2 cm in length, and most are represented only by a clump of fibers found in the touch hole of their respective cannons. To prevent the rinsing and treatment process from potentially causing them to fragment they were lightly rinsed in deionized water, then slowly dried between pieces of blotting paper.

Cartridges

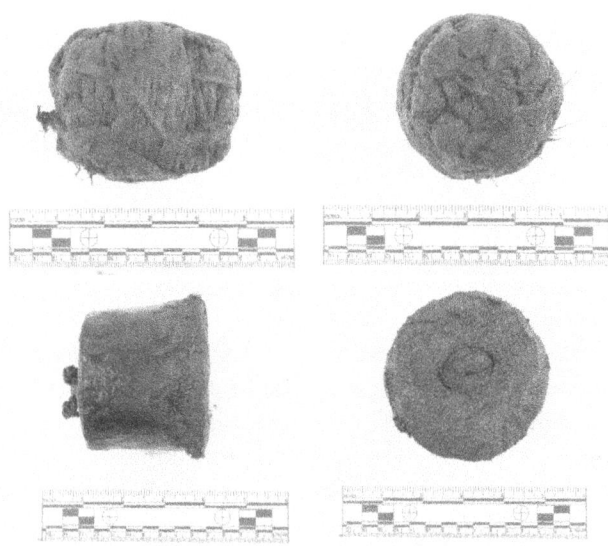

FIGURE 2. Top, a junk wad removed from cannon CT 07; bottom, a tampion removed from cannon CT05. (Photos by CRL, 2023.)

At the time of writing, 14 powder cartridges have been removed from the bores, and one cannon has not been fully cleaned of contents. Of these, five are mostly intact (missing only small fragments, if any), five are partially intact (represented by large fragments that could potentially be reassembled to form a cartridge), and five are fragmentary (represented by small pieces that cannot be reassembled). These are rare finds as such thin, organic material is usually moved away from a site by currents, eaten by marine pests, or simply degrades into nothing if not in a protective environment.

Cartridges are containers of black powder pre-measured to account for the load a cannon would be firing. Preparing cartridges ahead of time meant that gun crews did not have to measure out a load of black powder in the midst of battle, then ladle it into the bore and tamp it down. Removing these steps from the process allowed for rapid firing of cannons. There is some discrepancy on when cartridges were first used: Peterson (1969:27) states that cartridges were introduced in the second half of the 16th century, but McConnell (1988:282) states they were introduced in the early 17th century. Regardless, by the time this collection of cannons was operational the use of cartridges would have been fairly commonplace.

Since their introduction, cartridges have been made of a variety of materials, including canvas, linen, wool, paper, and parchment. Flannel was the material recommended by experts on the topic (Norton 1628; Muller 1768:200–201), as more of the material burned up during the firing reaction. This meant that flannel was ultimately safer and more efficient, as it was less likely to leave behind still-burning fragments that could cause the next round to fire unexpectedly. However, flannel was not the default material for cartridges—for British forces, at least—until well into the 19th century. Up to that point, cartridges could be made of any of the above materials or a mix of them, such as parchment or paper cartridges with flannel bottoms (McConnell 1988:282). Cartridge material was often soaked in a size (a dilute adhesive) to give them some stiffness, then folded and glued or sewn into a cylindrical or conical shape. Once filled with the correct measure of black powder, the top could be folded and glued, sewn, or tied off.

Conservators photographed the cartridges as they were unfolded (Figure 3). No signs of thread or sewing holes are visible, indicating these cartridges were folded, and possibly glued. As much black powder as possible was removed from each cartridge and stored in the refrigerator for future analysis. At this stage, the cartridges were stained black from the black powder, or orange from iron staining where the black powder did not reach. Conservators carefully transferred each cartridge to flexible plastic mesh screens to support them during the rinsing process. The cartridges were immersed in shallow baths of tap water for minutes then hours and days at a time to slowly and gently rinse out the powder.

In general, if not exposed to the elements or pests, textiles do well in water, and the treatments for waterlogged textiles are water-based. During pre-conservation photography and early rinsing, conservators noticed regular patterns on the cartridges that looked like the warp and weft of textiles. However, after several weeks of rinsing, the first three cartridges were not behaving as expected for textile. The pattern mistaken for the warp and weft of textile was in fact the lines left by paper molds (Hunter 1978:117–133).

This realization led to immediate changes in treatment plans. The first three cartridges had, at this point, been soaking in water for weeks. With guidance from Texas A&M University Libraries' conservator Jeanne Goodman, the cartridges were sandwiched between layers of Hollytex and plastic and stored flat in the refrigerator until she could assist CRL conservators with the drying process. From there, the cartridges were examined wet and arranged between layers of Hollytex, then dried between layers of blotting paper under light pressure.

FIGURE 3. The cartridge removed from cannon CT 01, before conservation. (Photo by CRL, 2023.)

For cartridges removed after March 2023, conservators established the following process: photograph cartridges as quickly as possible after removal from the bore, and remove as much black powder as possible while damp. Conservators then thoroughly rinse cartridges in tap water using the same method as before, but if the rinsing process may take multiple days, then the cartridge is stored overnight in the refrigerator. Conservators changed the water more frequently to reduce the time the paper was in water. The goal for rinsing is to reach the point where rinse water does not turn so black that the paper is obscured. The cartridges are then dried between layers of Hollytex and blotting paper.

Once dried, conservators took measurements of the paper. The intact sheets measure between 40.4–48.0 cm (15.90–18.89 in.) on the long side, 31.0–33.0 cm (12.20–12.99 in.) on the short side, and 0.34–0.71 cm (0.13–0.27 in.) thick. The weight of the intact sheets varies the most, from 23.5–50.5 g, or an average of 34.9 g. Some of the difference in weight may be due to slight variations in the dimensions of the paper, and some may be due to the presence of thin concretion on the paper.

The five intact cartridges were also inspected for the folding pattern, labeled in Figure 4, as these are the only artifact numbers that have both ends fully represented; folds are present on other artifact numbers, but are only represented as fragments. All of the intact cartridges have one end with very clear creases from being folded, and one end with possible, but very indistinct, folds. The folded ends are approximately 6.2–6.4 cm (2.44–2.51 in.) long. Interestingly, all edges with obvious folds also have a single, second fold line, approximately 9.3–9.8 cm (3.66–3.85 in.) from the edge, or 2.9–3.4 cm (1.14–1.33 in.) from the primary folds. At this time, conservators are unsure what this second fold may indicate. Since this secondary fold line is represented on all paper with primary folds, the second fold does not appear to be an accident; it possibly represents the fold line for a different charge of powder. The indistinct creases on the opposite end of the intact cartridges have no pattern, and may represent wrinkles that developed after deposition. The lack of distinct creases indicates that the upper ends were likely twisted, tied, or more loosely folded than the bottom, similar to the way cartridges for small arms are tightly folded on the bottom, and simply gathered and folded over on the top.

Fiber samples were taken from the edge of each cartridge for microscopic analysis. Unfortunately, most fibers are so clogged with black powder that it is difficult to see them well enough for identification, although strands of cotton are visible in some. Additional samples will be removed once the paper is clean.

Currently, CRL conservators are working to remove the remaining black powder, and as much iron residue as possible, using dry cleaning techniques. This primarily involves grating erasers into a fine dust and gently rubbing the dust into the paper to pick up particles of black powder, dirt, and iron residue. Some of the paper has "crusty" areas where concretion has started to form; these sections are reduced or removed using a scalpel.

Before cleaning, all cartridges are dark from black powder residue, and most have become distorted and wrinkled from deposition and treatment. Dry cleaning removes much of the black powder residue and some of the iron staining beneath it. Once the dry cleaning phase is complete, conservators will begin a second wet cleaning phase in order to further reduce the iron staining, remove wrinkles, and reposition any paper that has become warped over time or during treatment. Following wet treatment, the paper will be carefully dried one last time, and conservators will repair tears as necessary.

Throughout the cleaning process, conservators are careful to note any oddities. Cartridge CT 07.06 is the only cartridge to have cut shapes at each end: small and rectangular at the bottom; large and trapezoidal at the top. If cut intentionally, this may have facilitated a spark to reach the black powder. Cartridge CT 16.06 has a puncture hole at the bottom between the primary and secondary fold lines. The area was surrounded by concretion, indicating more iron was corroding there than other areas around the cartridge, but no iron was found in the cartridge or in the surrounding concretion. Since no rope fragments were found in the touchhole, an iron pick may have punctured the cartridge and either broke off, or was left in the touch hole and corroded away. At the time of writing, no evidence of written or printed text is apparent on any of the paper. Paper in the 18th and 19th centuries commonly had a watermark, a mark transferred to the paper from the paper mold that became visible when held up to the light (Hunter 1978:258–280). Like a maker's mark, a watermark could indicate where and when the paper was manufactured. While covered in black powder and iron residue, no watermarks are visible, but could become visible once clean.

FIGURE 4. The cartridge removed from cannon CT 01, after dry cleaning, with the primary folds (A), secondary fold (B), and indistinct top folds (C) labeled; laid lines can be seen in patches across the surface. (Photo by CRL, 2024.)

Conclusion

This assemblage provides clear evidence of the role environmental factors play in artifact preservation. Cannons without an intact tampion had no, or very fragmentary, contents, while those cannons with intact tampions had contents that were remarkably well preserved. Careful sampling and documentation of the organic material has already allowed researchers to prepare samples for radiocarbon dating, which may provide support for a later date of origin for the cannons, and further tests can be conducted as needed with the quantity of material sampled. Additionally, few extant examples of intact junk wads or paper cartridges remain from this period. Such a large collection represents a unique opportunity to study their respective manufacturing methods and preparation for use in the cannons, and to compare the archaeological artifacts to historic texts.

References

CARPENTER, ALYSSA
2024 Physical Characteristics of Seventeen Cannon from the Savannah Harbor Expansion Project (SHEP). Paper presented at the 57th Conference on Historical and Underwater Archaeology, Oakland, CA.

HUNTER, DARD
1978 *Papermaking: The History and Technique of an Ancient Craft.* Dover, New York, NY.

JAMES, STEPHEN R., WILLIAM WILSON, AND GORDON P. WATTS
2022 Submerged Cultural Resources Data Recovery of Site 38JA1178 and Artifact Recovery of Site 9CH1552 Savannah Harbor Expansion Project Savannah, Georgia. Report to U.S. Army Corps of Engineers Jacksonville District from Commonwealth Heritage Group, Inc.

MCCONNELL, DAVID
1988 *British Smooth-Bore Artillery: A Technological Study.* National Historic Parks and Sites Environment Canada – Parks, Ottawa, Canada.

MULLER, JOHN
1768 A Treatise of Artillery. Printed for John Millan, Whitehall, England. <https://play.google.com/books/reader?id=vylEAAAAYAAJ&pg=GBS.PP1&hl>. Accessed 4 June 2024.

NORTON, ROBERT
1628 The gunner shevving the vvhole practise of artillerie. Printed by A. M. for Humphrey Robinson, London, England. <https://quod.lib.umich.edu/e/eebo2/A08347.0001.001>. Accessed 4 June 2024.

PETERSON, HAROLD L.
1969 *Round Shot and Rammers: An Introduction to Muzzle-Loading Land Artillery in the United States.* Bonanza, New York, NY.

• • • • • • • • • • • • • • • •

Karen Martindale
Conservation Research Laboratory
Department of Anthropology
Texas A&M University
Anthropology Building
340 Spence St, Suite 234
College Station, Texas 77840

Arnold's Bay Project: Material Culture and Connections from a Colonial Battlefield in Lake Champlain

Cherilyn Gilligan

A little-known battlefield from the American War of Independence lies in Arnold's Bay in Panton, Vermont. In October of the 1776 campaign season, British troops made their way south from Fort St. Johns in a last attempt for the year to defeat the American fleet on Lake Champlain. The warring fleets met at Valcour Bay on 11 October and the overall engagement ended at Arnold's Bay on 13 October. This paper explores the battlefield site on land and in water, where General Benedict Arnold burned five vessels to prevent their capture and escaped with his remaining soldiers by land to Crown Point and Fort Ticonderoga. This ongoing archaeological investigation conducted by the Lake Champlain Maritime Museum was funded by the American Battlefield Protection Program and the Museum worked in collaboration with Stockbridge-Munsee Community Band of Mohican Indians, and partnered with the Advanced Metal Detecting for the Archaeologist (group.

Un campo de batalla poco conocido de la Guerra de Independencia de Estados Unidos se encuentra en Arnold's Bay en Panton, Vermont. En la campaña de octubre de 1776, las tropas británicas se dirigieron hacia el sur desde Fort St. Jean en un último intento de ese año por derrotar a la flota estadounidense en el lago Champlain. Las flotas enemigas se encontraron en la bahía de Valcour el 11 de octubre y la escaramuza general terminó en la bahía de Arnold el 13 de ese mes. Este artículo explora el lugar del campo de batalla en tierra y en agua, donde el general Benedict Arnold quemó cinco embarcaciones para evitar su captura y escapó con los soldados restantes por tierra a Crown Point y Fort Ticonderoga. Esta investigación arqueológica en curso realizada por el Museo Marítimo del Lago Champlain fue financiada por el Programa Estadounidense de Protección de Campos de Batalla y el Museo trabajó en colaboración con la Comunidad Stockbridge-Munsee, y se asoció con el grupo de Detección Avanzada de Metales para Arqueólogos.

Un champ de bataille peu connu de la Guerre d'indépendance américaine se trouve à Arnold's Bay à Panton, dans le Vermont. En octobre de la campagne de 1776, les troupes britanniques se dirigèrent vers le sud à partir du fort Saint-Jean dans une dernière tentative de l'année pour vaincre la flotte américaine sur le lac Champlain. Les flottes belligérantes se rencontrèrent à Valcour Bay le 11 octobre et l'escarmouche générale se termina à Arnold's Bay le 13 octobre. Cet article explore le site du champ de bataille sur terre et sous l'eau, où le général Benedict Arnold a brûlé cinq navires pour empêcher leur capture et s'est échappé avec ses soldats restants par voie terrestre à Crown Point et Fort Ticonderoga. Cette enquête archéologique en cours menée par le Musée maritime du lac Champlain a été financée par l'American Battlefield Protection Program et le Musée a travaillé en collaboration avec la communauté de Stockbridge-Munsee, et le groupe Advanced Metal Detecting for the Archaeologist.

Introduction

In 2020, the Lake Champlain Maritime Museum (the Museum) was awarded an American Battlefield Protection Program grant (P20AP00204) to investigate a little-known battlefield from the American War of Independence in Arnold's Bay, Panton, Vermont. Starting a project of this scale during the first year of the pandemic was a great challenge, but one benefit COVID-19 brought was time to help the Museum launch their first (now annual) Virtual Archaeology Conference to showcase research. Additional details about the last few years of the Arnold's Bay Project can be found at Lake Champlain Maritime Museum's YouTube channel where viewers can find recordings of past presentations.

The Arnold's Bay Project was carried out in collaboration with the Stockbridge-Munsee Community Band of Mohican Indians (SMC), and through a partnership with the Advanced Metal Detecting for the Archaeologist (AMDA) group in 2021 for a terrestrial course in metal detection of the shoreline and farmed fields that border the bay. The project obtained permission from private landowners for the terrestrial class, worked under Vermont State permits to access the bottomlands of the bay, and under permit from the Naval History and Heritage Command (NHHC) to access the row galley

Congress. Fieldwork in 2023 on the extant remains of *Congress* was funded by an anonymous donor, and allowed project staff to pursue the original research goals that were interrupted by the ongoing global pandemic. Under agreements with Vermont State and the Navy, the Museum will serve as a repository for these collections. Once the artifacts are conserved, the collections will be made available to the public for research. This article provides a site orientation, presents the research goals, and summarizes the last few years of the project with highlights.

The Battle of Lake Champlain

The action that took place in Arnold's Bay marked the end of a running battle up Lake Champlain and was the last naval engagement in the northern theater of the conflict in the year 1776. To place this battle in a more detailed context, the summer of 1776 during the American War of Independence had turned into a naval arms race on Lake Champlain after American forces retreated from their failed attack on Canada and returned to Lake Champlain in June. American forces began expanding their fleet in Skenesborough, present-day Whitehall, New York, while their troops regrouped to Crown Point and Fort Ticonderoga. British forces reestablished themselves at Fort St. Johns (present-day Fort St. Jean) and restarted shipbuilding efforts there (Bellico 2001:135). Control of the lake meant control of the major transportation route into the northern colonies, the ability to reach plentiful natural resources, and access to major cities in the colonies. If the British took control of Lake Champlain, they could essentially split the colonies and effectively divide and conquer the colonial forces. In defense, the Americans accelerated building a fleet that could secure their hold on the lake; in response, the British raced to reinforce their fleet for invasion.

The Americans began building more gondolas, or gunboats like *Philadelphia* and *Spitfire* (Morgan 1970:701, 731). These were flat-bottomed boats with a square mainsail and topsail on a single mast that could also be rowed with long oars or sweeps. These boats were not nimble navigators, but one great advantage to this vessel class was they could be maneuvered into shallow waters where the much larger British vessels could not follow. American gunboats were generally built around 54 ft. (feet((16.5 meter [m]) long by 15.5 ft. (4.7 m) wide and carried one large cannon on the bow (12- or 9-pounder); two smaller cannons on either side, generally 9-pounders; and eight swivel guns (Lake Champlain Maritime Museum 1995; Bellico 2001:138). American shipbuilders were also instructed to build larger row galleys, measuring between 72.0–80.0 ft. (22.0–24.4 m) in length and around 18.0 ft. (5.5 m) wide. These vessels had two masts equipped with lateen sails, and were outfitted with larger 18- and 12-pounder cannon in the bow and stern, 9-pounders or 6-pounders in the sides, and up to 16 swivel guns (Fadden 1776; Lake Champlain Maritime Museum 1995; Bellico 2001:139). Row galleys had the same advantages as the American gunboats of being able to maneuver in shallow waters and being easier to sail.

On the morning of 11 October 1776, General Benedict Arnold, with his new fleet of 15 vessels, some bateaux, and around 500 men, most of whom had little or no sailing experience, spotted the British fleet around 8:00 a.m. from their position between Valcour Island and the New York shoreline. Their unique position kept them from view of the British until they had sailed past Valcour Island, forcing them to tack and sail upwind in order to engage in battle (Fadden 1776; Morgan 1972:1235–1236; Bellico 2001:147–150).

The handful of extant primary sources about this event describe the British fleet to have had 20–28 armed warships to the Americans' 15, as well as a greater number of accompanying bateaux and soldiers. Their force included a troop of Hessian soldiers, allied Indigenous warriors, and Canadians who joined the battle from the New York shore, as well as the shores of Valcour Island (Morgan 1972:1228–1230,1235–1236; Bellico 2001:151).

The American fleet was badly damaged by the end of the first day, with their flagship *Royal Savage* crashed and burned on the southern tip of Valcour Island. The row galleys *Congress*, *Trumbull*, and *Washington* had taken significant damage to their hulls and sailing rigs. The gunboat *Philadelphia* sank from the damage caused by a cannon ball strike to its bow (Bellico 2001:153). A reported 60 Americans were killed or wounded at Valcour, and they had depleted three quarters of their ammunition. That night, what was left of the damaged American fleet was able to slip out of the bay to the south and through the British line with the aid of fog and the distraction of the burning *Royal Savage*.

The fleet continued through the night, 7.5 mi (12.0 km) to the south to Schuyler Island. Some boats stopped briefly and then continued south towards Fort Ticonderoga, but others including the row galleys *Congress* and *Washington*, needing to fix sails and leaks, took extra time. The gunboat *New Jersey* was partially scuttled at Schuyler Island and the gunboat *Spitfire* was sunk in deep water after the bulk of the fleet began moving southward once more (Morgan 1972:1275–1277).

By the evening of 12 October, the British resumed their pursuit, while the Americans struggled to row their battered fleet through the night. In the early morning of 13 October, with the help of a northern wind, the superior British vessels *Inflexible*, *Carleton*, and *Maria* came alongside the badly damaged American fleet and engaged them once again. The row galley *Washington* was overwhelmed quickly because of the damage it had already suffered, and the captain and crew struck the vessel's colors before their capture. The running battle began at Split Rock and continued over 9 miles (14.5 kilometers) south to where the row galley *Congress*, along with the gunboats *Boston*, *Connecticut*, *New Haven*, and *Providence*, were run aground in a shallow bay and ordered burned with their flags flying so they could not be captured (Baldwin 1906:80–81; Morgan 1972:1274–1275). This bay was known as Ferris Bay for the Ferris family who had a homestead there; it is located in present-day Panton, Vermont, and is now known as Arnold's Bay.

Arnold ordered his men overboard to shore to set up a line of defense against the British, who continued to fire on them from beyond the mouth of the bay (Wilkinson 1816:91; Bellico 2001:157). The large British boats could not follow into the shallow bay, measuring about 15 ft. (4.6 m) at the deepest part of the mouth. When the boats were burned beyond use, Arnold and his remaining men, along with the Ferris family from the homestead on the bay, fled on foot toward Crown Point and eventually to Fort Ticonderoga.

Project Goals, Site Formation, and Previous Archaeology

The main research goal for this project was to produce site boundary data and feature data in order to modernize our understanding of this battlefield site. This battlefield spans across land and water, requiring the development of differing methodologies to archaeologically test sample areas across the surrounding farmland, the shoreline, and along the bottomlands of the bay extending from the known location of the row galley *Congress*'s articulated remains. Primary features of interest included attempting to locate the American line of defense on land and the burning locations for the gunboats in the bay. Primary documents utilized included diary entries and letters from American and British soldiers who lived through this event (Wells 1879; Baldwin 1906; Morgan 1970, 1972, 1986; Snyder 1974; Cometti 1976; Commager and Harris 1983:222-224; Cohn 1987; Wickman 1996; Pippenger 2018). Contemporary summaries of the event written by people who were not there are extant, as are accounts from people who experienced the event as children and wrote about it in detail much later in their lives (Wilkinson 1816; Lossing 1851; von Eelking 1868; Everest 1963; Maguire 1978). Data from these sources were compared to the archaeological data generated from the 1980s excavations of the Ferris Homestead, the 1960s excavation of *Congress*, and the new data from the Arnold's Bay Project in order to determine whether they confirm or refute written accounts. All three archaeological collections mentioned are housed at the Lake Champlain Maritime Museum (Starbuck 1989; Lake Champlain Maritime Museum 1997).

Post-depositional disturbance of this site has been immense over the last nearly 250 years and began almost immediately with the British salvaging what they could off the ruined boats shortly after their burning. Locals commonly took wood from these wrecks and made mementos with it, represented today in objects like canes, rulers, gavels, and wood fragments claiming to be from *Congress* in historical societies all around Vermont and New York. It is also rumored that one of the gunboats was floated and used by the Ferris family for a time shortly after the battle (*Vermont Watchman & State Journal* 1858:1). Newspaper articles are a plentiful resource for references to the site, with notices of recovered materials from these wrecks over the course of time (Tucker 1861a:1; Tucker 1861b:1; *Vergennes Vermonter* 1866:1, 1883:1; *The Lamoille News* 1878:2; *The Yonkers Herald* 1892:7; *The Rockwood Publications* 1934:5). Three gunboats were removed from the bay by 1859 and a sail ferry began operating from the bay to the New York shore (Cohn 2001:3).

In the 1890s, an attempt to remove *Congress* from the bay broke the ship apart and approximately 30 ft. (91 m) of the stern end was dragged on shore. This piece was eventually moved to Chimney Point where it rotted away, though two floor timbers from this wreckage are in the Museum's collection. The same fate is unfortunately true for the four gunboats removed from the site, the last of which was taken out in the 1950s. The Museum houses photographs from the removal of the last gunboat along with a few sparse notes from the operation within the Peter Barranco Research Papers collection.

The first systematic exploration of Arnold's Bay occurred in 1960 and 1961 when avocational archaeologist William Leege and his team (Beverly Leege, Bob Leahy, and Oscar Bredenberg) spent a week dredging a portion of the remains of Congress and recovered a collection of artifacts. Leege donated the bulk of that archaeological collection to the Museum in 1997. In 1984, the Champlain Maritime Society (CMS, the Museum's former iteration) investigated the remains of *Congress* after consulting with Leege. The bow of the wreck was identified using Leege's locational information, remote sensing equipment, and underwater visual surveys and a dredge was employed to clear sediment. The following year, CMS continued a visual survey of the bay to locate unknown cultural features relating to the site and disarticulated remains were noted but not recovered. In 2001, the Museum returned to Arnold's Bay to inspect the site, reporting that more of the hull was exposed than was previously recorded in 1984 and that invasive zebra mussels had colonized about half of the exposed timber surfaces (Cohn 2001).

The latest research goals were focused on the row galley *Congress*. Through investigating the wreck, researchers hoped to determine what portion of the vessel remained, discover how intact that portion of the vessel was, and see if anything could be determined about the ship's construction. At this time, *Congress* is the only known row galley example that still exists, making this wreck of great interest to maritime archaeologists.

Methodology, Fieldwork, and Preliminary Conclusions

During 2021, archaeological investigations took place on land by means of a metal detecting course through the farmed fields behind Arnold's Bay and along the shoreline of the bay. The Museum partnered with the AMDA group to teach their Register of Professional Archaeologists (RPA)-certified course in chosen sample areas of the terrestrial portion of the battlefield site. In general, metal detecting in an archaeological setting is not always the best tool. In this specific case, metal detecting turned out to be an ideal tool to address the research goals of the project. A metal detecting survey allowed researchers to see the ammunition scatter across this site, which will help to determine site boundaries as well as feature data. The Museum also partnered with the SMC during this part of this project, but the COVID-19 pandemic prevented tribal members from traveling to Vermont and taking this course. Fortunately, the SMC Tribal Historic Preservation Officer (THPO) was able to join the class on site and provided a conference paper on the Stockbridge Militia and their involvement in the American War of Independence. This recorded presentation was part of the Museum's 2022 Virtual Archaeology Conference and can be found on the Museum's YouTube channel.

Sample areas for the metal detecting course were chosen and GPS points were taken at each corner of these roughly rectangular areas. Wooden stakes and twine were used to establish lanes 4.9 ft. (1.5 m) apart to maximize efficiency and to enable standardized coverage with metal detectors. The team flagged metal targets with plastic pin flags as students cleared lanes, and teams excavated targets using handheld pinpointing metal detectors if needed. GPS points were taken for each located target and artifact tags were bagged with objects containing identifying numbers, depth in centimeters, date, and initials of excavators. This survey technique was used across the surrounding farm fields, behind the Ferris homestead, and across the transitional shoreline, reaching as close to the waterline as possible.

The AMDA survey produced 276 cataloged artifacts, 131 of which were identified to be the correct time period. The survey located objects including musket balls, case shot in various sizes, a lead jaws pad or flint wrapper, a bayonet scabbard belt hook, buckle fragments, and buttons. These are all examples of personal items that might have fallen from soldiers' clothing and gear as they scrambled ashore and ran for cover as the British fired upon them from the mouth of the bay. By spatially mapping these data, we were able to see artifact density of these types of personal items in specific areas, which infers the main route that soldiers took upon reaching land after abandoning their boats. Case shot in the fields confirms the primary accounts of cannon fire in certain directions by British vessels at the mouth of Arnold's Bay. Terrestrial investigations did not determine an American line of defense, but did determine an area of the surrounding field that had been cut and filled in the recent past, possibly destroying the remains of such a feature on the battlefield. Alternatively, the remains of a line may be too ephemeral to withstand the two and a half centuries of farming that came afterwards.

During the 2021 field season, two 50.0 ft. (15.2 m) long underwater transects were established roughly north to south in orientation within close proximity to the known location of *Congress*, one to the northwest of the wreckage and one to the southeast. GPS points were taken on the north and south points, marked by buoys.

Along these transects, underwater metal detectors were used east and west of the lines, extending 3 ft. (0.9 m) in each direction, and covering the center line. Individual targets were located and dug immediately instead of using pin flags, and locational measurements along the centerline, and east or west of the lines, were recorded on underwater slates along with matching bag numbers to secure and stow finds along the way. All underwater work in the bay was carried out under a permit from the Vermont Division for Historic Preservation. Object locations were plotted using Google Earth Pro GIS mapping tools with recorded measurements. From the data gathered along these two transects, the team formed a hypothesis for the possible orientation of *Congress* before it was broken apart in the 1890s, and potentially a location for one of the burned gunboats based on the presence of melted lead and a large space of negative data along a transect. Objects found in 2021 included numerous musket balls, examples of iron case shot, a cannon ball, and a cupreous shoe buckle.

The 2022 season expanded the underwater investigations; more transects were established in-shore of the known *Congress* wreckage and existing lines were extended 50 ft. (15.2 m) farther south. Transects were placed roughly 25 ft. (7.6 m) apart. A tapering of artifact density was seen to the southern and northern ends of the transects, giving the impression of battlefield boundary lines through the density of located period-correct materials. The transect lying farthest west was closed to investigation after finding what may have been more articulated timbers potentially related to *Congress*. At that point in the project, the Museum did not yet have the necessary permit from the NHHC to be able to investigate *Congress*, so time was spent investigating site boundaries and clues about other vessel locations in the interim. Among the several hundred artifacts cataloged in 2022, examples of personalized items were found including a spoon handle engraved with the initials 'A.P.,' as well as a glass-lined cupreous inkwell, a hand grenade with the wooden fuse still in place, two bayonet examples, a two-tined fork with a bone handle, and the cupreous hinge from a folding ruler, among many more. In addition to mapping all located metal objects, the ballast pile to the north of *Congress*'s remains was also mapped in the GIS. This pile was apparently moved off the wreckage during the 1960s underwater investigation.

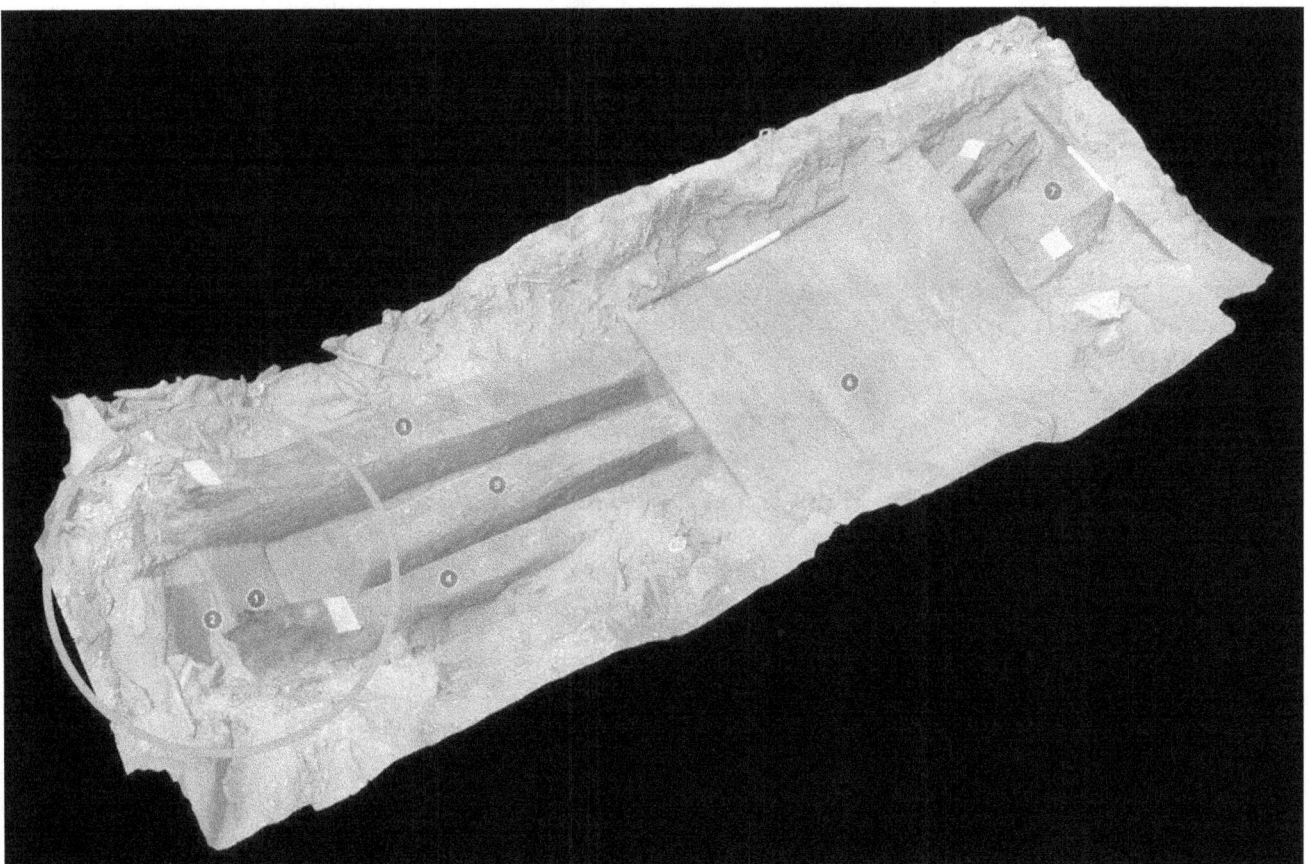

FIGURE 1: Photogrammetry model of *Congress*, Trench 2022, keel circled in red. (Courtesy of Lake Champlain Maritime Museum, Vergennes, Vermont.)

FIGURE 2: Photogrammetry model of the extent of dredge work, 2023. (Courtesy of Lake Champlain Maritime Museum, Vergennes, Vermont.)

During the last week of the project in 2022, the Museum received the NHHC archaeological permit needed to investigate the remains of *Congress*. In the following five days, a single trench across the wreckage was excavated using an induction dredge. The team recovered and documented artifacts in situ, and locational data for objects found in spoil bags were recorded using diver dredging locations. This single trench revealed that the assumed orientation of the wreckage was incorrect. The two sets of visible frame tips were not each side of the vessel with a keel at the center, but instead the keel was located to one side of the frame tips, where the side of the vessel broke away from the keel. The 3D photogrammetry model of the trench excavated in 2022 can be seen in Figure 1 where the keel is circled in red.

In 2023, the crew worked to uncover more of the remaining side of the vessel and to determine how much of the keel was present along the intact portion. The crew was also able to lay two additional underwater transects perpendicular to the others (east to west) that could test farther west of the site than previously reached. The second transect was positioned across an area hypothesized to be a location of one of the burned gunboats. The final photogrammetry model of *Congress*, produced by Chris Sabick, can be seen in Figure 2.

This imagery shows that *Congress* was built using an open framing technique, not uncommon for the time period, where many of the framing components are not attached to each other, and instead are fastened only to the hull and ceiling planking. Using the final photogrammetry model of the extent of the dredge work from 2023, *Congress*'s hull shape was extracted and compared to the historical lines drawing produced from its twin ship, *Washington* (Coleman 1776). This exercise helped to determine that the excavated portion of *Congress* is the forward section of the starboard side of the hull, which extends aft to near amidships.

A total of 245 objects were produced from the excavation of *Congress*, including animal bones, seeds, a cupreous scabbard tip, buckle fragments, melted lead, musket balls, glass, nails, brick, a trigger guard, buttons, a boot, and more. Artifacts are still being examined and conserved, meaning reported numbers may change as more data are generated. Further research is pending on the musket ball collection and more information will be shared through Lake Champlain Maritime Museum's social media accounts and detailed reports about the Arnold's Bay Project.

References

BALDWIN, THOMAS WILLIAMS
1906   The Revolutionary Journal of Col. Jeduthan Baldwin, 1775–1778. C.H. Glass & Company, Bangor, ME. <https://www.loc.gov/item/07001320/>. Accessed 17 May 2024.

BELLICO, RUSSELL P.
2001   *Sails and Steam in the Mountains: A Maritime and Military History of Lake George and Lake Champlain, Revised Edition.* Purple Mountain Press, New York, NY.

Cohn, Art

1987   An Incident Not Known to History: Squire Ferris and Benedict Arnold at Ferris Bay, October 13, 1776. *Vermont History* 55(2):95–112.

2001   Galley Congress Inspection Report. Report to Naval Historical Center, Department of Defense Legacy Resource Management Program, Washington Navy Yard, Washington DC, from Lake Champlain Maritime Museum, Vergennes, VT.

COLEMAN, JONATHAN
1776   *Washington Ship Plans.* National Maritime Museum Collections, Greenwich, UK.

COMETTI, ELIZABETH
1976   *The American Journals of Lt. John Enys.* Syracuse University Press, Syracuse, NY.

COMMAGER, HENRY STEELE, AND RICHARD B. MORRIS
1983   *The Spirit of Seventy-Six: The Story of the American Revolution As Told By Participants.* Bonanza Books, New York, NY.

EVEREST, ALLAN S.
1963   A British View on The Battle of Valcour. North Country Notes Issued Occasionally by the Clinton County Historical Association 13(April):2-3. Clinton County Historical Association, Plattsburgh, NY. <www.clintoncountyhistorical.org/files/newsletters>. Accessed 17 May 2024.

FADEN, WILLIAM
1776   *The Attack and Defeat of the American Fleet under Benedict Arnold by the King's Fleet Commanded by Sir Guy Carleton, Upon Lake Champlain in "11th of Octr." 1776.* Manuscript, Library of Congress, Washington, DC.

LAKE CHAMPLAIN MARITIME MUSEUM
1776   *A Return of the fleet belonging to the United State of America on Lake Champlain under the Command of Brigadier General Arnold together with the Names of the Capt.'s, Vessels, ye Ticonderoga, October 22, 1776.* Document on file, Lake Champlain Maritime Museum Collection, Vergennes, VT.

1995   Lake Champlain, Lake George, and Upper Richelieu River Naval and Military Vessel Inventory *1742–1836.* Digital document, Peter Barranco Research Papers, Lake Champlain Maritime Museum Collection, Vergennes, VT.

1997   Bill Leege Collection. Archaeological Objects and Research Papers, Lake Champlain Maritime Museum Collection, Vergennes, VT.

LOSSING, BENSON J.
1851   *The Pictorial Field-Book of the Revolution: Or Illustrations, by pen and pencil, of the history, biography, scenery, relics, and traditions of the war for independence, Vol. 1.* Harper & Brothers, New York, NY. <https://babel.hathitrust.org/cgi/pt?id=miun.abp1224.0001.001&seq=11>. Accessed 17 May 2024.

MAGUIRE, ROBERT J.
1978   Dr. Robert Knox's Account of the Battle of Valcour, October 11–13, 1776. *Vermont History* 3:141–150.

MORGAN, WILLIAM J. (EDITOR)
1970   *Naval Documents of the American Revolution, Vol. 5, American Theatre: May 9, 1776–July 31, 1776.* Naval History Division, Department of the Navy, Washington DC.

1972   *Naval Documents of the American Revolution, Vol. 6, American Theatre: Aug.1, 1776–Oct.31, 1776; European Theatre: May 26, 1776–Oct. 5, 1776.* Naval History Division, Department of the Navy, Washington DC.

1986   *Naval Documents of the American Revolution, Vol. 9, American Theatre: June 1, 1777–July 31, 1777; European Theatre: June 1, 1777–Sept. 30, 1777; American Theatre: Aug. 1, 1777–Sept.30, 1777.* Naval History Division, Department of the Navy, Washington DC.

PIPPENGER, C. E.
2018   Finding Edward Wigglesworth's Lost Diary. Journal of the American Revolution website. <https://allthingsliberty.com/2018/10/finding-edward-wigglesworths-lost-diary/>. Accessed 17 May 2024.

SNYDER, CHARLES M.
1974   With Benedict Arnold at Valcour Island: The Diary of Pascal De Angelis. *Vermont History: The Proceedings of the Vermont Historical Society* 42(3):195–200.

STARBUCK, DAVID R.
1989   *The Ferris Site on Arnold's Bay: A Research and Educational Program of the Lake Champlain Maritime Museum.* Lake Champlain Maritime Museum, Vergennes, VT.

THE LAMOILLE NEWS
1878   Man-of-War Sunk. *The Lamoille News* 3 April, 1(51):2. Hyde Park, VT.

The Rockwood Publications
1934　Find Old Cannon in Lake at Arnold's Bay, Anchor and Cannon Ball of Revolutionary Days also Discovered. *The Rockwood Publications* 24 August:5. Orwell, VT.

The Yonkers Herald
1892　Benedict Arnold's Flagship. *The Yonkers Herald* 8 December:7. Yonkers, NY.

Tucker, Philip C.
1861a　General Arnold and the *Congress* Galley. *The Vermonter* 8 February. Vergennes, VT.

1861b　For the Vermonter: No. II. *The Vermonter* 15 March. Vergennes, VT.

Vergennes Vermonter
1866　General Arnold and the Congress Galley. *Vergennes Vermonter* 14 September, 12(21):1. Vergennes, VT.

1883　Revolutionary Incidents. *Vergennes Vermonter* 27 July, 29(17):1. Vergennes, VT.

Vermont Watchman & State Journal
1858　Historical. From the Vergennes Citizen, Local History, Revolutionary Scenes, 1775. *Vermont Watchman & State Journal* 26 February, 52(14):1. Montpelier, VT.

von Eelking, Max
1868　*Memoirs and Letters and Journals, of Major General Riedesel, During His Residence in America, Vol. 1*, William L. Stone, translator. J. Munsell, Abany, NY.

Wells, Bayze
1879　Journal of Bayze Wells of Farmington: May, 1775–February, 1777, At the Northward and in Canada. *Collections of the Connecticut Historical Society* 7:241–296. Providence College Digital Commons, Providence, RI. <https://digitalcommons.providence.edu/primary/21/>. Accessed 17 May 2024.

Wickman, Donald
1996　A Most Unsettled Time on Lake Champlain: The October 1776 Journal of Jahiel Stewart. V*ermont History: The Proceedings of the Vermont Historical Society* 64(2):89–98.

Wilkinson, James
1816　*Memoirs of My Own Times*. Abraham Small, Philadelphia, PA.

• • • • • • • • • • • • • • • •

Cherilyn Gilligan
Lake Champlain Maritime Museum
4472 Basin Harbor Road
Vergennes, Vermont 05491

Wrecks and Williwaws: Archival Identification of Shipwrecks in Shemya and the Semichi Islands, Alaska

Kendra Kennedy

The history of World War II is replete with stories of famous maritime losses such as Arizona, Royal Oak, Bismarck, *and* Yamato; *these names are etched into our collective memory. But the losses of non-naval vessels are often less well known. This is especially true in distant theaters like the Aleutian Islands, which stretch for over 1,000 miles from Alaska almost to Russia's Kamchatka Peninsula. The Aleutian Campaign of World War II is sometimes called the Forgotten War so it is unsurprising that the identity of vessels wrecked around Shemya Island—now the home of Eareckson Air Station—had also been forgotten. Dedicated archival research, particularly at the Alaska State Historic Preservation Office, the University of Alaska Anchorage, and Alaska Pacific University (UAA/APU) Consortium Library in Anchorage, brought to light several vessels that met their end in the Semichi Islands on the far reaches of the Aleutian chain.*

La historia de la Segunda Guerra Mundial está repleta de historias de famosas pérdidas marítimas. Arizona, Royal Oak, Bismarck, Yamato; *estos nombres están grabados en la memoria colectiva. Pero las pérdidas de buques no navales suelen ser menos conocidas. Esto es especialmente cierto en teatros distantes como las Islas Aleutianas, que se extienden por más de 1.000 millas desde Alaska casi hasta la península rusa de Kamchatka. La campaña de las Aleutianas de la Segunda Guerra Mundial a veces se llama la Guerra Olvidada. Por lo tanto, no sorprende que también se haya olvidado la identidad de un naufragio en el puerto de Alcan, en la isla Shemya (ahora sede de la estación aérea Eareckson). Una investigación de archivo en la Oficina de Preservación Histórica del Estado de Alaska y la Biblioteca del Consorcio UAA/APU en Anchorage, sacó a la luz la desgarradora historia de un barco de suministros que encalló en el puerto rocoso justo antes de la Navidad de 1943 y encontró su final durante una tormenta de enero de1944 en una gran tormenta de las Aleutianas conocidas como williwaw.*

L'histoire de la Seconde Guerre mondiale regorge d'histoires de pertes maritimes célèbres. Arizona, Royal Oak, Bismarck, Yamato; *ces noms sont gravés dans la mémoire collective. Mais les pertes de navires non militaires sont souvent moins bien connues. Ceci est particulièrement vrai sur des théâtres éloignés comme celui des îles Aléoutiennes, qui s'étendent sur plus de 1 000 miles de l'Alaska presque jusqu'à la péninsule russe du Kamtchatka. La campagne des Aléoutiennes de la Seconde Guerre mondiale est parfois appelée la guerre oubliée. Il n'est donc pas surprenant que l'identité d'une épave dans le port d'Alcan, sur l'île Shemya—qui abrite aujourd'hui la base aérienne d'Eareckson—ait également été oubliée. Des recherches archivistiques dédiées, en particulier au Alaska State Historic Preservation Office et à la UAA/APU Consortium Library à Anchorage, ont mis en lumière l'histoire déchirante d'un navire de ravitaillement qui s'est échoué dans le port rocheux juste avant Noël 1943 et a connu sa fin en janvier 1944 lors d'un Williwaw, une tempête majeure des Aléoutiennes.*

Introduction

Eareckson Air Station (EAS), located on Shemya Island in Alaska, serves as a trans-Pacific communications hub and an emergency diversion airfield for both military and civilian aircraft. The host unit for the base is the Pacific Regional Support Center under the command of Pacific Air Forces. Shemya Island belongs to the Semichi Islands, which include Alaid and Nizki Islands as well as two islets, Lotus Island and Hammerhead Island. The Semichi Islands form part of the Near Islands, together with Attu and Agattu Islands (Figure 1). The Near Islands, in turn, form part of the Aleutian Islands chain, which stretches over 1,000 miles from Alaska almost to Russia's Kamchatka Peninsula.

On behalf of the United States Department of the Air Force (DAF), Argonne National Laboratory (Argonne) conducted research into shipwrecks around Shemya and the Semichi Islands to determine the potential for historic maritime archaeological sites, particularly shipwrecks, in ALCAN Harbor at EAS. The research was conducted to aid EAS in managing historic properties under its jurisdiction as required by the National Historic Preservation Act of 1966, as amended, as well as Department of Defense and DAF instructions, manuals, and policies.

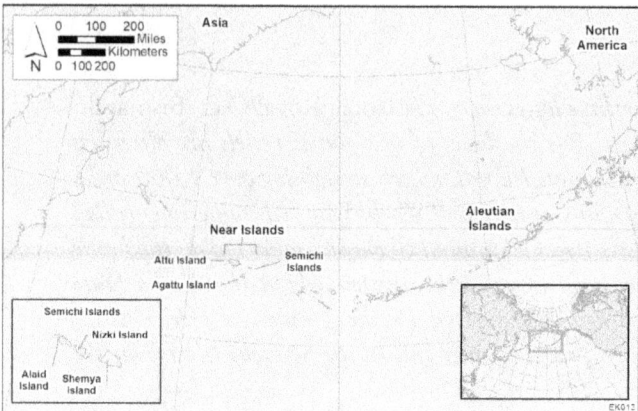

FIGURE 1. Map of the Near Islands, Aleutian Island Chain, Alaska (Argonne 2024.)

History of Shemya Island

Despite the isolated location of the Near Islands in the vastness of the Pacific Ocean and Bering Sea, Shemya has a fascinating history. Settlement of the Near Islands by Aleut people appears to have occurred sometime between 2,550 and 550 B.C., relatively late for the Aleutian Islands, which were gradually settled westward starting around 7,050 B.C. Russian exploitation of the Near Islands began in A.D. 1745 and continued through 1867, when the United States (U.S.) purchased Alaska (Corbett et al. 2010; Argonne 2021). Japan's surprise invasion of Attu and Kiska Islands during the Battle of Midway in June 1942, only six months after the attack on Pearl Harbor, turned America's attention to the Aleutian Islands. The American military responded with new bases in the Aleutians (Morrisette 1988; Lancaster 1990). By early 1943, Shemya Island—Code name: Voluble, APO 729—was chosen for construction of an airfield because of its proximity to Attu, its flat topography, and its comparatively long stretches without heavy fog (Ross 1969; Morrisette 1988).

As the battle on Attu was coming to an end in May 1943, U.S. Army 4th Infantry and 18th Engineer Regiments landed on Shemya to begin construction of an airfield. Tank landing ships (LSTs), tank landing crafts (LCTs), tank landing barges (BTLs), and power barges—or barges, self-propelled (BSPs)—unloaded the troops and supplies needed to construct a landing strip, harbor facilities, and more (Argonne 2021). Once airfield construction was underway, focus turned to breakwaters and docks to facilitate transport of supplies to the island. Until docks could be completed, supplies had to be transferred from ships to shallow-draft lighters, BSPs, or LSTs and then unloaded onto the beach or ramps. Work barely ceased, since the desolate island had to be supplied with almost all necessities.

Almost no sooner than ramps, breakwaters, or docks could be constructed, severe Aleutian storms, called williwaws, washed them away and construction began anew (Rust 1944; Van Arsdol 1983; Morrisette 1988). The official history of the 420th Port Company on Shemya addresses the harbor's failings: "Shemya's harbor was completely unprotected from the northwest, from the north, from the northeast, and opened out directly on the trackless expanses of the Bering Sea, one of the stormiest stretches of water in the world" (Van Arsdol 1983:17). Through the war years, construction of harbor facilities continued unabated but with the end of all hostilities in August 1945, Shemya Air Base was rapidly demobilized.

From the end of WWII to 1949, only limited personnel remained on Shemya and construction of new facilities ceased. Shemya provided critical missile tracking and test monitoring facilities during Russia's missile testing activities from 1957 to the end of the Cold War. Phased array radars were constructed in the 1970s and replaced conventional radars at the installation. Designated Cobra Dane, these arrays could track missiles with multiple warheads and saw significant use until the end of the Cold War. Shemya Air Force Station was renamed EAS in 1994 and converted to contractor operations and maintenance in 1995 (Argonne 2021). Today, EAS continues to be operated and maintained for the DAF with contractor support.

Methods

During the course of the project, Argonne reviewed numerous published and DAF documents; historical United States Coast and Geodetic Survey (USCGS) and National Oceanic and Atmospheric Administration (NOAA) charts (NOAA 2023); unpublished sources; and several shipwreck databases and websites, including the Bureau of Ocean Energy Management's (BOEM) "Alaska Shipwreck table" (BOEM 2011) and the "Alaska Shipwrecks" website (Good 2023). The author conducted dedicated research at the Alaska Office of History and Archaeology in Anchorage, which serves as the State Historic Preservation Office, and the University of Alaska Anchorage/Alaska Pacific University Consortium Library, which includes collections from several former

Shemya military personnel. Additional information was obtained from national and regional repositories. This research resulted in the identification of a shipwreck in ALCAN Harbor as well as evidence that at least five other vessels are known to have wrecked near Shemya Island. These results are summarized below.

Results

Potential Wrecks Near Shemya Island

Potential wrecks off Shemya Island identified in archival collections include one J-boat and at least one barge. The J-boat overturned and sank in late 1943 or early 1944 during salvage of a wreck in ALCAN Harbor (Rust 1944). Sources do not indicate exactly where the J-boat sank other than within the harbor. The barge, or barges, were photographed by two individuals stationed on Shemya at different times.

Cesare Carlucci, who served with the 18th Engineer Regiment on Shemya Island during World War II, took one of the photographs sometime between May 1943 and 1945. In Carlucci's photo, a barge is clearly grounded and numerous individuals are visible both on the barge and next to it (Figure 2). A few of the men next to the barge appear to be carrying a long, narrow object. It is not clear whether they are removing the item or bringing it to the barge (Carlucci [1943–1945]). The barge's exact location on Shemya's coast cannot be ascertained because the photograph lacks any unique reference points. Henry Frese, a photographic laboratory technician and aerial photographer at Shemya Air Base from December 1944 to March 1946, took the other photograph, which apparently shows a wrecked landing barge on a shoal (Frese [1944–1946]a). The barge, marked with a white arrow, is barely visible in the foreground. The barge pictured in Frese's photograph is possibly the same as that shown in Carlucci's photograph, but not enough details are visible to confirm. Since the photograph shows Alaid and Nizki Islands in the distance, triangulating the location of the wreck in ALCAN Harbor today may be possible to investigate whether any structure remains.

These vessels may have been refloated and put back into service after they wrecked. Regardless, these records demonstrate that the wrecks of smaller craft and barges may still be present in ALCAN Harbor, especially considering the many small vessels used in difficult weather conditions during Shemya's hectic WWII years.

FIGURE 2. Barge washed ashore, Shemya Island, ca. 1943 to 1945 (Carlucci [1943–1945].)

Lotus Island Wreck

An unknown wreck off Lotus Island, an islet between Shemya and Nizki Islands, was noted on charts but could not be definitively identified during this study. A 1945 USCGS chart of Shemya Island first depicts what appear to be a small pier and a wreck off the southeast portion of Lotus Island. The pier and the wreck are also depicted on a 1947 chart of Shemya Island and on a 1948 chart of Alaid and Nizki Islands. Neither the pier nor the wreck appear on a 1950 chart of Shemya nor on a 1969 chart of Alaid and Nizki Islands (USCGS 1945, 1947, 1948, 1950, 1969). Based on the information provided on the chart, the wrecking event probably occurred in 1943 or 1944.

Since the pier and wreck no longer appear on charts after 1950, the pier and wreck may have been removed or simply deteriorated to such an extent that they were no longer visible and/or no longer served as hazards to navigation. Archival research online and in various repositories did not reveal any mention of a pier or wreck off Lotus Island. Since the first use of the name "Lotus Island" appears to date to a 1948 chart, any primary accounts of the construction of the pier and the wrecking event might not utilize the island's name (USCGS 1948). Additional research is needed to determine the construction history of the pier and the identity of the Lotus Island wreck.

Russian Shitik Sv. Petr i Pavel

Petr i Pavel was a Russian fur-trading shitik, a type of broad-bottomed vessel used for coastal trade and initial Russian exploitation of the Aleutian Islands. *Petr i Pavel* made several trips to the Near Islands to collect furs in the 1750s and early 1760s. The vessel was captained by Petr Bashmakov and owned by merchants Andrei Serebrennikov and Ivan Rybinskii (from Moscow) and Stepan Tyrin (from Yaroslavl) when it wrecked off Shemya Island in 1762. The *Petr i Pavel* that wrecked on Shemya may be the same shitik that was built from the wreck of *Ieremiia* (or *Ieremiya*) in 1753. The shitik *Ieremiia*, also skippered by Bashmakov and owned by Serebrennikov and Rybinskii, wrecked off an unknown island (possibly Adak) on 2 September 1753. The crew survived and were able to return home on a ship they built from the wreck of *Ieremiia*, which they named *Petr i Pavel* (Makarova 1975; Grinëv and Bland 2011).

From 1756 to 1761, Bashmakov made successful fur-trading trips to the Aleutian Islands on a vessel named *Petr i Pavel*, possibly the same vessel built from *Ieremiia* or another with the same name. In 1762, during another fur-trading trip, *Petr i Pavel* wrecked close to shore on Shemya Island; Bashmakov and the crew survived. Some built a baidara, a large skin boat, that they sailed to Attu Island, while others remained on Shemya. The survivors who made it to Attu were rescued by *Zakhari i Elizaveta*; those who remained on Shemya were picked up by *Ioann Ustiuzhskii* in 1763 (Makarova 1975; Black 1983; Black and Desson 1986; Grinëv and Bland 2011). Available sources do not indicate exactly where *Petr i Pavel* wrecked, but since what is now known as ALCAN Harbor was one of the few sheltered anchorages, *Petr i Pavel* possibly wrecked in the harbor. Further research into Russian archives could potentially provide more information about the location of the shipwreck.

American Schooner Trilby

Another known wreck near the Semichi Islands is the American schooner *Trilby*, which wrecked off Alaid Island in 1914 (McKenzie 1964). Information from available wreck databases and websites lists only "Semichi Island" as the wrecking location for *Trilby* (BOEM 2011; Good 2023). Since the Semichi Island group is made up of Alaid, Nizki, and Shemya Islands, research was conducted to determine whether the wreck occurred off Shemya Island.

According to U.S. Department of Commerce, Bureau of Navigation (BN) annual lists of merchant vessels, the 12-ton wooden schooner *Trilby* was built in 1901 in Anacortes, Washington, at 51.5 ft. in length and 12.3 ft. in breadth with a depth of hold of 4.2 ft. The vessel carried a crew of two and was originally homeported out of Juneau, Alaska (BN 1914, 1915). The official wreck report (Larsen 1916) indicates that *Trilby* sailed out of Unalaska on 20 August 1913, with a crew of two bound for Attu Island. The master was A. B. Somerville (also spelled "Sommerville" and "Summerville"), owner and manager of the village store on Attu. According to the report, the wreck occurred in November 1914 on "Semechie Island. 21 miles from Attu," when the vessel stranded after drifting onto the beach during a night of heavy wind and swells. Although the crew threw out two anchors, they could not control the vessel. *Trilby* was valued at $1,000 and was carrying a cargo of about two tons of general merchandise worth $500. Although the report indicates the crew survived and no cargo was lost or damaged, the vessel itself was a total loss (Larsen 1916). A microfilm copy of the wreck report contains additional written annotations, which specify that the wreck occurred on the "western extremity" of the islands (U.S. Coast Guard 1916).

Further research revealed several errors in the wreck report as well as more details about the wrecking. According to the BN annual lists, *Trilby*'s official number was 145688, but the wreck report lists the official number as 145876 (BN 1914, 1915; Larsen 1916). In addition, *Trilby* probably left Unalaska in August 1914, not 1913, and the vessel wrecked in the Semichi Islands in August or September of 1914, not in November 1914. Although the wreck report records that no assistance was rendered to *Trilby*, the survivors were rescued and aid was provided by the U.S. Revenue Cutter (USRC) *Tahoma*. According to the account of Dan J. McKenzie, a young coal passer on USRC *Tahoma*, Captain Richard O. Crisp and the crew of *Tahoma* arrived at Attu Island in September 1914 and learned that *Trilby* had been missing for three weeks. The crew of *Tahoma* searched for three days and found *Trilby* stranded on Alaid Island. Attempts were made to refloat the vessel, but when these efforts were unsuccessful *Tahoma* transported Captain Somerville and his crew of 10 Aleuts to Attu Island (McKenzie 1964).

Shortly after assisting *Trilby*'s crew, *Tahoma* itself wrecked on an uncharted reef east of Shemya Island and south of Buldir Island. The crew and passengers managed to escape on *Tahoma*'s small boats (McKenzie 1964). After about 60 hours of constant rowing in variable weather, McKenzie and 25 others on the sailing launch found themselves just off the eastern end of Alaid Island. McKenzie's (1964:52) account clarifies that the crew members knew the island because *Tahoma* had assisted the schooner *Trilby* at that location:

> We recognized the island because we had been there a short time before with the ship. There was a small harbor about ten miles from where we were and there a 100-ton schooner, the TRILBY, had blown ashore in a storm. We had anchored not far from the harbor while some of the officers and men of the TAHOMA tried unsuccessfully to salvage the schooner. So we knew where we were, even if nobody else did.

Trilby was still beached on the shore, so the survivors of *Tahoma* used the remains of *Trilby* and its cargo for shelter and supplies until they were able to signal a passing freighter, the Alaska Steamship Company's *Cordova*. *Cordova* took the sailing launch survivors onboard, where they quickly learned that the steamer had already rescued survivors from three of *Tahoma*'s other small boats. The remaining crew members were rescued by the USCGS ship *Patterson* (McKenzie 1964). Despite conflicting information, the various accounts of *Trilby*'s stranding and salvage efforts indicate that it likely wrecked on the southeastern side of Alaid Island.

American Steam Screw Scotia

Built by the Manitowoc Ship Building Company of Manitowoc, Wisconsin, in 1919, SS *Scotia* was a 2,711-ton, 1,500-horsepower, steel-hulled steam screw with a triple-expansion steam engine from the Nordberg Manufacturing Company. The vessel began its life as SS *Lake Galewood*, measuring 253.5 ft. in length and 43.9 ft. in breadth, with a depth of hold of 25.9 ft. The vessel's draft ranged from 10.75 ft. in ballast to 24 ft. when fully loaded. The vessel had two decks, two masts, a rounded or elliptical stern, and a crew of 41. Intended for service as an ocean freighter for the U.S. Shipping Board (USSB), the vessel's official number was 219120. The vessel carried 199,386 gallons of fuel oil, could attain a speed of 9.5 knots, and had a dead-weight capacity of 4,050 tons (Collector of Customs [CC] 1944).

Once launched and registered in 1919, *Lake Galewood* made its way from Manitowoc to Cleveland, Ohio, then to Montreal, Quebec, then to Baltimore, Maryland, where it participated in the coasting trade. In 1926, the USSB sold *Lake Galewood* to the Peninsular State Steamship Corporation (PSSC) of New York for $25,000 (USSB 1926). Frank W. Irvine, Vice President of the PSSC, sailed *Lake Galewood* to New York City. From June 1926 to late 1929, *Lake Galewood* hauled freight along the Atlantic and Gulf coasts for the PSSC (CC 1944). In December 1929, Benjamin S. Free purchased the vessel on behalf of Robert C. Sudden of San Francisco. *Lake Galewood* arrived in San Francisco in April 1930 (CC 1944).

Robert C. Sudden transferred ownership of *Lake Galewood* to the Pacific Lumber Company (PLC) in October 1934. The PLC was one of the largest lumber companies in Humboldt County, California, with the company logging town of Scotia located on the Eel River about 250 mi north of Sacramento (Wilson 2001). The PLC changed the vessel's name to *Scotia* in December 1934. From 1934 to 1939, *Scotia* (Figure 3) traveled up and down the Pacific coast hauling lumber for the PLC to the ports of San Francisco, Oakland, Eureka, and Los Angeles; records indicate the vessel made 82 voyages for the company (CC 1944; Doolaege 1962).

After 1939, the PLC chartered the vessel to Grace Lines for use in the Central American coffee trade, and to Coastwide Lines. In July 1941, the vessel was chartered

FIGURE 3. *Scotia* (name visible on bow), location unknown, post-1934 (Alaska State Library Historical Collections [1930s].)

by the War Shipping Administration and allocated a year later to the War Department, Transportation Corps (Doolaege 1962). *Scotia* made 20 voyages between 1941 and 1943, including 3 trips to Alaska. No details are available about the vessel's January 1942 trip. In May 1943, *Scotia*, carrying a load of airfield landing mats, was involved in the invasion of Attu Island. From July to September 1943, *Scotia* was drydocked in Seattle, Washington, while the government spent $500,000 outfitting the vessel for war (Doolaege 1962). *Scotia*'s last trip to Alaska in September 1943 would also be the vessel's final voyage.

In September 1943, *Scotia* accepted a load of lumber in Seattle and headed to the Aleutians. The lumber was offloaded on Attu Island and *Scotia* accepted a partial load of general cargo for Shemya Island, which included three reels of lead-sheathed marine copper cable to be used for completing the cable line from Dutch Harbor to Attu, a movie projector for the base theater, holiday wrist watches, Christmas beer for the military personnel on Shemya, and fresh rations. *Scotia* entered ALCAN Harbor on 23 December 1943 in weather that was fast worsening; winds had begun to increase, and slow, heavy swells were rolling into the harbor (Doolaege 1962; Van Arsdol 1983). Just as *Scotia* steamed past the harbor's submarine net, heading for the small barge dock, "a heavy swell lifted her up and carried her past the end of the pier. The skipper put his helm hard to port to get away from the beach and it looked like the vessel was in the clear when another large swell lifted her up dramatically and she settled down on a hitherto unknown submerged rock pinnacle" (Van Arsdol 1983:19). SS *Scotia* had made its last voyage.

Upon grounding, *Scotia* listed immediately and waves began crashing over the vessel (Figure 4). Personnel on Shemya Island scrambled to assist the grounded *Scotia* in the harbor. As darkness fell, the heavy seas worsened and icy sleet began falling. Shemya personnel, including men of the 420th Port Company, set out in small dories and lighters to rescue *Scotia*'s crew. As vessels pulled alongside, crews threw ropes up to men on *Scotia*, who held tight as their fellow crewmembers jumped onto the pitching decks of the small boats. After numerous trips, all 52 men aboard *Scotia* were saved (Rust 1944; Doolaege 1962; Van Arsdol 1983). Despite the howling winds, lashing sleet, and heaving seas, no lives were lost.

Once *Scotia*'s crew were all accounted for, salvage began in earnest. The aft hatches had filled with water,

FIGURE 4. Wreck of the *Scotia*, ALCAN Harbor, ca. 1943 (Suckling [1943–1944]).

while the forward hatches were partially flooded. The aft hatches were filled with supplies for the Post Exchange (PX), including radios and watches. The men of the 420th Company were tasked with removing the deck load from the aft hatches and salvaging anything they could from the forward hatches. Since steam power and winches were unavailable, all cargo had to be removed by hand. Salvage continued through Christmas Day and New Year's Day, despite near constant storms. Work continued even at night; anti-aircraft searchlights were set up on the bluff towering over the beach to illuminate the scene. Salvagers used gas lanterns and flashlights to light the interior of the ship, but efforts were made to provide better illumination. The J-boat mentioned above overturned and sank while attempting to supply generators for lighting purposes (Rust 1944; Van Arsdol 1983).

At some point, *Scotia*'s bow broke off and sank but work continued, ceasing only when the ship broke in half in early January 1944. By that time, over 600 tons of freight had been removed by sliding materials over the side on planks or rolling it down nets, all by hand. Salvaged items included *Scotia*'s 20-mm machine guns, radio equipment, an expensive gyrocompass, sinks, wash basins, bedding, windows, furniture, dishware, piping, and the crew's personal belongings. Salvaged cargo included huts, rations, coal, lumber, mattresses, and property destined for the 18th Engineer Regiment on Shemya. Only heavy items, like safes for the finance department, could not be removed (Rust 1944; Van Arsdol 1983). Anything portable that could be "reached in its holds or torn from its interior [was removed]. The ship was literally stripped" (Van Arsdol 1983:20–21). Even so, some items remained. Shemya personnel lamented the loss of the Christmas beer *Scotia* was carrying and the watches intended for the PX appear to have been unreachable as well. An early 1944 account of the wrecking dared intrepid Shemya personnel to dive down to the wreck to get themselves a watch (Rust 1944; BOEM 2011). If any portion of the wreck remains in situ on the floor of ALCAN Harbor, the presence or absence of various ship's fittings and cargo matching those specified in these detailed accounts would assist in the vessel's definitive identification.

After *Scotia* broke in half in early January 1944, the wreck was still visible in the harbor for several years. Hank Frese remembered the masts sticking out of the water through at least 1945 (Frese [1944–1946]b).

Morrisette's Project Warrior report states that the vessel was still "on the reef" (likely the pinnacle rock on which the vessel grounded) as late as April 1947, but was subsequently blown off by a storm and came to rest in 45 ft. of water in the center of the harbor (Morrisette 1988:18). Exactly when the wreck disappeared beneath the waves is unclear, but *Scotia* and some of its cargo likely still lie silent under the waters of ALCAN Harbor.

Conclusions

Archival research revealed information about numerous shipwrecks around the Semichi Islands, including several potential unknown wrecks consisting of at least one J-boat andup to two barges, the Lotus Island wreck, the Russian shitik *Sv. Petr i Pavel*, the American schooner *Trilby*, and the American steam screw *Scotia*. Some of these wrecks are well documented, while others are barely visible in the historical record. The extreme conditions and weather events to which the Semichis are continually subjected and the highly dynamic nature of coastal waters in the Aleutian Islands means that historic shipwreck sites in the region are likely subjected to constant deterioration. While some of the wrecks identified during this study may forever remain historical phantoms, additional archival and archaeological research has the potential to lead to the identification of shipwrecks and illuminate the stories of vessels that played a role in the development of the Semichis, Shemya Island, and EAS.

Acknowledgments

The study upon which this article is based was conducted by Argonne National Laboratory (Argonne) for the Pacific Regional Support Center (PRSC) with funding from the Air Force Civil Engineer Center. Thank you to Karlene Leeper, PRSC Cultural Resources Manager, and Konnie Wescott, Argonne Sociocultural Systems Department Head, for their support and guidance. My thanks also to my former colleagues at Argonne who made my time at the lab both a privilege and a pleasure. Finally, thank you to the Alaska Office of History and Archaeology for the work they do to preserve and promote Alaska's rich cultural heritage and to the University of Alaska Anchorage/Alaska Pacific University Consortium Library for their stewardship of significant historical collections that provide a deep view of the history of Alaska.

References

Argonne National Laboratory (Argonne)
2021   Integrated Cultural Resources Management Plan for Eareckson Air Station, Shemya Island, Alaska, 2021–2026. Prepared for 611th Civil Engineer Squadron, Joint Base Elmendorf Richardson, AK, by Argonne, Lemont, IL.

2024   Shipwrecks and Williwaws: Archival Investigation of Shipwrecks in Shemya and the Semichi Islands for Eareckson Air Station, Shemya Island, Alaska. Argonne Report No. ANL/EVS-23/26. Prepared for the Air Force Civil Engineer Center, Joint Base San Antonio, Lackland, TX, by the Environmental Science Division, Argonne, Lemont, IL.

Alaska State Library Historical Collections
[1930s]   *Scotia*, post-1934. Photograph. Item 211, PCA 134, Robert DeArmond Photograph Collection, Ships, Shipwrecks and Miscellaneous Alaskan Views, Historical Collections, Alaska State Library, Juneau.

Black, Lydia T.
1983   Record of Maritime Disasters in Russian America, Part One: 1741–1799. In *Proceedings of the Alaskan Marine Archeology Workshop,* May 17–19, 1983. Sitka, AK.

Black, Lydia T., and Dominique Desson
1986   Early Russian Contact. *Studies in History* No. 191. Alaska Historical Commission, Anchorage.

Bureau of Navigation (BN)
1914   *Forty-Sixth Annual List of Merchant Vessels of the United States*. Department of Commerce, Bureau of Navigation, Washington, DC.

1915   *Forty-Seventh Annual List of Merchant Vessels of the United States*. Department of Commerce, Bureau of Navigation, Washington, DC.

Bureau of Ocean Energy Management (BOEM)
2011   Shipwrecks Off Alaska's Coast. BOEM Office of Communications, Washington, DC. <https://www.boem.gov/about-boem/shipwrecks-alaskas-coast>. Accessed 21 May 2024.

Carlucci, Cesare
[1943–1945]   Barge Washed Ashore. Photograph. uaa-hmc-0083-7, Item 7, Cesare Carlucci Photographs (HMC-0083), Archives and Special Collections, Consortium Library, University of Alaska Anchorage, Anchorage.

COLLECTOR OF CUSTOMS (CC)
1944   Steam Screw *Lake Galewood / Scotia*, File 219120, Entry 126, Official Number Files, 1867-1958, Records of the Bureau of Marine Inspection and Navigation, 1774-1982 (NAID 370), Record Group 41, National Archives Building, Washington, DC.

CORBETT, DEBRA, DIXIE WEST, AND CHRISTINE LEFÈVRE (EDITORS)
2010   The People at the End of the World: The Western Aleutians Archaeology Project and the Archaeology of Shemya Island. *Aurora Monograph Series* No. 8. Alaska Anthropological Association, Anchorage.

DOOLAEGE, CLARICE
1962   Historical Record of the Vessels of the Pacific Lumber Company. In *Humboldtiana: A Collection of History of Humboldt and Her Neighboring California Counties*, Eureka City Schools, Adult Education Department, Eureka, CA.

FRESE, HENRY K.
[1944–1946]a   Alaid & Oubeloi, Arrow Shows Wrecked Land'g Barge. Photograph. uaa-hmc-0862-b2-f12-photo1, Folder 12, Box 2, Henry K. "Hank" Frese Papers (HMC-0862), Archives and Special Collections, Consortium Library, University of Alaska Anchorage, Anchorage.

[1944–1946]b   Shemya & Attu WWII Recreations. Folder 10, Box 2, Henry K. "Hank" Frese Papers (HMC-0862), Archives and Special Collections, Consortium Library, University of Alaska Anchorage, Anchorage.

GOOD, WARREN
2023   Alaska Shipwrecks: A Comprehensive Accounting of Alaska Shipwrecks and Losses of Life in Alaskan Waters. <https://alaskashipwreck.com/>. Accessed 21 May 2024.

GRINËV, ANDREI V., AND RICHARD L. BLAND
2011   Russian Maritime Catastrophes during the Colonization of Alaska, 1741–1867. *Pacific Northwest Quarterly* 102(4):178–194.

LANCASTER, STEVE
1990   Shemya Island, Alaska and the History of Eareckson Air Station. Manuscript, Operations Office, Eareckson Air Station, AK.

LARSEN, EDWIN
1916   Wreck Report No. 31 (American Schooner *Trilby*). Page 87, Folder 5, Box 1, SEAL-822, Casualty and Wreck Reports, 1905-1943, Records of the U.S. Customs Service (NAID 4529617), Record Group 36, National Archives at Seattle, WA. <https://catalog.archives.gov/id/4710226>. Accessed 21 May 2024.

MAKAROVA, RAISA V.
1975   *Russians on the Pacific, 1743–1799*, Richard A. Pierce and Alton S. Donnelly, translators and editors. Limestone Press, Kingston, Ontario, Canada.

MCKENZIE, DAN J.
1964   The Wreck of the *Tahoma*. *Alaska Sportsman* 30(6):8–12, 51–56.

MORRISSETTE, STEPHEN
1988   Shemya: If You've Seen One Pacific Island You've Seen Them All. Project Warrior Report. Shemya, Aleutian Islands, AK: The "Black Pearl" of the Aleutians. <https://www.hlswilliwaw.com/aleutians/shemya/>. Accessed 21 May 2024.

NATIONAL OCEANIC AND ATMOSPHERIC ADMINISTRATION (NOAA)
2023   Historical Map and Chart Collection. Office of Coast Survey, National Ocean Service, Silver Spring, MD. <https://historicalcharts.noaa.gov/>. Accessed 21 May 2024.

ROSS, JAMES L.
1969   *Construction and Operation of a World War II Army Air Force Forward Base: Shemya, Alaska, May 1943-December 1945*. Elmendorf Air Force Base, Office of History, Alaskan Air Command, Anchorage.

RUST, FRED
1944   Unloading with the Port Company, *Williwaw Wail* 1(4):5. Call Number: UG634.5.E27 W55 1944. Jerome Sheldon Papers, Archives and Special Collections, Consortium Library, University of Alaska Anchorage, Anchorage.

SUCKLING, ROY
[1943-1944]   Wreck of the *Scotia*. Photograph. uaa-hmc-1220-b1-f3-11, Roy Suckling Photographs (HMC-1220), Archives and Special Collections, Consortium Library, University of Alaska Anchorage, Anchorage.

UNITED STATES COAST AND GEODETIC SURVEY (USCGS)
1945   *Chart No. 9125: Alaska - Aleutian Islands, Semichi Islands - Shemya Island*, March 1945, Historical Map and Chart Collection. Office of Coast Survey, National Ocean Service, Silver Spring, MD. <https://historicalcharts.noaa.gov/>. Accessed 21 May 2024.

1947   *Chart No. 9125: Alaska - Aleutian Islands, Semichi Islands - Shemya Island,* 3rd edition, February 1947, Historical Map and Chart Collection. Office of Coast Survey, National Ocean Service, Silver Spring, MD. <https://historicalcharts.noaa.gov/>. Accessed 21 May 2024.

1948   *Chart No. 9130: Alaska - Aleutian Islands, Semichi Islands - Alaid and Nizki Islands*, 1st edition, October 1948, Historical Map and Chart Collection. Office of Coast Survey, National Ocean Service, Silver Spring, MD. <https://historicalcharts.noaa.gov/>. Accessed 21 May 2024.

1950   *Chart No. 9125: Alaska - Aleutian Islands, Semichi Islands - Shemya Island*, 4th edition, October 1950. Historical Map and Chart Collection. Office of Coast Survey, National Ocean Service, Silver Spring, MD. <https://historicalcharts.noaa.gov/>. Accessed 21 May 2024.

1969   *Chart No. 9130: Alaska - Aleutian Islands, Semichi Islands - Alaid and Nizki Islands*, 2nd edition, July 1969, Historical Map and Chart Collection. Office of Coast Survey, National Ocean Service, Silver Spring, MD. <https://historicalcharts.noaa.gov/>. Accessed 21 May 2024.

UNITED STATES COAST GUARD (USCG)
1916   Wreck Report No. 31 (American Schooner *Trilby*), File 1542, Records of the Surface Facilities Branch, Record Group 26.5.8, *U.S. Coast Guard Casualty and Wreck Reports, 1913–1939*, Microfilm Publication T925, National Archives Building, Washington, DC.

UNITED STATES SHIPPING BOARD (USSB)
1926   *Tenth Annual Report of the United States Shipping Board*. USSB, Washington, DC.

VAN ARSDOL, TED (EDITOR)
1983   *27 Months in Alaska: History of the 420th Port Company, World War II*. Vancouver, WA.

WILSON, PAUL G.
2001   *The Legacy of the Log Boom: Humboldt County Logging from 1945 to 1955*. California State Polytechnic University, Humboldt, Arcata.

• • • • • • • • • • • • • • • •

Kendra Kennedy
Wisconsin Historical Society
816 State Street
Madison, Wisconsin 53706

World War II Survey in Green Cove Springs, Florida

Dorothy Rowland

A maritime survey of Green Cove Springs, Florida, was conducted to look for evidence of the area's World War II history as a naval air station and reserve fleet mooring location. Work included surveying over 2,000 acres of the river and diving on six targets, including a shipwreck and a previously found F4F Wildcat aircraft. Three of the sites had connections to World War II and artifacts were found at two. The project ended with many questions that could be investigated in future projects.

Green Cove Springs fue el sitio de un aeródromo naval de la Segunda Guerra Mundial y albergó a más de 300 barcos de la Flota Atlántica después de la guerra. Hay dos sitios conocidos en el área, con la creencia de que existe una alta probabilidad de que existan otros sitios. En 2022, el Programa Marítimo Arqueológico del Faro (LAMP) realizó un estudio de buceo y teledetección de una sección del río St. Johns que abarcaba gran parte de la antigua zona de amarre en un intento por encontrar sitios adicionales.

Green Cove Springs était le site d'un aérodrome naval de la Seconde Guerre mondiale et abritait plus de 300 navires de la flotte de l'Atlantique remisés après la guerre. Il y a deux sites connus dans la région, avec la croyance qu'il y a une forte probabilité d'autres sites dans cette zone. En 2022, le Lighthouse Archaeological Maritime Program (LAMP) a effectué des prospections de télédétection et de plongée dans une section de la rivière St. Johns qui englobait une grande partie de l'ancienne zone d'amarrage dans le but de trouver des sites supplémentaires.

Introduction

Green Cove Springs, Florida, has a rich maritime history that includes a World War II Naval Air Station and a post-World War II mothball fleet mooring area. In 2022, the Lighthouse Archaeological Maritime Program (LAMP) surveyed the St. Johns River in Green Cove Springs. The project was funded by a small matching grant from the Florida Department of State, Division of Historical Resources, and included both remote sensing and diver investigations. The project attempted to identify sites relating to this history and visited two previously identified sites from the era.

Historical Background

The Green Cove Springs area has a long history surrounding the river as it was used by both Native Americans and early Europeans as an important route of transportation. The near-by St. Johns River was the main route of transportation during both peace and war. The addition of the railroad to the area limited the amount of traffic on the river. As the railroad expanded from the 1880s to the 1920s, river traffic continued to dwindle, further exacerbated by several hard winter freezes during this timeframe that made river travel extremely difficult. This was followed shortly by the arrival of the car, which signaled the end of most river traffic in this area (Mueller 1979).

Lee Naval Air Station was commissioned in September 1940 in response to the start of World War II. It was one of several naval air stations that opened in the area for training and the training flights sometimes transited between the different air stations. Lee Naval Air Station was active throughout the war until its closure in 1962. Although it was an air station, its location along the banks of the St. Johns River created an opportunity following the end of the war as the nation's requirement for naval ships drastically diminished. To lessen the number of ships in use that required upkeep while retaining a supply of ships if tensions escalated, the excess ships were "mothballed" or stored in reserve fleets. For the Atlantic Reserve Fleet, the St. Johns River at Green Cove Springs was chosen to store mostly destroyers, destroyer escorts, and fleet auxiliary vessels. Thirteen 1,500-foot-long piers were built to house these ships (Davis 2017). To add even more storage space for the ships, concrete blocks with chains were sunk in the river to provide moorings. At the peak, over 600 ships were moored as part of the mothball fleet, with the docks holding as many as four ships moored together and the blocks in the river mooring up to eight ships. These ships faced various fates with some being reactivated for the Korean War and some sold to other countries, but a majority were scrapped. The last of the mothball fleet left the area in 1962 (Davis 2017). The docks and airfield that once belonged to the Navy were given to the City of Green Cove Springs, with some of that land later being sold into private hands. The docks built by the Navy are still extant, though their conditions vary greatly. The docks still are in use for various purposes with several dedicated to industrial work and others converted to marinas. One of the marinas has several old casino ships moored there that are no longer in use, but are waiting to be either bought or scrapped.

Two significant areas of previous research informed the plans for the project. In 2019, SEARCH, Inc. conducted surveys and diver investigations in the area around the Shands Bridge, which resulted in the discovery of what is believed to be a Higgins landing craft (Grinnan et al. 2019). The second project was a St. Johns County Sheriff's Office investigation that was initiated in 2017 by a fisherman reporting a downed plane near the St. Johns County shore. After a diving investigation recovered several items, the lead investigator, Thomas Keisler, determined it to be an F4F Wildcat. This investigation was thorough and included the investigators finding a fingerprint on the recovered navigation board. The information from the navigation board and the state of the aircraft led to the determination that this aircraft had gone down during the time the naval air station was active (Keisler 2018).

Investigation Plan and Execution

The project field work occurred from the last week in March to the first week in May 2023. This timeline allowed one month of survey, one week of initial data processing, and one week of diver investigations. The planned survey area was chosen to encompass the area near the docks, the channel in the center of the river, and the two mooring areas. The areas near the docks and the two mooring areas were determined to be a priority as the channel is maintained to a minimum depth of 13 ft. and was unlikely to have high-priority targets. The eastern mooring area was also the closest area to both of the known historic sites.

Due to poor weather conditions, the survey operations extended into the last week of April. The several days of weather interruption were used to begin processing data, with a primary focus on identifying targets from the side-scan sonar data. The interruptions in the survey caused the planned week break between the survey and diving sections to be repurposed to complete the survey and prepare for diver investigations, which occurred during the final week. All of the four survey areas were completely covered as well as short surveys over the known F4F Wildcat and landing craft locations (Figure 1). The diver investigations allowed six targets to be investigated before the project time expired. These dives included the recovery of some artifacts likely related to the World War II (WWII) activity in the area.

Survey Results

Though project staff had high hopes for what might be found in the area immediately off the docks based on oral histories from local citizens about debris being pushed into the water, the survey results were mostly inconclusive. The docks themselves covered possible magnetic signatures, and the water depth showed that the area around the docks is much shallower than it had been historically as the area is no longer being dredged to accommodate large ships. The side-scan sonar detected a couple of targets, but the main contact seen on the side-scan survey in this area was determined to be logs.

The channel survey area was, unsurprisingly, mostly clear of features in the side-scan sonar data. This was expected as much of the area is dredged to maintain the channel depth. No side-scan targets were chosen in either area for diver investigation. A few targets were identified in both of these areas, but they were lower probability and did not rank high enough to be investigated in the short time frame available for diver investigations.

Both mooring field survey areas showed several targets on the side-scan data. The eastern mooring field contained a shipwreck, along with most of the high-priority targets. These targets included several with distinctive features and some that appeared to be chains related to the mooring blocks. The western mooring field had what initially looked to be an exciting find, with a crater appearing as a contact. After ensonifying it on several passes, its oval shape made it appear to be most likely natural, possibly caused by a spring seep. This section also had a large number of logs and many crab traps. The magnetometer readings for these sections had a high rate of detections, as the mooring blocks sunk to create the mooring field clearly appear in the readings (Figure 2).

The survey of the four sections was completed halfway through one day, so the remaining time was used to conduct follow-up surveys at the F4F Wildcat and at the landing craft. The plane had not been previously archaeologically surveyed and side-scan sonar data of this area showed a possible secondary piece of the plane approximately 10 m from the plane wing (Figure 3).

FIGURE 1. Survey areas covered for World War II Green Cove Springs project. (Map created by author, 2024)

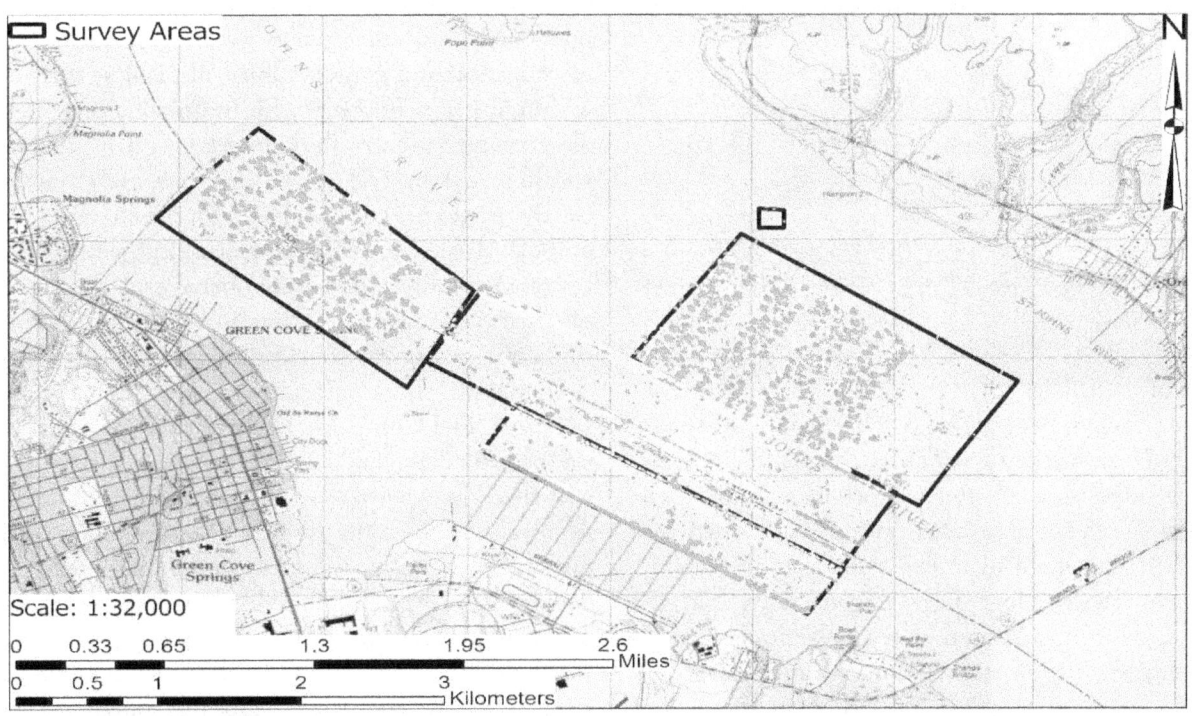

FIGURE 2. Magnetic anomalies recorded during survey. The high positive readings are represented by the red (darker) contours while the blue (lighter) contours represent strong negative readings. (Map courtesy of Lighthouse Archaeological Maritime Program, 2024.)

As no previous investigation had been conducted for this piece, it was labeled a priority for diving. The sonar images of the landing craft previously identified by SEARCH, Inc., appeared similar to their sonar images of it, and it was determined to be low priority and was not chosen for further diver investigations.

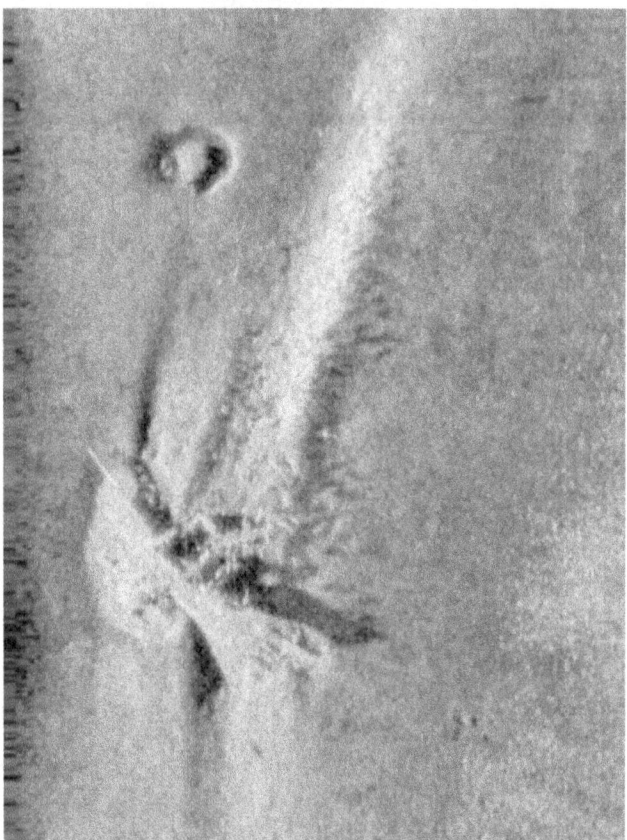

FIGURE 3. Sonar imagery of F4F Wildcat with secondary contact (Sonar image by Lighthouse Archaeological Maritime Program, 2024.)

One of the challenges of the survey was watching for the many buoys marking crab traps that were spaced throughout all of the survey areas outside of the channel. The side-scan sonar showed a similar, if not larger, number of derelict crab traps no longer attached to a buoy. The other item identified frequently in the side-scan sonar data was logs. In total, sonar identified 392 contacts, with only 42 considered possible targets. Of the 42 targets, only 6 were subject to diver investigations.

Diver Investigations

The overall time for investigation dives was limited. Targets were chosen based on size and distinct characteristics as viewed on the side-scan sonar results. The short interval between the survey and diving portions of the project meant the magnetometer results were not considered when choosing targets for investigation. The magnetic data were processed after fieldwork was completed.

Visibility was minimal in the St. Johns River due to its tannic nature, with 1–2 feet maximum visibility and no visibility at the bottom of the river, which had liquid mud extending one foot into the water column. Several targets investigated barely protruded out of the mud layer, while three were completely covered by it.

A shipwreck was the first target subject to diver investigations, with three total dives conducted on the target with varying levels of success. Two of the dives were spent investigating the boat's distinctive features including a wood hull with a metal frame. Phillips-head screws were used to attach the wood. Some of the wood was still intact showing a thickness of less than 1 inch, but wood did not survive in several areas. In the mud within a foot of the boat was a box of rubber or asphalt tile; none were brought to the surface for closer examination. One of the three dives did not investigate the boat, but instead found several artifacts including two USN steel mess trays, an Alka Seltzer bottle, a ketchup bottle, a shoe heel, half of a Buffalo China Company bowl, and a pool cue ball. These artifacts were recovered for further investigation and conservation. All of these artifacts fit within the timeframe of the mothball fleet and may have some relation to the shipwreck as they were found within 2 meters (m) of it. The steel mess trays were clearly related to the Navy based on the engraved 'USN' on both (Figure 4). They were also readily identified by a veteran volunteer who remembered eating many meals off such trays during his time in the Navy. The partial Buffalo China bowl also clearly related to Navy activity as it was the china pattern made for the Navy by the Buffalo China Company. Unfortunately, the portion of the pattern that would indicate the rank of personnel who used the bowl was on the missing half of the bowl. Archival research after the field work to find candidates for sunken boats in the area proved unsuccessful. No determination on the period of the boat or type was made, and more investigation is needed.

One other target dive yielded results in the form of artifacts, chosen because it appeared on the side-scan sonar with multiple circular features. The target did not protrude above the mud layer, and was found to be a debris scatter with a mix of WWII-era related and unrelated artifacts. A rectangular iron box with an oval hole for a handle at one end was found, but left in place due

FIGURE 4. One of the United States Navy mess trays found during diver investigations. (Photo by author, 2022.)

to its size. The box was below the mud layer, so divers were unable to look for markings. The most exciting find was half of a ceramic cup with a maker's mark of 'Carr China Co. Grafton, W. VA 45.' The '45' refers to the year made, 1945, and the Carr China Co. supplied the Navy during WWII. Other finds in the scatter included two large drill bits with an uncommon connection style that seemed likely to date to WWII; these artifacts were returned to the location found. A second dive to this target found a gauge cover made of copper and fiberglass; however, patent information on the object dated it to the 1980s. The gauge cover likely is intrusive as active boating takes place in the area and, due to its nonhistorical date, it was removed as trash.

Three of the targets chosen for diver investigation turned out to be logs, crab traps, or a combination of logs and crab traps. The sharp lines created by the combination of the two made several convincing targets. As the survey showed, the area was littered with derelict crab traps that, in some cases, were stacked, were multiple in number, were right next to logs, or were on top of logs. These targets helped to refine the data processing once field work was done, but consumed limited dive time.

The F4F Wildcat aircraft was the last target for diver investigations in the area. As the previous investigation had focused on the larger portion of the wreck easily visible on the side-scan sonar with the cockpit and wings, the main goal for the dive was to locate and determine if the second part of the side-scan image was possibly part of the missing tail section of the plane. Diver orientation was slightly challenging due to the low visibility and fragmented nature of the site. The dive team conducted a partial circle search in the quadrant where the secondary feature was believed to be. The search was successful and the target from the side-scan survey was found. As this target was completely under the liquid mud layer of the bottom, visual confirmation was not possible, but based on texture and feel the divers agreed it was likely aluminum and a portion of the plane. One of the divers also reported a further description of the section as being approximately 1.5 m across and 'roundish' aluminum skin with wiring inside, similar to a F4F Wildcat tail found at another site they had previously encountered. Whether this piece is the full tail piece of the plane is unknown, but is a good subject for further investigation.

Conclusion

Green Cove Springs has a rich maritime history that has only partially been explored. While conditions make it somewhat challenging underwater, historic sites in the area have strong potential for further investigation and research. Both the landing craft and plane could benefit from further investigation, especially what is believed to be a secondary section of the plane. Because the shipwreck was not definitively dated or identified, further investigation is recommended. Components from an F4F Wildcat ammunition can were found two miles upriver from the investigation area by a crab fisherman, possibly indicating additional aircraft in the river. This survey achieved the goal of discovering more about the WWII maritime history of the area, but clearly more could be investigated and discovered.

References

Davis, Ennis
2017 The Ghosts of Green Cove Springs. ModernCities.com. <https://www.moderncities.com/article/2017-mar-the-ghosts-of-green-cove-springs>. Accessed 3 June 2024.

Grinnan, Joseph J., Nicholas J. Linville, and Jeffrey M. Enright
2019 Submerged Cultural Resource Assessment Survey for the State Road 16 Shands Bridge Over the St. Johns River, St. Johns and Clay Counties, Florida. Report prepared for RS&H, Inc., Jacksonville, FL, by SEARCH, Inc., Pensacola, FL. FDOT Financial Management No. 422938-1, SEARCH Project No. T19059, FLMSF Survey No. 26413.

Keisler, Thomas
2018 St. Johns Plane Report: F4F Wildcat. Manuscript, St. Johns County Sheriff's Office, St. Augustine, FL.

Mueller, Edward A.
1979 *Steamboating on the St. Johns*. South Brevard Historical Society, Melbourne, FL.

• • • • • • • • • • • • • • • •

Dorothy Rowland
2510 Golden Lake Loop
St. Augustine, Florida 32084

Shells and Shifting Shorelines: Paleoenvironmental Reconstruction in the Western Gulf of Mexico Outer Continental Shelf

Emma Graumlich, Hope Bridgeman, Kaitlin Decker, Ramie Gougeon, Amanda Evans, August Costa

*In 2019, a team of archaeologists and marine geologists designed a project funded by the National Oceanic and Atmospheric Administration to characterize the now-submerged paleolandscape associated with the shoreline stand ca. 8,000 yrs BP through piston core sampling. This landscape was available to early migratory human populations in the northwestern portion of the Gulf of Mexico's outer continental shelf. Graduate students at the University of West Florida analyzed samples rich in Atlantic Rangia (*Rangia cuneata*) shell as part of high-impact educational practices offered to train basic analytical techniques. This paper outlines the methods used and preliminary results. Sizes and conditions of Rangia identified in the sample may indicate a natural population (i.e., not a human created midden). While Rangia predominate the processed samples, other species present in the cores (including botanical and faunal remains) may point to specific environmental conditions at these locations.*

Se diseñó un proyecto financiado por una subvención de la National Oceanic and Atmospheric Administration para crear caracterizaciones de referencia del paleopaisaje ahora sumergido asociado con el limite costero ca. 8.000 años A.C. que habrían existido para las primeras poblaciones humanas en la plataforma continental exterior del noroeste del Golfo de México. En la primavera de 2020 se tomaron muestras mediante vibracore de varios lugares con una alta probabilidad de evidencia de uso prehistórico de la tierra. Estudiantes de posgrado de la Universidad de West Florida analizaron muestras de núcleos ricas en conchas como parte de prácticas educativas de alto impacto destinadas a ofrecer capacitación en técnicas analíticas básicas. Este artículo describe los métodos utilizados en este estudio y los resultados preliminares. Los tamaños y condición de las conchas Rangia identificados en la muestra pueden indicar una población natural (es decir, no un basurero creado por humanos). Si bien Rangia predomina en las muestras procesadas, otras especies presentes en los núcleos (incluidos restos botánicos y de fauna) pueden indicar condiciones ambientales específicas en estos lugares.

Un projet financé par une subvention de la National Oceanic and Atmospheric Administration a été conçu pour créer des caractérisations de base du paléopaysage maintenant submergé associé au peuplement riverain d'environ 8 000 ans avant aujourd'hui qui aurait été disponible pour les premières populations humaines dans le nord-ouest du plateau continental étendu du golfe du Mexique. Plusieurs endroits présentant une forte probabilité de preuves d'utilisation préhistorique des terres ont été échantillonnés avec un équipement par vibration (vibracore) au printemps 2020. Des étudiants diplômés de l'University of West Florida ont analysé des échantillons de carottes riches en coquillages dans le cadre de pratiques éducatives à fort impact visant à offrir une formation aux techniques analytiques de base. Cet article décrit les méthodes utilisées dans cette étude et les résultats préliminaires. La taille et l'état des Rangia identifiés dans l'échantillon peuvent indiquer une population naturelle (et non des dépôts anthropiques). Alors que les rangia prédominent dans les échantillons traités, d'autres espèces présentes dans les carottes (y compris les restes botaniques et fauniques) peuvent indiquer des conditions environnementales spécifiques à ces endroits.

Paleolandscapes in the Gulf of Mexico

Archaeologists continuously grapple with captivating and contentious inquiries about human migration and settlement across the Americas. Scholars have crafted diverse models of early human movement grounded in terrestrial evidence, yet challenges arise due to evolving insights into climate shifts and sea-level changes. Given archaeologists' current knowledge of sea level rise and the ever-growing repository of archaeological evidence, which frequently moves the "peopling of the Americas" timeline earlier and earlier (Stright 1999; Waters et al. 2011; Halligan et al. 2016; Letham 2024), we know that extensive portions of the modern outer continental shelf (OCS) (nearly 40 million acres in the Gulf of Mexico) once appeared as dry land during those ancient migrations. These paleolandscapes exist over the majority of the North American continental shelves of both coastlines and are likely to contain evidence of human occupation and activity from the late Pleistocene through the early Holocene (Faught 2004). This subaerially exposed land constituted both a cultural and physical landscape that early Americans created, cultivated, and exploited. The modern submerged OCS preserves the signatures of those landscapes. This project investigates the physical signature created over 8,000 years ago by the environment on what is now the northwestern Gulf of Mexico's (GOM) OCS. The project aims to explicate the environmental backdrop for future investigations of the contemporaneous cultural landscape.

Despite the potential for areas like the OCS to reveal crucial information about prehistoric human life, continental shelves are rarely targeted for prehistoric archaeological investigation. As of the 2019 project that prompted this article, only two previous studies had conducted archaeological testing of submerged landscapes on the GOM OCS (Pearson et al. 1986; Evans 2016). Together, these two studies collected 106 10-centimeter (cm) diameter cores ranging from 6 to 12 meters (m) in length. Put in perspective, the sediment in the recovered cores makes up a surface area of 0.827 square meters (m^2) across the entire GOM OCS. In recent years, the continental shelf has been heavily developed to support oil and natural gas extraction, and though this development poses a risk to these cultural and physical signatures, the clearance and compliance work required by United States (U.S.) law offers archaeologists an opportunity to investigate them. Using a combination of predictive modeling (Coastal Environments Inc. 1977; Gagliano et al. 1982; Pearson et al. 1986) and geophysical technologies (Gaffney 2008), such as sub-bottom profilers, magnetometers, and bathymetric sonar, archaeologists identify probable areas of occupation and take core samples to locate evidence of human activity.

Even with the aid of predictive modeling techniques, locating cultural material from the early American migrations using a piston core can be akin to finding a needle in a haystack. When cultural material evidence is not discovered during archaeological investigations, archaeologists can still use the evidence they collected to piece together characteristics of the physical landscape where humans lived. Paleoenvironmental reconstruction aims to use environmental proxies that may be recovered during archaeological investigation such as botanicals (such as plant remains, pollen spores, and diatoms), faunal remains (like invertebrates, insects, mollusks, and other fossil remains), soil systems, and raw materials that contain vital environmental clues. When these materials are analyzed, general environmental qualities are revealed, punctated by events like storms, droughts, and fires, as well as longer-term changes like sea level rise and shifts in the pattern of human-environment interactions (Rapp and Hill 2006).

In the spring of 2019, the National Oceanic and Atmospheric Administration's (NOAA) Ocean Exploration (OER) funded a team of marine archaeologists and geophysicists headed by Dr. Amanda Evans to explore the OCS in the northwestern part of the GOM to identify submerged paleolandscapes and to provide an initial characterization of these sites. The team surveyed a 606 km² area within the Sabine Pass and High Island federal lease areas, which had previously been investigated by Evans (2016). The team sought paradigm-shifting evidence of human life on the paleolandscapes that had been submerged after the Last Glacial Maximum (LGM) ended nearly 20,000 years ago. The 2019 project recovered a total of 39 cores from areas of high occupation probability (Figure 1). Four of the 39 cores that contained visible Atlantic Rangia (*Rangia cuneata*) shell material were entrusted to graduate students at the University of West Florida (UWF) for further paleoenvironmental investigation. Analysis of shell material aimed to answer questions about the state of the hydrological regime in the northwest GOM, including the status of the local river deltas and the sea level.

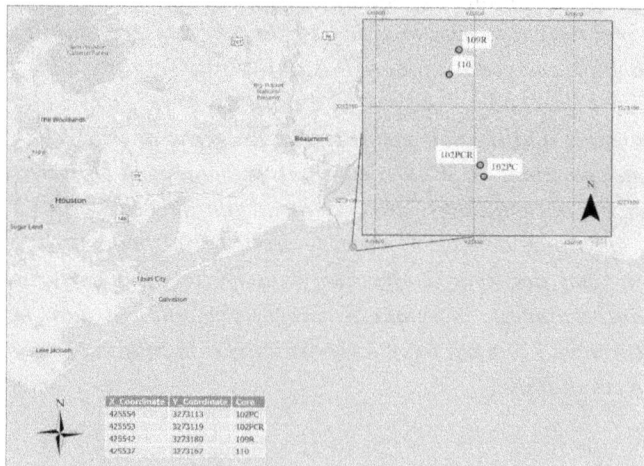

FIGURE 1. Image depicting Evan's 2019 project area in the Gulf of Mexico and locations of University of West Florida SP6 core samples processed. (Map by authors, 2023.)

The Utility of Shells in Paleolandscape Analysis

Archaeologists study shell material from prehistoric sites to gain insight into a variety of human activities including subsistence practices, art and tool technologies, and environmental data. Mollusks' utility to archaeologists lies in their aptitude for preservation, their ubiquitous presence in submerged settings, and their sensitivity to environmental change (Butler et al. 2019; Torben 2023). This project considers how bivalves, like Rangia, may be used as a proxy record to investigate prehistoric environments. The calcium carbonate shell that a mollusk builds during its lifetime acts as an archive of the organism's growth patterns and can indicate environmental characteristics that remained stable or changed over the years (Claassen 1998). Shell growth reflects the complex interactions of biological and physiological processes such as light/dark cycles, tidal exposure, temperature variations, salinity, water depth, and dissolved oxygen content, among others (Butler et al. 2019; Torben 2023). The state in which archaeologists recover the shells reflects the way they were deposited, which provides information about water level, water turbidity, and sediment deposition (Rapp and Hill 2006).

Rangia, a brackish-water clam commonly found in coastal river-influenced estuary sites, have specific environmental tolerances that reveal basic environmental characteristics. These organisms thrive in estuarine environments with soft substrate bottoms (sand, clay, and plant matter), low salinity, and high turbidity that are typically less than 20-feet deep (U.S. Fish and Wildlife Service 2012). They tolerate salinity measurements between 0 and 18 parts-per-trillion (ppt) and temperatures of up to 91 degrees Fahrenheit (°F) but require a stable salinity of between 2 and 15 ppt and a water temperature between 64 to 90°F to reproduce (Smithsonian Environmental Research Center 2022). Rangia can be classified as juvenile until they reach between 14 and 25 millimeters (mm). Adult shells typically measure between 25 to 60 mm in length and live for an average of four to five years. In stable environments they may grow up to 110 mm and live for up to 15 years (U.S. Fish and Wildlife Service 2012).

In addition to simply determining the presence/absence of Rangia shell to infer approximate water qualities, this project considered five different qualities of shell samples that can act as environmental indicators: their whole or fragmentary nature, the size of whole shells, the presence of the shell valve, the sided-ness of those valves, and the presence of weathering on the shells. The information gathered by taking these qualities into consideration can aid in determining depositional processes, landscape change, and their associated climatic factors.

Methods

The 2019 team surveyed the GOM OCS for two weeks using a chirp sub-bottom profiler, magnetometer, bathymetry, and a parametric sonar to record the seafloor and its underlying strata (Evans 2020). A piston-coring system was used to acquire sediment samples from areas that would have been part of a freshwater river delta during the LGM approximately 20,000 yrs BP. Four of the 39 cores collected in the Sabine Pass (SP6) survey area were delivered to UWF graduate students for analysis in compliance with the NOAA OER grant's education and outreach requirement. These cores totaled over 17 meters of sediment, which students processed between 2022 and 2023 (see Evans 2020 for discussion about field procedures).

The OER 102-PC, 102-PCR, 109-R, and 110 core samples were cut into approximately 1 m long sections and rough-sorted according to fraction size (4.75 mm, 2.0 mm, 1.0 mm, and <1.0 mm) into arbitrary 10 cm levels by Dr. Gus Costa prior to their transport to UWF. Students sorted, identified, photographed, and logged the material in these levels according to categories provided by the project principal investigators (PI): shell, bone, charcoal, macrobotanical remains, sediment aggregates, lithic debitage, and miscellaneous material. Of all this material, students prioritized classifying the Rangia shell. Core materials were photographed, counted, weighed in grams, then bagged separately with labels for their specific OER core number, section, and level.

These methods for analysis were all discussed and established by the graduate students based on their understanding of how the data might aid the PIs' paleo-landscape research. This project provided an opportunity for students to learn how archaeological lab procedures and analyses are performed within an academic setting and within the wider field of archaeology itself. The collaborative experience of designing spreadsheets for data collection, creating a uniform tray layout for sorting and photography, and establishing a system of bag identification provided a valuable opportunity in understanding how laboratory methodology is created and utilized for accurate analysis.

Project Results

The data recovered during this project allow researchers to draw broad conclusions about the character of the environment that shaped the lives of prehistoric humans. This data include sediment, Rangia shell, bone, botanical remains, and burned material. Relative percentages of these categorized materials within the cores were organized according to arbitrary geological zones created by the project PIs (Figure 2; Table 1). Within these zones, trends appear when materials are compared according to count (n) and weight (g). This section will first reference results regarding fraction size and then material categories. Lab work to sort, categorize, and analyze materials from the 1.0 mm and <1.0 mm sized samples is ongoing and will be included in the final published report for this project.

4.75 mm Fraction

When compared relatively, whole and fragmentary Rangia shell material dominated each geological zone, making up over 80% of the 4.75 mm fraction total by both count and weight (Figure 3). This is to be expected, as the shell is prone to both preservation and fragmentation, and average weights are heavier than the other materials measured. Among the Rangia, students measured relative amounts of fragmented shells, fragmented shells with valves, whole shells that were left-sided, and whole shells that were right-sided. Fragmented shells made up the majority of the Rangia samples by count. Valves made up the majority by weight across all geological zones. The most shell material was recovered in Zone 5 by weight and by Zone 6 by count.

Graduate students identified charcoal in Zones 4 and 6. When compared to other materials that make up the sample, charcoal constituted 14.29% of Zone 4 and 0.62% of Zone 6. Further investigation of this charcoal is warranted, as the known history of natural wildfires in the area (Liu et al. 2017) has implications for how prehistoric humans would have occupied and utilized the area. Sediment aggregates were found in proportions between less than 1% and nearly 10% throughout the samples by both count and weight. Students did not recover bone or macrobotanical remains in the 4.75 mm sized fraction. The methodology classified some materials as "Miscellaneous," which included ferrous concretions in Zone 6.

Students recovered no relevant material in the 4.75 mm fraction in Zone 3, nor did they recover any obvious evidence of human activity; no lithic debitage was identified and no shells were determined to be worked. Additionally, students did not identify any shell that was obviously altered by above-water processes like weathering or burning.

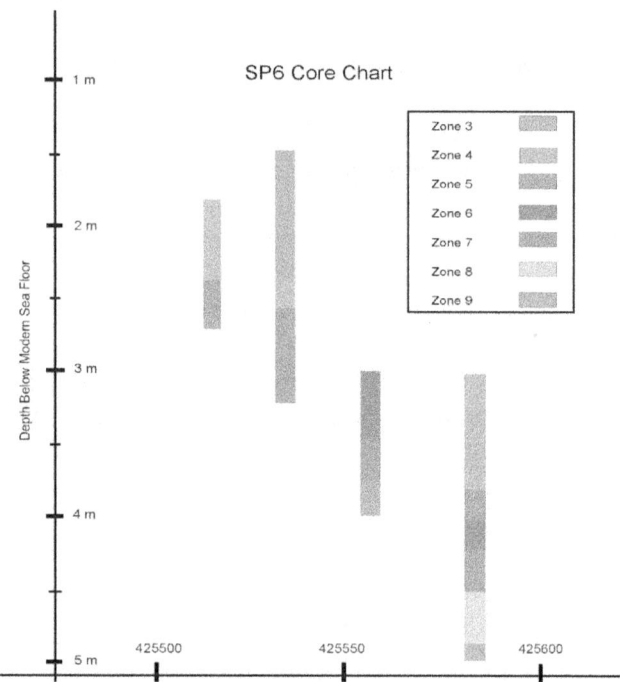

FIGURE 2. SP6 project area core chart. (Chart by authors, 2023.)

Geological Zone	Description	OER SP6 Core	Material Dated	Radiocarbon Years BP	Calibrated Years BP
3	Dark greenish gray (10GY4/1), dense massive clay, few oxidized inclusions (mottles). Faintly laminated.	106	Humic Lamination	7980 +/- 30	8995–8717
4	Dark greenish gray (10GY4/1) gleyed sandy clay. May include burrows and *Rangia* shell.	106	Humic Lamination	8690 +/- 30	9715–9543
5	Dark greenish gray (10GY4/1) clay with few fine (<2mm) sandy laminations. In cores 102PC and 102 PCR this zone is a dense shell bed including *Rangia*.	103R	Peat	8200 +/- 30	9275–9025
6	Very dark greenish gray (5GY3/1) laminated sandy clay, organic rich laminations. May also present as a darker gray (5Y4/1).				
7	*Rangia* dense across all cores that have this zone. Sandy granular matrix surrounding some valves (black 5Y2.5/2), diffuse dark organic-like matter around some shells and matrix, gleyed clay matrix (greenish black 5GY2.5/1) mottling, granular debris looks like worm castings.	109-PC	Rangia	8270 +/- 30	9274–7849
8	Dark greenish gray (10GY4/1) sandy clay to clayey sand, coarser laminations of clay, small shell fragments. May be categorized in some locations further as 8a, 8b, and 8c which differ in color.	109-PC	Peat	8490 +/- 30	9538–9467
9	Very dark greenish gray (5GY3/1) clayey peat, very dark gray to black (2.5Y3/1 to N2.5/) organic matter. Shell hash in SP6-110.	109-PC	Peat	8530 +/- 30	9543–9483

TABLE 1. Geological zone descriptions. (Table by authors, 2023.)

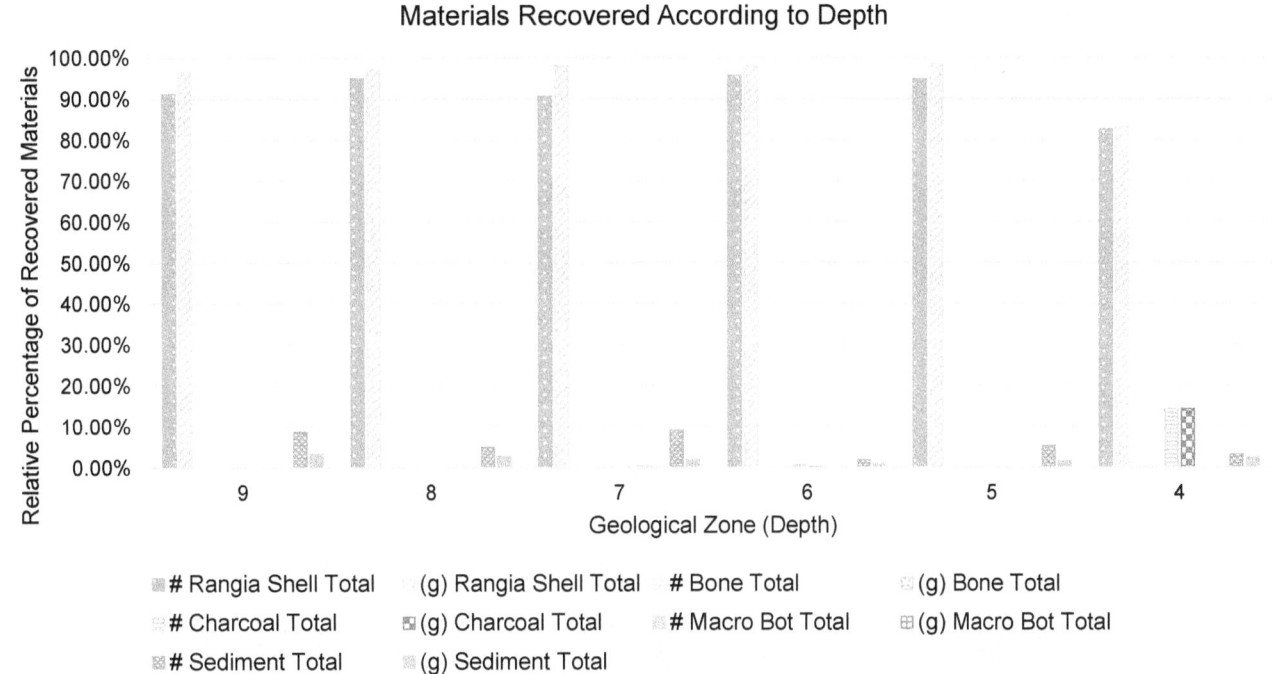

FIGURE 3. Environmental indicators recovered, according to depth. (Chart by authors, 2023.)

2.0 mm Fraction

The 2.0 mm fraction results are similar to the 4.75 mm fraction in that shell dominates most of the sample, but the smaller-sized mesh size trapped samples of non-shell material that will be used for further paleoenvironmental analysis. Whole and fragmentary Rangia shells made up most of the sample by both count and weight, except for Zone 4 where sediment constituted more of the sample's weight (Figure 4). Zone 5 hosted the majority of shell material by both count and weight (between 70% and 80% of the samples by count and weight, respectively). Sediment in the form of aggregates and Rangia shell casts made up 16–20% the sample by both weight and count, respectively. Graduate students identified fish bone throughout Zones 4, 5, and 6. The students found minimal amounts of macrobotanical remains in Zones 4 through 7, which were broadly identified as wood, grass, and unidentified seeds. Charcoal was also identified by students in minimal amounts (less than 1% by weight and less than 3% by count) in Zones 5 through 7. The Miscellaneous category consisted of one non-Rangia bivalve in Zone 5. Students recovered no relevant material in the 2.0 mm fraction in Zones 3, 8, and 9.

Rangia Shell

Students paid extra attention to Rangia shell during sample analysis; after sorting the shell from other sample materials, students classified each shell as either being whole or fragmentary, identified whether it had an intact valve, and then sided the valve. The PIs developed four categories to classify Rangia: (1) fragmented, (2) fragmented with a valve, (3) whole with a left-facing valve, and (4) whole with a right-facing valve; whole shells were measured during the classification process. This sorting method was designed to assist in extracting environmental information, as the qualities of the shells combined with the clam's environmental tolerances may reflect environmental characteristics.

The quantities and locations of whole and fragmented shells and ages of the sediments where they are found provide information about water turbidity and sediment deposition. Turbid conditions are more likely to churn the substrate, which may break shells apart, and rapid sediment deposition may crush shells. Valves are the bulkiest part of the shell and thus are more likely to be preserved. Siding the valves identifies whether the assemblage experienced any preservation bias; cultural assemblages tend to have equal ratios of left- and right-sided valves, as humans collect, open, and dispose of intact clams. Natural assemblages tend to vary in their left-to-right side ratio as the assemblages do not reflect humans' preferences for collecting and breaking apart whole shells. Further, preservation may be biased by hydrological and sedimentation processes. Whole shells were measured to determine their relative age and, at times, health of the shell given modern Rangia growth

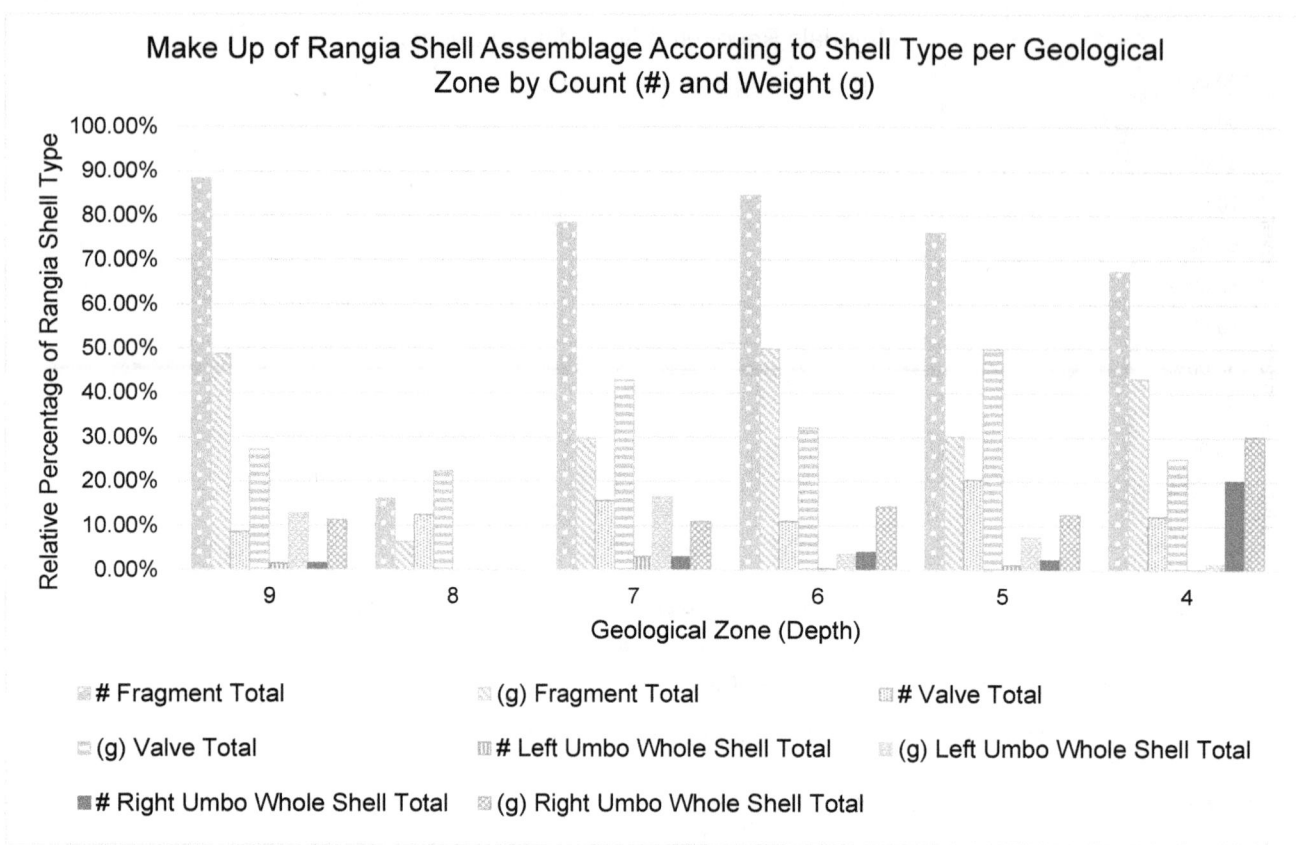

FIGURE 4. Make-up of Rangia shell assemblage, according to depth. (Chart by authors, 2023.)

rates. Modern Atlantic Rangia can be classified as juvenile until they reach between 14 and 25 mm. Adult shells typically measure between 25 to 60 mm in length and live for an average of four to five years.

Whole shells were recovered in the 4.75 mm fraction only, and occur throughout the samples in Zones 4, 5, 6, 7, and 9. Zone 5 had the most whole shells, which averaged 32.4 mm in length. The largest shells were found in Zone 6, averaging 34.6 mm in length. Zone 9 had the fewest and smallest whole shells, whose lengths averaged 26.3 mm. Of all the whole shells across the geological zones, nearly 63% were right-sided. Similar right-sided valve discrimination is found among fragmented shells as well. Among the fragmented shells with valves, students found a 41% preservation preference for right-sided shells and 35% preservation of left-sided; 24% of shells were too damaged for their direction to be determined. Overall, right-sided shells represent the majority of the valved Rangia sample.

Paleoenvironmental Conclusions

The aims of this project were two-fold. First, this project aimed to offer graduate students an opportunity to learn about the potential for paleolandscape research in the Gulf of Mexico and the paleoenvironmental data analysis used to study it. Second, the PIs of this project plan to use these data to draw broad conclusions about the state of the prehistoric environment in the survey area. Results of the preliminary analysis of the amounts, locations, and state of Rangia shells were married with knowledge of the organism's ecological tolerances, the state of sea level rise, sedimentary analysis, and radiocarbon dating of the geological zones. Given these ecological preferences, their presence in these cores reveals they were submerged beneath a fully estuarine ecotone or a low-salinity oceanic ecosystem. In either case, Rangia populations would have survived and continued to reproduce as the water levels rose until they were buried by the gradual sedimentation process associated with sea level rise in this area.

The project results highlight three heavily concentrated shell layers that contain whole and fragmentary adult and juvenile Rangia in Zones 5 and 6, and significantly smaller shells in Zone 7. Given the cores' depth, geological characterization, and contextualization with radiocarbon dates taken by other projects (Evans 2016), the 2019 cores recovered from the Sabine Pass Area represent Early Holocene deposits ranging from approximately 10,000 to 8,700 BP. Radiocarbon dates for these deposits will be provided in a forthcoming publication. The middle and later Texas and Louisiana Paleoindian periods encompass this timeframe, as they span broadly from 13,450 BP to 8,000 BP (Evans 2016:26). During this period, the Gulf of Mexico's sea level oscillated between approximately 20 m and 35 m lower than it is today (Evans 2016:18). Sea level curves for the Sabine Pass area characterize the sea level as being around 19 m to 22 m lower than its modern level (Nelson and Bray 1970:67–70). During this time, the Sabine Pass area would have been characterized by muddy estuarine/bay sediments and a fluctuating salinity as freshwater rivers infiltrated the retreating sea. These shell deposits likely developed during and just after that period of re-entrenchment

Whole shells in every zone measure as juveniles or young adults grown just over half of their potential maximum size. Their growth may have been cut short due to changes in a variety of water factors including salinity, temperature, available oxygen, available sunlight, water turbidity, and sediment deposition. Fragmentary shells made up a majority of many of the samples from these zones (over 50% by count and between 40% and 50% by weight). As mentioned earlier, shell fragmentation can occur through different modes including high water turbidity and rapid sediment deposition. As these shell layers formed during a period of river delta re-entrenchment, both potential causes are plausible. Results from sedimentary analysis such as grain size analysis and magnetic susceptibility will allow further interpretation of the whole-to-fragmented shell ratio.

In summary, given the graduate students' understanding of the temporal brackets of the geological zones with Rangia deposits and existing sea-level data for the GOM, we can conclude that these shell deposits developed in a brackish water environment (though the exact salinity is unknown given the shell data alone). The significantly smaller size of some shells in Zones 7 and 9, the lack of fully grown adult shells in Zones 5 and 6, and the lack of observable mixed adult and juvenile sized shells suggest two environmental possibilities. First, that environmental conditions such as fluctuating salinity, oxygen content, and temperature limited the clams' growth and capacity to reproduce. Second, that post-depositional environmental conditions such as high-water turbidity or rapid sediment deposition fragmented the smaller shell enough that graduate students could not observe the true range of the Rangia's size. In either case, the side discrimination and lack of both worked shells and lithic material in any of the zones suggest this shell deposit developed naturally, without human intervention. However, Rangia environmental tolerances suggest the shells developed in an environment like a tidal estuary that would have been accessible by humans in the area for purposes other than collecting Rangia.

The interpretation of this data is ongoing, as the results from proxy records like shell are most soundly understood when compared to other proxy records. The team will investigate the results of magnetic susceptibility testing, grain size analysis, and other sedimentary analysis to further characterize the estuarine environment in which these shell deposits formed. Further radiocarbon dating of the geological zones containing Rangia may be completed in order to more closely contextualize these layers. Graduate students will continue to process the 1.0 mm and <1.0 mm fraction throughout their Spring 2024 and Fall 2024 semesters; these analyses will be added to a final published report.

The purposes of this project were two-fold. First, students aimed to contribute to the ever-growing understanding of early North American human populations and how they arrived here, in accordance with outreach and education goals of the 2019 NOAA grant project. Second, students refined essential methodological skills while exploring the concepts of submerged paleolandscape data and theory. Both project goals advance the participating graduate students' professional development as it allowed them to engage in a dynamic process of applying newly learned theoretical frameworks and interdisciplinary material to a hands-on research opportunity, which fosters a foundation for future professional pursuits.

References

Butler, Paul, Pedro Freitas, Meghan Burchell, and Laurent Chauvaud
2019 Archaeology and Sclerochronology of Marine Bivalves. In *Goods and Services of Marine Bivalves*, Aad C. Smaal, Joao G. Ferreira, Jon Grant, Jens K. Petersen, Øivind Strand, editors, pp. 413-444. Springer, Cham, Switzerland. <https://doi.org/10.1007/978-3-319-96776-9>. Accessed 17 May 2024.

Claassen, Cheryl
1998 *Shells*. Cambridge Manuals in Archaeology. Cambridge University Press, Cambridge, MA.

Coastal Environments, Inc.
1977   Cultural Resources Evaluation of the Northern Gulf of Mexico Continental Shelf. Coastal Environments, Inc., Baton Rouge. Submitted to the National Park Service, U.S. Department of the Interior, Washington, DC <https://espis.boem.gov/Final%20Reports/4227.pdf>. Accessed 17 May 2024.

Evans, Amanda
2016   Examining and Testing Potential Prehistoric Archaeological Features on the Gulf of Mexico Outer Continental Shelf. U.S. Department of the Interior, Bureau of Ocean Energy Management, Gulf of Mexico OCS Region, New Orleans, LA. OCS Study BOEM 2016-015. <https://espis.boem.gov/final%20reports/5557.PDF>. Accessed 17 May 2024.

2020   Submerged Paleolandscapes of the Northwestern Gulf of Mexico. Sponsored Projects: The NOAA Office of Ocean Exploration and Research. *Oceanography* 33(1):90–99. <https://oceanexplorer.noaa.gov/explorations/20paleolandscapes-gomex/background/plan/plan.html>. Accessed 17 May 2024.

Faught, Michael
2004   The Underwater Archaeology of Paleolandscapes, Apalachee Bay, Florida. *American Antiquity* 69(2):275–289. <https://doi.org/10.2307/4128420>. Accessed 17 May 2024.

Gaffney, Chris
2008   Detecting trends in the prediction of the buried past: A review of Geophysical techniques in archaeology. *Archaeometry* 50(2):313–336. https://doi.org/10.1111/j.1475-4754.2008.00388.x. Accessed 15 June, 2024.

Gagliano, Sherwood M., Charles E. Pearson, Richard A. Weinstein, Diane E. Wiseman, and Christopher M. McClendon
1982   Sedimentary Studies of Prehistoric Archaeological Sites: Criteria for the Identification of Submerged Archaeological Sites of the Northern Gulf of Mexico Continental Shelf. Coastal Environments, Inc., Baton Rouge, LA. Submitted to U.S. Department of the Interior, National Park Service, Division of State Plans and Grants, Washington, DC. Contract No. C35003(79). <https://ntrl.ntis.gov/NTRL/dashboard/searchResults/titleDetail/PB88178017.xhtml>. Accessed 17 May 2024.

Halligan, Jessi J., Michael R. Waters, Angelina Perrotti, Ivy J. Owens, Joshua M. Feinberg, Mark D. Bourne, Brendan Fenerty, Barbara Winsborough, David Carlson, Daniel C. Fisher, Thomas W. Stafford Jr., and James S. Dunbar
2016   Pre-Clovis Occupation 14,550 Years Ago at the Page-Ladson site, Florida, and the Peopling of the Americas. *Science Advances* 2(5). <https://www.science.org/doi/full/10.1126/sciadv.1600375>. Accessed 17 May 2024.

Letham, Bryn
2024   Perspectives on a Post-White Sands Coast: Re-Evaluating Research into Early Peopling of the Northwest Coast of North America. *PaleoAmerica* 1–9. <https://doi.org/10.1080/20555563.2024.2318129>. Accessed 17 May 2024.

Liu, Kam-biu, Houyuan Lu, and Caiming Shen
2017   A 1200-year Proxy Record of Hurricanes and Fires from the Gulf of Mexico Coast: Testing the Hypothesis of Hurricane-Fire Interactions. *Quaternary Research* 69(1):29–41. <https://doi.org/10.1016/j.yqres.2007.10.011>. Accessed 17 May 2024.

Nelson, Henry F., and Ellis E. Bray
1970   Stratigraphy and History of Holocene Sediments in the Sabine-High Island Area, Gulf of Mexico. In *Deltaic Sedimentation, Modern and Ancient*, J. P. Morgan, editor, pp. 48-77. Society of Economic Paleontologists and Mineralogists Special Publication No. 15, Tulsa, OK <https://doi.org/10.2110/pec.70.11.0048>. Accessed 17 May 2024.

Pearson, Charles E., David B. Kelley, Richard A. Weinstein, and Sherwood M. Gagliano
1986   Archaeological Investigations on the Outer Continental Shelf: A Study Within the Sabine River Valley, Offshore Louisiana and Texas. OCS Study MMS 86-0119. Coastal Environments, Inc., Baton Rouge, LA. Submitted to Minerals Management Service, U.S. Department of the Interior, Reston, VA. <https://www.boem.gov/sites/default/files/boem-newsroom/Library/Publications/1986/86-0119.pdf>. Accessed 17 May 2024.

Rapp, George, and Christopher Hill
2006   *Geoarchaeology: The Earth-Science Approach to Archaeological Interpretation*. Yale University Press, New Haven, CT.

Smithsonian Environmental Research Center
2022   *Rangia cuneata*. NEMESIS, Smithsonian Environmental Research Center, Edgewater, MD. <https://invasions.si.edu/nemesis/species_summary/80962>. Accessed 17 May 2024.

STRIGHT, MELANIE J.
1999 Spatial Data Analysis of Artifacts Redeposited by Coastal Erosion: A Case Study of McFaddin Beach, Texas. Doctoral dissertation, Department of Anthropology, American University, Washington DC. University Microfilms International, Ann Arbor, MI. <https://www.proquest.com/docview/304520204>. Accessed 17 May 2024.

TORBEN, RICK C.
2023 Shell Midden Archaeology: Current Trends and Future Directions. *Journal of Archaeological Research*. <https://doi.org/10.1007/s10814-023-09189-9>. Accessed 17 May 2024.

U.S. FISH AND WILDLIFE SERVICE
2012 Atlantic Rangia (*Rangia cuneata*) Ecological Risk Screening Summary. Web Version. U.S. Fish and Wildlife Service, Washington, DC. <https://www.fws.gov/sites/default/files/documents/Ecological-Risk-Screening-Summary-Atlantic-Rangia.pdf>. Accessed 17 May 2024.

WATERS, MICHAEL R., STEVEN L. FORMAN, THOMAS A. JENNINGS, LEE C. NORDT, STEVEN G. DRIESE, JOSHUA M. FEINBERG, JOSHUA L. KEENE, JESSI HALLIGAN, ANNA LINDQUIST, JAMES PIERSON, CHARLES T. HALLMARK, MICHAEL B. COLLINS, AND JAMES E. WIEDERHOLD
2011 The Buttermilk Creek Complex and the Origins of Clovis at the Debra L. Friedkin Site, Texas. *Science* 331(6024):1599–1603. <https://pubmed.ncbi.nlm.nih.gov/21436451/>. Accessed 17 May 2024.

. . . .

Emma Graumlich
11000 University Parkway
Pensacola, Florida 32514-5750

Hope Bridgeman
11000 University Parkway
Pensacola, Florida 32514-5750

Kaitlin Decker
11000 University Parkway
Pensacola, Florida 32514-5750

Ramie Gougeon
11000 University Parkway
Pensacola, Florida 32514-5750

Amanda Evans
11000 University Parkway
Pensacola, Florida 32514-5750

August Costa
11000 University Parkway
Pensacola, Florida 32514-5750

Abandoned, But Not Forgotten: The Systemic and Archaeological Context of *Hildegarde*

Paul Willard Gates

Lake Champlain is the repository of a considerable number of submerged cultural resources and shipwrecks representing over 12,000 years of human occupation in the region. While archaeologists have collated a substantial amount of data on the vessels, the histories of many have yet to be fully understood. Hildegarde *is a case study of a vessel with a complete historic background from its launch in 1876 to its abandonment in 1937. This article explores the systemic context of the vessel with a focus on its uselife through lateral cycling during its pre-depositional context. The post-depositional context is explored when the vessel was abandoned in the Pine Street Barge Canal Breakwater Ship Graveyard along the shore of Burlington, Vermont. Cultural and non-cultural site formation processes are discussed along with potential correlations between ship abandonment and trends in maritime commerce, economics, population, and technological trends*

El lago Champlain es el depósito de un número considerable de recursos culturales sumergidos y de naufragios que representan más de doce mil años de ocupación humana en la región. Si bien los arqueólogos han recopilado una cantidad sustancial de datos sobre vasijas, la historia de muchas aún no se ha comprendido completamente. Hildegarde *es un estudio de caso de una embarcación con antecedentes históricos completos desde su botadura en 1876 hasta su abandono en 1937. Este artículo explora el contexto sistémico de la embarcación con un enfoque en su vida útil a través de ciclos laterales durante su contexto previo al depósito. También se explora el contexto posterior al depósito cuando el barco fue abandonado en el cementerio de barcos rompeolas del canal de barcazas de Pine Street a lo largo de la costa de Burlington, Vermont. Se discuten los procesos de formación de sitios culturales y no culturales junto con las posibles correlaciones entre el abandono de barcos y los patrones en el comercio marítimo, la economía, la población y tendencias tecnológicas.*

*Le lac Champlain est le dépositaire d'un nombre considérable de ressources culturelles submergées et d'épaves représentant plus de douze mille ans d'occupation humaine dans la région. Bien que les archéologues aient rassemblé une quantité importante de données sur les navires, l'histoire de beaucoup d'entre eux n'a pas encore été entièrement comprise. L'*Hildegarde *est une étude de cas d'un navire avec un contexte historique complet de son lancement en 1876 à son abandon en 1937. Cet article explorera le contexte systémique du navire en mettant l'accent sur sa vie d'utilisation par le biais d'un cycle latéral au cours de son contexte pré-déposition. Le contexte post-déposition sera également exploré lorsque le navire a été abandonné dans le cimetière de navires du brise-lames du canal de barges de la rue Pine le long de la rive de Burlington, au Vermont. Les processus de formation de sites culturels et non culturels seront discutés, de même que les corrélations potentielles entre l'abandon de navires et les tendances du commerce maritime, de l'économie, de la population et des tendances technologiques.*

Introduction

The Pine Street Barge Canal and Breakwater are ideal examples of a historic industrial area along the waterfront of Burlington, Vermont. As an inland canal used for offloading lumber and other raw materials, the canal and basin within the breakwater were heavily used in the 19th and early 20th centuries. Over the years, a cluster of five shipwrecks accumulated in this area. While rudimentary research has already been conducted on these vessels, they have yet to be examined through the theoretical paradigm of behavioral archaeology. Additionally, the abandoned vessels have not been adequately placed in their historical and local contexts.

The study of ship graveyards provides a wealth of data on the use-lives of abandoned vessels, especially when analyzing the broader impacts on maritime culture and commerce. The vessels interred within the Pine Street Barge Canal Breakwater Ship Graveyard represent a microcosm of Burlington's maritime industrial era. The purpose of this article is to focus on the history and use life of *Hildegarde* (VT-CH-794) as a case study of a singular vessel in this ship graveyard.

The systemic context of the vessel is explored through lateral cycling within its pre-depositional context. The post-depositional context also is explored, which is the history of the vessel abandoned in the Pine Street Barge Canal Breakwater Ship Graveyard along the shore of Burlington. Cultural and non-cultural site formation processes are discussed along with potential correlations between ship abandonment and trends in maritime commerce, economics, population, and technological trends. The study also adds essential information to the underrepresented study of freshwater abandonment sites and underwater archaeology in this geographic region.

Ship Graveyards in Lake Champlain and Theoretical Interpretations of their Development

To understand how the ship graveyard formed, it is important to explore the history of the area. As an ideal location for a maritime port along Lake Champlain, Burlington developed into a commercial center starting in the late 18th century (Hemenway 1867; Rann 1886; Cohn 2003). Historically, the Pine Street Barge Canal area was known as "the cove," where the beach formed a natural breakwater and mooring for vessels (Hemenway 1867:669). The area was used by master builder Richard Fittock to keep his stores and cargo and to provide lighter services for deep-water ships. Lighter services were provided by smaller vessels, typically barges, to offload or "lighten" larger cargo ships with deep drafts that were unable to dock in shallower areas along the shore. Eventually, the Rutland and Burlington Railroad Company established a depot and railyard in the area. The development of the waterfront was further propelled by the increase in commerce created by the canals, steamships, and railroads in the 19th century.

Traditional lake sailing vessels used before the creation of the Champlain and Chambly Canals were employed for heavier bulk cargoes in this era. However, the use of canal boats (later, sailing canal boats) replaced most traditional sailing vessels as a more efficient and cost-effective freight service after the canals were established. Much of the Burlington waterfront was used by canal boats and, by the 1860s, a breakwater, small canal, and a turning basin were developed in "the cove." After these additions, it was officially named the Pine Street Barge Canal. This small inland canal facilitated the loading and unloading of canal boats. The canal also serviced firms such as the Kilburn & Gates Lumber Mills and other companies in the late 19th century (Kane et al. 2008:51–52, 88).

The lumber mill and railroad industry continued to build up around the area into the 20th century, including the establishment of a coal-gasification plant and the expansion of the Rutland and Burlington Railroad enterprise. The area immediately surrounding the Barge Canal area eventually fell into disuse (Kane et al. 2008:54). The development of petroleum engines along with automobiles and airplanes in the 20th century marked a notable decline in maritime commerce on the lake. Many of the older sailing, canal, and steam vessels further fell into disuse.

In 1937, *Hildegarde* was abandoned within the canal breakwater entrance's southern pier. As a result of the coal-gasification plant waste product in-flows, the Pine Street Barge Canal eventually became a designated toxic site and was listed on the Superfund National Priorities List by the Environmental Protection Agency in 1983 (Kane et al. 2010). Other boats were eventually discarded into this derelict area and the ship graveyard was formed.

Because the graveyard constitutes a complex underwater archaeological site with a long history, understanding the site's formation processes is extremely important. For contemporary researchers to have a better understanding of the archaeological and historical record, a better understanding of systemic and archaeological contexts is needed. The systemic context reflects artifacts when they are actively engaged in a behavioral system. On the other hand, artifacts that interface with the natural environment in a depositional setting are regarded as existing in an archaeological context. In general, objects move from the systemic to the archaeological context, but in some instances objects move back and forth between both contexts (Schiffer 1987:3–4).

The factors responsible for generating the historical and archaeological records are known as formation processes (Schiffer 1987:7). Two distinct operations affect the depositional record accordingly. Cultural formation processes are "processes of human behavior that affect or transform artifacts after their initial period of use in a given activity" (Schiffer 1987:7). This process preserves artifacts in their systemic context, meaning it reflects artifacts when they are actively engaged in a behavioral system to create the historical record through reuse. As an example of a cultural formation process, reuse is when an artifact or artifacts change ownership from one user to another or from one social group to another without the artifact changing in its intended use or form (Schiffer 1987:28). Artifacts are preserved in the archaeological context (artifacts that interface with the natural environment in a depositional setting) through the deposition of artifacts and any consequent cultural alterations of material in both records (Schiffer 1987:7).

The second part of site formation processes includes non-cultural formation processes. Non-cultural formation processes are influenced by all occurrences in the natural environment that affect the archaeological record. Variability exists within all levels of environmental formation processes with effects like deterioration, decay, alteration, and modification (Schiffer 1987:143). Natural, non-cultural formation processes can physically, biologically, or chemically change the characteristics of artifacts or entire sites. They affect artifacts in systemic and archaeological contexts by influencing decay patterns, changes in sedimentation, natural disturbances, and the accumulation of ecological evidence that can be used to ascertain historic environmental conditions.

The theoretical concepts of site formation processes have been modified and applied to the study of underwater archaeological sites over the years. Academic studies in maritime archaeology also focus on ship graveyards and how these processes, especially related to abandonment practices, influence the creation of sites (Muckelroy 1978a, 1978b; Stewart 1999; Ward et al. 1999; Gibbs 2006; Richards and Staniforth 2006; Seeb 2007; Richards 2008; Gates 2019). Applying these concepts to the study of *Hildegarde* and the other vessels in the Pine Street Barge Canal Breakwater Ship Graveyard yielded comprehensive data and contributed to a broader understanding of abandonment practices.

Use-Life and Abandonment: A Case Study of *Hildegarde* and its Systemic Context

Historical data on *Hildegarde* were found from the listings of the Merchant Vessels of the United States, which aided in outlining the vessel's systemic context. The American Yacht List and Lloyds Register of American Yachts provided additional information. Formerly known as *Niantic*, *Hildegarde* has the official number of 130070 and the call number K.C.F.S. (United States Bureau of Navigation 1877:198, 1880:86, 1884:152, 1885:162, 1886:158; Olsen 1881:41; Lloyds Register of Shipping 1903:216). *Hildegarde*'s original configuration was as a centerboard sloop yacht with one deck and one mast. The gross tonnage was 37.91 while the net tonnage was 36.02. The length of the vessel was 58.2 feet (ft.) (17.7 meters [m]), the breadth was 19.2 ft. (5.8 m), and depth was 6 ft. (1.8 m). Figure 1 depicts a model of *Hildegarde* made from historic photographs and the digitized lines of a comparative model of the yacht *Pocohontas* (Historic New England 1887, 1889; Gary 2019).

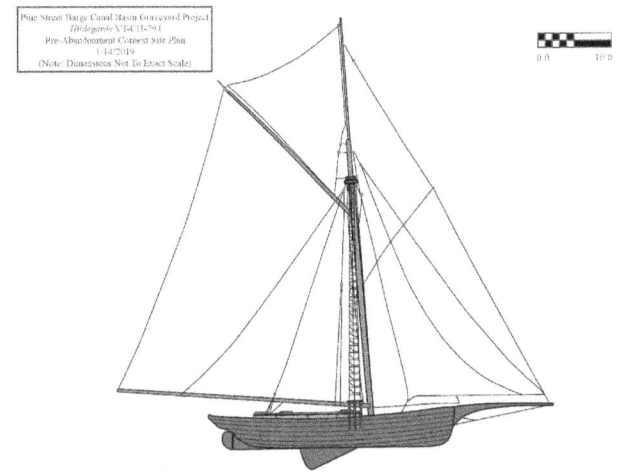

FIGURE 1. Model of *Hildegarde*. (Image by author, 2019.)

Hildegarde is listed as being built by A. E. Smith in 1876 at Islip, New York, with the home port of New York City. On 14 June 1880, the name of the vessel was officially changed from *Niantic* to *Hildegarde* (United States Congress 1880:197). *Hildegarde* was originally built as a sailing yacht and was a member of several yacht clubs, including the New York Yacht Club, the Atlantic Yacht Club, the Larchmont, the Riverton, Shelter Island, and the San Francisco Yacht Club (Olsen 1882:44, 1883:46, 1884:58, 1885:62, 1886:75, 1891:41, 1896:117). *Hildegarde* enjoyed an early career as a racing yacht and took part in America's Cup races and trial matches from 1876 to 1885 (Cozzens 1887:79, 89, 92, 94–95).

James C. Bergen was listed as the owner of *Hildegarde* in 1889 (United States Bureau of Navigation 1889:48–138). Ownership changed again to W. W. Butcher in 1906 (Lloyds Register of Shipping 1906:259). The register from 1925 lists a new owner as the Westport-Vergennes Ferry Co. (New York), with a home port in Rouses Point, New York, and the address of the owner in Westport, New York (United States Bureau of Navigation 1925:100–101). At this time, *Hildegarde* was converted to a car ferry by the Westport-Vergennes Ferry Company. In 1930, ownership of *Hildegarde* once again changed, and the new and final owner was listed as Herbert Pashby, who lived at 398 St. Paul Street in Burlington, Vermont (United States Bureau of Navigation 1930:88–89). Pashby operated the vessel as a tugboat for a stone barge from Fiske's Landing in Isle La

Motte to Burlington Harbor (Lake Champlain Maritime Museum 2014:52). The final listing of *Hildegarde* is in the 1937 register of The Merchant Vessels of the United States, which lists the vessel as being abandoned due to age or deterioration (United States Bureau of Marine Inspection and Navigation 1937:531).

Understanding *Hildegarde*'s Systemic Context

During the vessel's primary mercantile phase, *Niantic* (changed to *Hildegarde* in 1880) was used as a racing yacht and took part in several matches. One of the primary transformation processes that *Hildegarde* had undergone is the reuse process termed lateral cycling (Schiffer 1987:27). The activity of reuse maintains items within the systemic context until they are discarded and become part of the archaeological record. Table 1 lists the series of owners and the year of ownership that *Hildegarde* had during its use-life.

Owner	Year
Herman Oelrichs	1881
James C. Bergen	1889
W. W. Butcher	1906
Westport – Vergennes Ferry Company	1935
Herbert Pashby	1930

TABLE 1. Ownership history of *Hildegarde* (VT-CH-794) (Olsen 1881:41; Manning 1889:48–13; United States Bureau of Navigation 1906:259, 1925:100–101, 1930:88–89).

Additionally, the vessel had undergone physical changes in length, breadth, and depth. The increase in tonnage is another indicator that the vessel changed in configuration over time in conjunction with changes in ownership. The purpose of the vessel also changed from a sloop yacht to a gas screw-equipped ship, to steam screw ship listed for freight service. Within the systemic pre-depositional context, *Hildegarde* underwent primary and secondary modification and conversion processes (Richards 2008:102). These reuse processes are associated with secondary use, where the object (in this case a ship) assumes a new use and function due to modifications (Schiffer 1987:30). Modifications to *Hildegarde* required a substantial amount of work, effort, time, and money in order to adapt it from a sailboat to a gas screw, and then to a steamship.

The changes that occurred to the vessel related to modifications in the hull dimensions and materials along with modifications to the propulsion system. Modification in the hull dimensions and materials usually are variations in a vessel's overall measurements and tonnage (Richards 2008:124). From the first documents that record measurements, the dimensions of *Hildegarde* include a length of 58.2 ft. (17.7 m), a breadth of 19.3 ft. (5.8 m), a depth of 6.5 ft. (1.9 m), and a volume of 36.02 net tons (United States Bureau of Navigation 1884:152, 1885:162). However, in 1894 the length increased to 64 ft. (19.5 m) and the breadth decreased to 19.2 ft. (5.8 m), while the tonnage increased to 40.09 net tons and 42.19 gross tons (United States Bureau of Navigation 1894:143). As mentioned above, a significant amount of effort, financial investment, energy, and time was put into the modification of the vessel. The internal and external structural components changed drastically, likely due to economic and technological considerations.

In 1918, the tonnage of *Hildegarde* increased again to 46 gross tons with a net tonnage of 39. This change is in relation to the modification of the propulsion system from sail to a gas-powered screw with an indicated 100 horsepower engine. The centerboard for the ship was removed to make room for the engine and related components. Other modifications likely were applied to the outer hull, the framing, and even the keel, keelson, sister keelsons, and reinforced stern and bow sections for towing. The vessel also changed its function from a sailing ship to a ship intended for freight service (United States Bureau of Navigation 1918:246). This process of *Hildegarde*'s primary mercantile phase as a sloop yacht changing to a gas screw freighter is known as the secondary mercantile phase and is indicative of the owner's wish to maintain the ship in operational condition (Richards 2008:119–120). In 1924, another modification was made to the vessel when it was converted from a gas screw to a steam screw-equipped with an indicated 75 horsepower engine (United States Bureau of Navigation 1924:51).

Hildegarde underwent significant pre-depositional salvage when it was discarded and abandoned in 1937. This included stripping the ship of any material of value while the vessel was still in floating condition through primary salvage processes. Salvaged material could have included movable items, rigging elements, deck machinery, the pilot house, decking, the upper portions of the hull, and any machinery associated with a steam engine. Primary salvage of this material happened before the vessel was finally abandoned in its pre-depositional context (Richards 2008:155).

Post-Abandonment: The Archaeological Context of *Hildegarde*

Located at the southern entrance to the Pine Street Barge Canal, *Hildegarde* was identified during a Phase I archaeological study of the area in 1991 (Kane et al. 2008:93). The remains of *Hildegarde* are closest to the southern breakwater extension. The remains of a ferrous propeller are mentioned as well in the report, *Phase I Archaeological Survey of Burlington Harbor in Lake Champlain, Burlington, Chittenden County, Vermont* (Kane et al. 2008). Prior to its discovery, the only other known examination of this vessel was historical research conducted by Arthur Cohn in 1984 (Kane et al. 2010). Archaeological survey work completed in July 2018 found much of the vessel remains in poor condition. The remains of *Hildegarde* are oriented with the stern section facing west and the portside remains facing east. All extant remains are in a severe state of decay. Much more of the vessel may be buried underneath the sediment.

The remaining architectural features of *Hildegarde*, after the vessel underwent secondary salvage processes in its immediate post-abandonment context, include the keel, keelson, sister and rider keelsons, floor frames, frames, and bottom planking. Other elements include the stem, apron, stemson, bow cant timbers, propeller post, stern tube, stuffing box, stuffing box bulkhead, propeller, propeller hub, screw aperture, stern post, stern frames, and hull planking.

Figure 2 shows the archaeological site plan of *Hildegarde* with site formation signature locations. The remains of the iron rudder post assemblage, a large ferrous propeller, the stuffing box for the propeller shaft, the sternpost, and a steel pipe are also present. The extant assemblage also lies at an angle southwest over 10 ft. (3.04 m) away from the portside remains.

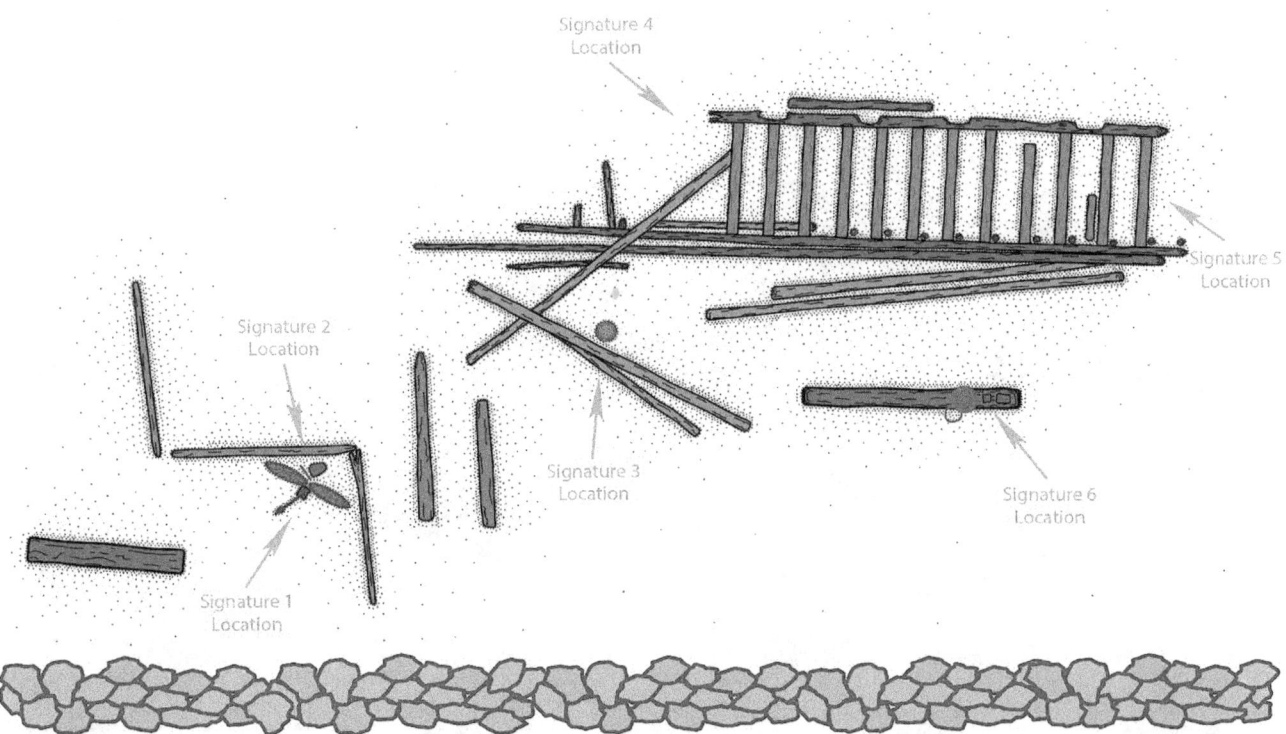

FIGURE 2. Archaeological site plan of *Hildegarde* with locations of site formation signatures: signature 1 is the remains of the iron rudder post assemblage; signature 2 is the remains of the propellor; signature 3 is remains of a steel pipe; signature 4 is the portside remains; signature 5 is the remains of the portside bow; and signature 6 is remains of the large, contorted ferrous ring and unidentified, large wooden structure. (Image by author, 2019.)

Additionally, a large intact wooden element with ferrous framing elements lies south of the portside remains near the southern breakwater pier foundations. A large contorted ferrous ring-shaped object lies just on top of the remains with the bottom section of an unidentified, large wooden structure. It is unclear if this is associated with *Hildegarde*.

Structural minimization processes are part of secondary salvage, where much of the vessel was reduced to its bottom-most parts. Because much of the vessel does not remain, all accessible material likely was removed before the vessel lost its ability to float. However, given the significant removal of material, finding evidence of pre-depositional salvage signatures on the present-day hull remains is difficult. There is the distinct possibility that much more of the bottom section of the hull from below the turn of the bilge is extant. Much of this section of the vessel is significantly buried under mud and any archaeological excavation could potentially reveal the remaining architectural features of *Hildegarde*.

Non-cultural site transformation processes are also present on the archaeological remains. The processes related to biological agents of deterioration are evident by the damage caused by zebra mussels. Pedoturbation processes of sedimentation buried most of the remnant structural features. Given the amount of mud and soil on the site, exactly how much of the ship is buried is unclear. There is evidence of floralturbation with the growth of invasive milfoil and grasses, which does not appear to affect the archaeological remains except to cover and obscure them. Figure 3 illustrates both the effects of secondary salvage processes where the remains of the partially buried and broken up rudder, propellor, and propeller post are still evident near the stern of *Hildegarde*. Non-cultural site formation processes related to biological agents, pedoturbation, and floralturbation are clearly seen affecting the remains of the vessel's stern.

Conclusions and Reasons for Abandonment

As acts of watercraft abandonment and salvage occur within the context of economic change, deliberate ship discard events potentially may correlate to broader historical trends in economic changes in Burlington's

FIGURE 3. Site formation signature location 1, photo GOPR5469. (Photo by author, 2018.)

waterfront. The introduction of innovative technologies, such as the sailing canal boat, trains, steam engines, and petroleum-fueled engines, are developments that impacted Vermont's broader maritime trade networks. To explain why *Hildegarde* was abandoned, potential reasons are explored through the analysis of correlational data relating to several key factors. These factors include economic and technological correlations. As a note, these reasons are limited from a much broader evaluation of correlations.

Data on the coal tonnage arriving in the port of Burlington from 1869 to 1920 correlate to *Hildegarde*'s abandonment. In 1869, the total amount of coal was 22,050 tons with the highest peak in trade listed in 1892 with 115,000 tons (United States Army Corps of Engineers 1869, 1892). The rest of the time period shows fluctuations in tonnages with 250 tons in 1920, the last registered year (United States Army Corps of Engineers 1920). Analysis of economic data on the decline in the coal trade led to uncertainty of any possible relational correlates to the abandonment of *Hildegarde*. As *Hildegarde* was a steam vessel, it would have relied on sources of coal to fuel the ship's boiler to produce steam for the engine. While the decline of the coal trade well before 1900 is evident from the research, it is plausible that the continuing decrease in coal coming into the port of Burlington may have led to the abandonment of *Hildegarde*.

The analysis of technological correlates like the replacement of traditional commercial sailing craft with the newer classes of canal boats provides the most plausible evidence of the decision to abandon *Hildegarde*. Vessels that ran on petroleum-based fuels made both sail and steam vessels obsolete. The use of these fuels replaced the need for coal-fired steam engines. This provides a plausible correlation for the abandonment of *Hildegarde*. A more credible and stronger correlation is the effects of the Great Depression during the 1930s. The economic downturn in the United States during the Great Depression was catastrophic and did not recover until the 1940s (PBS 2019). Research into the history of *Hildegarde* revealed that the vessel was abandoned in the 1930s due to economic hardship experienced by its owner, Clarence Morgan (Kane et. al. 2008:93). Given that Morgan could no longer afford to keep the vessel, it presents a highly plausible correlation for abandonment.

However, *Hildegarde* presents an interesting case of steam-powered vessels in use during an era when petroleum-powered ships replaced older vessels with coal-fired steam engines. Given that the last owners operated *Hildegarde* until its final abandonment in 1937, perhaps Morgan could not sell the vessel due to the demand for petroleum-powered vessels at the time. The decline of steam-engines in marine vessels is further supported by evidence regarding the downward trend in coal imports and correlates to abandonment from 1866 to 1970.

Future Considerations for Ship Graveyards in Lake Champlain

Research shows that the vessels within the basin are remnant products associated with commercial activities that rose and declined from the late 18th century into the 20th century. Each of these vessels had specific use-lives and reached a stage of obsolescence. The potential reasons for decisions made in the abandonment of the vessels in the Pine Street Barge Canal Breakwater Ship Graveyard are correlated to the changing social, economic, and technological trends of the Burlington Waterfront.

As stated by Seeb (2007:215), "Ships' graveyards are an underdeveloped and under-researched area of the subdiscipline of maritime archaeology." Research into the collection of abandoned vessels in the Pine Street Barge Canal area helps to provide information into this subdiscipline of maritime archaeology. Along with this collection of vessels including the abandoned canal boats in the canal itself (Kane et al. 2010), the entire Burlington waterfront is littered with the remains of vessels. While it is unclear if this larger collection of vessels was intentionally abandoned, they contribute to the archaeological and historical record of the maritime industry, commerce, and technological change in the port of Burlington. Research into this geographic area for ships' graveyards is minimal and the study of freshwater abandonment sites will augment the field of maritime archaeology.

The vessels found within the confines of the Pine Street Barge Canal Basin Ship Graveyard represent only a small portion of abandoned ships in Burlington Harbor, let alone in Lake Champlain. Previous research on the Shelburne Shipyard Steamboat Graveyard identified the remains of four 19th-century steamboats in the shallow waters adjacent to Shelburne Shipyard in Shelburne, Vermont (Kennedy and Crisman 2014; Kennedy 2015, 2016). Future investigations could study patterns of use and salvage on these vessels and generate a comparative analysis between them and the vessel remains in Burlington. Collaborative research on ship graveyards in Lake Champlain would contribute to the future of abandonment studies.

References

Cohn, Arthur B.
2003   *Lake Champlain's Sailing Canal Boats: An Illustrated Journey from Burlington Bay to the Hudson River.* Lake Champlain Maritime Museum, Ferrisburgh, VT.

Cozzens, Fred S.
1887   *Yachts and Yachting: With Over One Hundred and Ten Illustrations.* Cassell & Company, New York, NY.

Gary, Yves
2019   Pocahontas: Story and Specifications. America-scoop.com. <http://america-scoop.com/index.php?option=com_content&view=article&id=1354:pocahontas-story-and-specifications>. Accessed 17 May 2024.

Gates, Paul Willard
2019   What Lies Beneath at the Pine Street Barge Canal Breakwater Ship Graveyard: Site Formation Processes as a Document of Change in Burlington, Vermont (c. 1830–1960). Master's thesis, Department of History, East Carolina University, Greenville, NC.

Gibbs, Martin
2006   Cultural Site Formation Processes in Maritime Archaeology: Disaster Response, Salvage and Muckelroy 30 Years On. *International Journal of Nautical Archaeology* 35(1):4–19.

Hemenway, Abbie Maria (editor)
1867   *The Vermont Historical Gazetteer: A Magazine Embracing A History of Each Town, Civil, Ecclesiastical, Biographical and Military.* Miss A. M. Hemenway, Burlington, VT.

Historic New England
1887   Photograph of *Hildegarde* in America's Cup 1887. Nathaniel L. Stebbins Photographic Collection, PC047, Historic New England, Boston, MA.

1889   Photograph of *Hildegarde* in the Atlantic Yacht Club Regatta 1889. Nathaniel L.Stebbins Photographic Collection, PC047, Historic New England, Boston, MA.

Kane, Adam I., Christopher R. Sabick, and Joanne M. DellaSalla
2008   *Phase I Archaeological Survey of Burlington Harbor in Lake Champlain, Burlington, Chittenden County, Vermont.* Report to Environmental Analysis Section, U.S. Army Corps of Engineers from Lake Champlain Maritime Museum. Vergennes, VT.

Kane, Adam I., Joanne M. Dennis, Scott A. McLaughlin, and Christopher R. Sabick
2010   *Sloop Island Canal Boat Study: Phase II Archaeological Investigation in Connection with the Environmental Remediation of the Pine Street Canal Superfund Site.* Report to U.S. Environmental Protection Agency and the Vermont Division for Historic Preservation from Lake Champlain Maritime Museum. Vergennes, VT.

Kennedy, Carolyn
2015   Shelburne Shipyard Steamboat Graveyard: 2015. *Institute of Nautical Archaeology Quarterly* 42(2):12–17.

2016   Shelburne Shipyard Steamboat Graveyard: 2016. *Institute of Nautical Archaeology Quarterly* 43(1/2):12–17.

Kennedy, Carolyn, and Kevin Crisman
2014   Shelburne Shipyard Steamboat Graveyard. Institute of Nautical Archaeology Quarterly 41(2):16-21.

Lake Champlain Maritime Museum
2014   *Images of America: Lake Champlain.* Lake Champlain Maritime Museum, Basin Harbor, VT.

Lloyds Register of Shipping
1903   *Lloyds Register of American Yachts, Containing particulars of Yachts, Yacht Owners, Yacht Builders and Designers and Yacht Clubs of the United States and Canada for 1903-4.* Lloyds Register of Shipping, New York, NY.

1906   *Lloyds Register of American Yachts, Containing particulars of Yachts, Yacht Owners, Yacht Builders and Designers and Yacht Clubs of the United States and Canada for 1906-7.* Lloyds Register of Shipping, New York, NY.

Muckelroy, Keith
1978a   The Archaeology of Shipwrecks. In *Maritime Archaeology: A Reader of Substantive and Theoretical Contributions*, Larry Babits and Hans Van Tilburg, editors, pp. 267–291. Plenum Press (now Springer), New York, NY.

1978b   The Analysis of Sea-Bed Distributions Discontinuous Sites. In *Maritime Archaeology: A Reader of Substantive and Theoretical Contributions*, Larry Babits and Hans Van Tilburg, editors, pp. 471–489. Plenum Press (now Springer), New York, NY.

Olsen, Niels
1881   *The American Yacht List for 1881.* Henry Bessey, Steam Book and Job Printers, New York, NY.

1882   *The American Yacht List for 1882.* Henry Bessey, Steam Book and Job Printers, New York, NY.

1883 *The American Yacht List for 1883*. Henry Bessey, Steam Book and Job Printers, New York, NY.

1884 *The American Yacht List for 1884*. Henry Bessey, Steam Book and Job Printers, New York, NY.

1885 *The American Yacht List for 1885*. Henry Bessey, Steam Book and Job Printers, New York, NY.

1886 *The American Yacht List for 1886*. Henry Bessey, Steam Book and Job Printers, New York, NY.

PUBLIC BROADCASTING SERVICE (PBS)
2019 Surviving the Dustbowl. Article, The Great Depression. American Experience, Public Broadcasting Service, Arlington, VA. <https://www.pbs.org/wgbh/americanexperience/features/dustbowl-great-depression/>. Accessed 1 April 2024.

RANN, W. S. (EDITOR)
1886 *History of Chittenden County with Some Illustrations and Biographical Sketches of Some of Its Prominent Men and Pioneers*. D. Mason & Co., Syracuse, NY.

RICHARDS, NATHAN
2008 *Ships Graveyards: Abandoned Watercraft and the Archaeological Site Formation Process*. University Press of Florida, Gainesville.

Richards, Nathan, and Mark Staniforth

2006 The Abandoned Ships Project: An Overview of the Archaeology of Deliberate Watercraft Discard in Australia. *Historical Archaeology* 40(4):84–103.

SEEB, SAMI KAY
2007 Cape Fear's Forgotten Fleet: The Eagles Island Ships' Graveyard, Wilmington, North Carolina. Master's thesis, Department of History, East Carolina University, Greenville, NC.

SCHIFFER, MICHAEL B.
1987 *Formation Processes of the Archaeological Record*. University of Utah Press, Salt Lake City.

STEWART, DAVID J.
1999 Formation Processes Affecting Submerged Archaeological Sites: An Overview. *Geoarchaeology: An International Journal* 14(6):565–587.

UNITED STATES ARMY CORPS OF ENGINEERS
1869 *Annual report of the Chief of Engineers, United States Army, to the Secretary of War, for the year 1869*. U.S. House of Representatives, Washington, DC.

1892 *Annual report of the Chief of Engineers, United States Army, to the Secretary of War, for the year 1892, Part III*. U.S. House of Representatives, Washington, DC.

1920 *Annual report of the Chief of Engineers, United States Army, to the Secretary of War, for the year 1920, Part I*. U.S. House of Representatives, Washington, DC.

UNITED STATES BUREAU OF NAVIGATION
1877 *Merchant Vessels of the United States, Vol. 1876–1877*. U.S. Treasury Department, Washington, DC.

1880 *Merchant Vessels of the United States, Vol. 1879–1880*. U.S. Treasury Department, Washington, DC.

1884 *Merchant Vessels of the United States, Vol. 1883–1884*. U.S. Treasury Department, Washington, DC.

1885 *Merchant Vessels of the United States, Vol. 1884–1885*. U.S. Treasury Department, Washington, DC.

1886 *Merchant Vessels of the United States, Vol. 1885 - 1886*. U.S. Treasury Department, Washington, DC.

1889 *Merchant Vessels of the United States, Vol. 1888–1889*. U.S. Treasury Department, Washington, DC.

1894 *Merchant Vessels of the United States, Vol. 1893–1894*. U.S. Treasury Department, Washington, DC.

1918 *Merchant Vessels of the United States, Vol. 1917–1918*. U.S. Department of Commerce, Washington, DC.

1924 *Merchant Vessels of the United States, Vol. 1923–1924*. U.S. Department of Commerce, Washington, DC.

1925 *Merchant Vessels of the United States, Vol. 1924–1925*. U.S. Department of Commerce, Washington, DC.

1930 *Merchant Vessels of the United States, Vol. 1929–1930*. U.S. Department of Commerce, Washington, DC.

UNITED STATES BUREAU OF MARINE INSPECTION AND NAVIGATION
1937 *Merchant Vessels of the United States*. U.S. Department of Commerce, Washington, DC.

UNITED STATES CONGRESS
1880 An Act to Change the Name of yacht *Niantic* to that of *Hildegarde*, pp. 197. *The Statutes At Large of the United States of America*, 46th Congress, 2nd Session, Washington, DC.

Ward, Ingrid A. K., Piers Lacombe, and Peter Veth
1999 A New Process-Based Model for Wreck Site Formation. *Journal of Archaeological Science* 26(5):561–570.

• • • • • • • • • • • • • • • • •

Paul Willard Gates
Lake Champlain Maritime Museum
4472 Basin Harbor Road
Vergennes, Vermont 05491

Tides of Time: Climate Change and its Impact on the Maritime Archaeological Sites of Fort Mose and Tolomato Bar Anchorage, St. Augustine, Florida

Airielle R. Cathers, Bryce A. Peacher

This study delves into the intersection of climate change and maritime archaeology, focusing on two sites in St. Augustine, Florida: Fort Mose and the Tolomato Bar Anchorage. Archaeologists with the St. Augustine Lighthouse Archaeological Maritime Program charted the impact of shifting environmental conditions, illuminating the urgent threats they pose to our understanding of history. Drawing on geographic information systems and archaeological data, we contrast the distinct challenges faced by terrestrial and underwater sites in the era of climate change. Furthermore, we extrapolate these findings to predict future vulnerabilities and discuss adaptive strategies for preserving these invaluable portals to our past. This investigation not only illuminates the resilience and fragility of historical sites but also offers a blueprint for safeguarding our cultural heritage amidst our changing climate.

Este estudio profundiza en la intersección del cambio climático y la arqueología marítima, centrándose en dos sitios dentro de St. Augustine, Florida: Fort Mose y Tolomato Bar Anchorage. La investigación traza el impacto de las condiciones ambientales cambiantes, iluminando las amenazas urgentes que representan para nuestra comprensión de la historia. Utilizando datos meteorológicos y oceanográficos específicos del sitio, analizados a través de Sistemas de Información Geográfica, los investigadores contrastan los distintos desafíos que enfrentan los sitios arqueológicos marítimos cuando se ven afectados por grandes tormentas. Además, los hallazgos se extrapolan para pronosticar vulnerabilidades futuras en la región y discutir estrategias de adaptación para preservar estos invaluables portales a nuestro pasado. Esta investigación muestra tanto la resiliencia como la fragilidad de los sitios históricos y ofrece un plan para salvaguardar nuestro patrimonio cultural en medio de un clima cambiante.

Cette étude se penche sur l'intersection du changement climatique et de l'archéologie maritime, en se concentrant sur deux sites à St. Augustine, en Floride : Fort Mose et le mouillage de Tolomato Bar. La recherche trace l'impact des conditions environnementales changeantes, en mettant en lumière les menaces urgentes qu'elles posent à notre compréhension de l'histoire. À l'aide de données météorologiques et océanographiques propres au site, telles qu'analysées au moyen des systèmes d'information géographique, les chercheurs comparent les défis distincts auxquels les sites archéologiques maritimes sont confrontés lorsqu'ils sont touchés par des tempêtes majeures. De plus, les résultats sont extrapolés pour prévoir les vulnérabilités futures dans la région et discuter des stratégies d'adaptation pour préserver ces portails inestimables à notre passé. Cette enquête met en lumière la résilience et la fragilité des sites historiques et offre un plan pour la sauvegarde de notre patrimoine culturel dans un contexte de changement climatique.

Introduction

In 2020, the St. Augustine Lighthouse Archaeological Maritime Program (LAMP) received a Hurricane Irma National Park Service Subgrant to assess and mitigate, or recommend future mitigation activities, for maritime archaeological sites impacted by 2017's Hurricane Irma. The resulting project, the Hurricane Irma Damage Assessment and Mitigation Strategy (HIrmaDAMS), aimed to address major storm impacts to the First Coast region along northeast Florida, an ever-present issue in light of current climate change trends. Priority targets spanned 10 terrestrial, foreshore, and submerged archaeological sites, all varying in age and initial documented condition. Two of those sites, Fort Mose II and the Tolomato Bar Anchorage, have shown particularly interesting patterns in coastal erosion and site integrity in light of various recent environmental forces.

While fluctuations in global and regional temperatures have always occurred, there has been a notable rise in global air temperatures in the last decade. Recent research has modeled a mean air temperature rise of 1.6–6.6 degrees Celcius (°C) in the United States by the end of this century (Melillo et al. 2014). This global warming trend affects the temperature of the ocean's surface layer within the top 50 to 200 meters. With this warming, land-based ice sheets melt into the oceans, resulting in ocean water thermal expansion and increased mean sea-level rise. Some of the most pressing issues resulting from sea-level rise are coastal erosion, mass extinction of threatened and endangered species, salinity shifts, amplified wave and surge action, and more powerful storms. According to Lim et al. (2018) and the National Oceanic and Atmospheric Administration (NOAA)'s Geophysical Fluid Dynamics Laboratory (NOAA GFDL 2019), higher sea-surface temperatures in the eastern Marine Development Region combined with record-breaking ocean heat content are linked to more intense tropical cyclones. This is based on multiple models demonstrating an increase in the global proportion of tropical cyclones that reach Category 3, 4, or 5 on the Saffir-Simpson Hurricane Wind Scale. While the number of major hurricanes is expected to increase, the overall number of hurricanes each year should stay relatively the same, or even show a slight decrease (NOAA GFDL 2019). This increase in storm intensity is particularly detrimental to coastal and nearshore environments and populations where the damage probability is highest due to increased storm surge, wave action, and environmental erosion.

Extreme, high-energy events such as storms and hurricanes often cause high tides, strong currents, coastal flooding, and modern debris transport into the marine environment. These factors are major contributors to damage to both cultural and biological resources in the region of impact. Previous archaeological studies in the Gulf of Mexico and the Florida Keys have exposed varying levels of impacts to submerged archaeological sites in direct paths of major hurricanes (Gearhart et al. 2012; Emmons 2018; Cathers 2019, 2020). Forces such as wave action and strong currents have been documented to cause extensive sediment movement in the form of mass deposition and site scour, both submerged and terrestrially. With tidal surges at the magnitude often found during these events, fragmentation, and destruction of historic and archaeological sites are also not uncommon. The shallow or exposed high-energy environment within which most of St. Augustine's archaeological sites are situated faces an increased risk of disturbance and damage due to passing storms.

Hurricane Irma was a particularly devastating hurricane that initially formed over the Atlantic on 30 August 2017. By 4 September, Irma had grown from a Category 3 storm to a monster Category 5, with sustained winds over 185 mph, becoming the strongest hurricane ever observed in the Atlantic basin outside the Caribbean Sea and Gulf of Mexico (NOAA NESDIS 2018). Irma passed through the Leeward Islands just north of Puerto Rico as a Category 5 storm. Weakening slightly as it grazed the northern coastline of Cuba and then moving north, Irma made landfall on 10 September as a Category 4 hurricane on Cudjoe Key in the lower Florida Keys. Irma subsequently left a trail of destruction in its path as it moved up the western coast of Florida, causing an estimated $50 billion (USD) in damage to businesses, property, and infrastructure (NOAA NCEI 2018). Florida's north and northeast regions were spared the brunt of major damage but still dealt with a ripple of tropical storm-level impacts, particularly flooding. In June 2018, the National Hurricane Center produced a Tropical Cyclone Report on Hurricane Irma in conjunction with NOAA and the National Weather Service (Cangialosi et al. 2018). It states, "Even though Irma made landfall along the southwestern coast of Florida, the hurricane's large wind field produced significant storm surge flooding along the northeastern coast of Florida, where a maximum of 3.0–5.0 ft. (feet) (0.9–1.5 meters [m]) of inundation above ground level occurred from Cape Canaveral northward to the Florida-Georgia border" (Cangialosi et al. 2018:10).

Local to St. Augustine, a storm tidal sensor recorded a Hurricane Irma storm surge above 6.5 ft. (1.98 m) in the Matanzas River, and another sensor in St. Augustine South recorded over 10 inch (in.) (25.4 centimeters [cm]) of rainfall in a period of less than 24 hours. A report from the United States Geological Survey (USGS) highlights heavily impacted areas of the Palm Coast, Matanzas, South Ponte Vedra, Mayport, and Little Talbot Island, areas near or containing maritime heritage sites previously investigated and monitored by LAMP or other archaeologists (USGS 2018). The report compares aerial images of these locations before and after the impact of Hurricane Irma and states, "The combined effects of surge and storm-induced wave runup created elevated total water levels at the shoreline, causing extensive erosion of the beach and dunes" (USGS 2018:1). Dune erosion was indeed significant, especially considering the extreme erosion that local beaches had suffered from Hurricane Matthew just the year before. In addition, Irma caused widespread flooding in both Jacksonville and St. Augustine, impacting hundreds of local households and historic buildings.

Since Hurricane Irma and the resulting award of the HIrmaDAMS grant in 2020, multiple major storms and hurricanes have impacted the study region. This includes Michael in 2018, Dorian in 2019, Ian and Nicole in 2022, and Idalia in 2023. The primary research question for HIrmaDAMS encompassed Irma's general impacts on maritime archaeological sites in this region. This was lat–er expanded to include subsequent storm impacts. Of the 10 sites chosen for the grant—encompassing historic waterfront sites, beached shipwrecks, and submerged shipwrecks—two of the sites included African American working waterfront sites. These are the Tolomato Bar Anchorage and Fort Mose.

Tolomato Bar Anchorage

Tolomato Bar Anchorage (8SJ4801), located approximately 7 miles north of St. Augustine, is situated on the southward-facing Guana Peninsula and is framed by the Tolomato River to its west and the Guana River to the east. This strategic positioning on the Guana Peninsula is further defined by the establishment of a dam on the Guana River in the 1950s, which resulted in the creation of the Guana Reservoir and the formation of a land bridge that connects the peninsula to an eastern barrier chain. The landscape of the peninsula is rich in biodiversity, marked by a mix of tidal marshes and oak/pine forests, particularly in areas proximate to the project site.

The geological composition of the Guana Tolomato Matanzas National Estuarine Research Reserve (GTMRR), including the Anchorage area, is primarily made up of Holocene epoch sediments, including sand, clay, and shell fragments. Notably, the soil profiles within this archaeological region vary significantly along the short stretch of shoreline. The northern section is characterized by Pellicer sediment, commonly found in tidal marshes. These soils, originating from loamy and clayey marine sediments, are particularly notable for their poor drainage, position in lower landscape areas, and clay-like texture (USDA 2006). Conversely, the southern section of this shoreline is distinguished by Tavares soil, which is distinct in its characteristics: very deep, moderately well-drained, and rapidly/very rapidly permeable. This soil type predominantly occupies the lower slopes of hills and knolls and is formed from sandy marine or eolian deposits. These diverse soil types underpin a complex ecosystem in which this archaeological site resides (FL DEP 2024).

The Anchorage is formed and sheltered by a sandbar situated in the Tolomato River (Figure 1). Historical records have noted this sandbar, which has a navigable channel to its west and provides to its east a sheltered anchorage where the water depth at low tide can exceed 12 ft. Contemporary accounts suggest that any ship navigating past the bar at St. Augustine could reach this landing. This site is the first anchorage north of the St. Augustine Inlet next to a significant tract of usable land, making it historically significant for linking farming activities with regional and broader maritime commerce. A considerable portion of the peninsula was owned by James Grant, the first British governor of East Florida, who developed it into a plantation worked by enslaved Africans (Schafer 2000). Following the British Period (1763-1783), Minorcan settlers continued to utilize the wharf at this location as a vital transportation and agricultural export center (Beeson 2006).

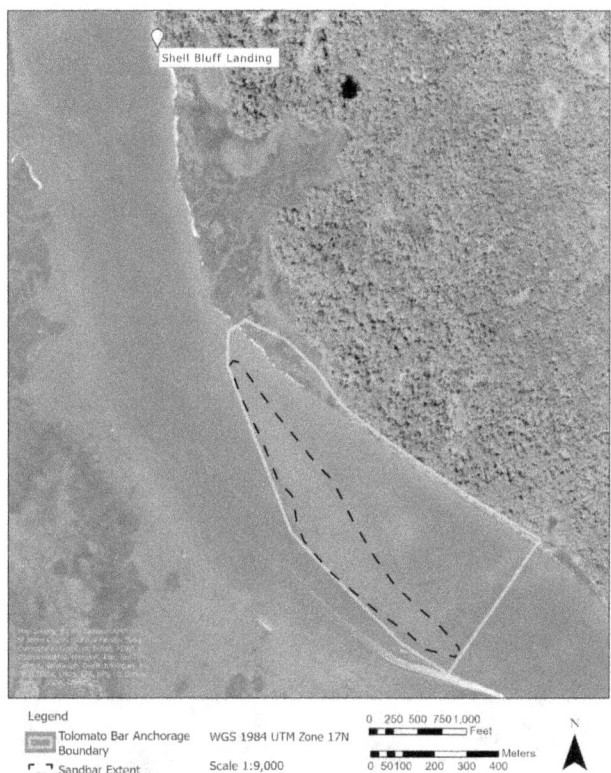

FIGURE 1. 2024 GIS site map of Tolomato Bar Anchorage showing site boundaries, sandbar extent, and the location of the Shell Bluff Landing archaeological site. (Map by Airielle Cathers, 2024.)

Tolomato has been documented by archaeologists over the past 20 years with, for the most part, little change noted, even after storms. This site is unique in St. Augustine with its excellent preservation of organic waterfront features dating to the colonial period. This study has identified particular features previously documented to compare their current condition with previous descriptions, scaled drawings, and photographs. The best example of this is the cribbing at the Area B pier. This feature is readily recognizable because of its distinctive form, and comparisons with previous photographs suggest it has survived with very little deterioration since it was initially photographed by LAMP in 2009 and again in 2022 (Meide et al. 2021). This is very promising, given that the cribbing is made up of delicate slats of wood. If these fragile slivers of wood have survived the impact of natural and human-created erosion events over the last 20 years, then the logs and larger timbers making up the piers, wharves, and hards are likely to prove resilient.

The level of preservation is largely due to the area's unique geography: the sandbar, which provided a sheltered anchorage, also serves to protect delicate archaeological resources from everyday erosion due to boat traffic on the Intracoastal Waterway that regularly produces powerful surges from boat wakes, and from the seasonal impact of hurricanes, including particularly destructive ones like Matthew in 2016 and Irma in 2017. Further evidence that the sandbar is naturally mitigating this damage can be gleaned from visiting sites upriver and downriver from the sandbar, where the effects of erosion are painfully apparent. As seen on the left of Figure 2, just a mile downriver from Tolomato Bar Anchorage is a tree with an almost fully exposed root system, a testament to the amount of shoreline that has eroded here without the protection of the sandbar. Almost two vertical meters of land have been swept away by boat wakes and storm action.

Perhaps more shocking is the damage to a neighboring archaeological site, Shell Bluff Landing (8SJ32). Located just upriver from the Tolomato Bar, Shell Bluff is named for the massive prehistoric shell midden and features a historic coquina well known locally as the "Minorcan well." Around 20 years ago, the top of the well was just at ground level. Over the last two decades, the earth around the well has been eroded, as seen on the

FIGURE 2. Left, photograph of a tree with eroded roots, downriver from the Tolomato Bar Anchorage site. The height of the exposed roots and bluff in the background make clear how much erosion this part of the shore has suffered. Right, photograph of the "Minorcan well" (behind protective fencing) and the eroded shoreline at the Shell Bluff Landing site (8SJ32), located just upriver from the Tolomato Bar Anchorage site. Extreme erosion has decimated the shoreline at this site, exposing a large portion of the coquina well that was once buried. (Photos by Chuck Meide, courtesy of Lighthouse Maritime Archaeological Program, 2022.)

right side of Figure 2. The original ground surface can be seen in the photograph, behind the almost fully exposed well, which now has protective fencing around it to help prevent it from collapsing. Again, a portion of the shoreline almost 2 m high is now missing. As with the historic cribbing, the sandbar has provided a barricade of protection for the site against storms like Hurricane Irma and the everyday impact of boat wakes. Researchers on site regularly saw the results of wakes from distant vessels, which produced powerful, repeated surges of water that pounded the shore even with the protection of the bar. It is, therefore, evident that potential still exists for erosion damage here.

Fort Mose II

Fort Mose, established in 1738 by Florida's Spanish governor, was a notable fortified settlement home to free Africans escaping slavery from the nearby British colonies (Landers 1990). Featuring two notable periods of habitation, the Fort Mose II site was a strategic defensive outpost for St. Augustine, located 2 to 3 miles to the south. It is situated along Robinson Creek, a minor offshoot of the Tolomato River that originates from tributaries in northern St. Augustine before converging into a main flow that moves northeastward from the edge of the tidal zone where marsh and dry land meet. Railroad magnate Henry Flagler purchased the land in the late 1880s and dredged the area to generate fill for the construction site of the Flagler Hotel (now Flagler College), transforming upland farms once belonging to Fort Mose's inhabitants into salt marshes (Landers 1990).

The terrain of Fort Mose Historic State Park, where Fort Mose II is located, is notably flat and lies within the Eastern Valley physiographic province (White 1970). Despite the presence of Cretaceous, Tertiary, and Quaternary limestones within this region (Brooks 1981), sand is the predominant surface cover. Beneath the surface, the region is composed of Holocene-era sediments characterized by quartz sands and small quantities of organic material and clay from lagoon sediments (Scott 1993). The landscape is largely the result of clastic sediment deposition during periods of higher sea levels and is marked by sediments from marsh formation in the lagoon behind the current barrier island and to the west of the Tolomato River. The site predominantly features Pellicer Silty Clay Loam, prone to frequent flooding with elevations ranging from sea level to about 7 ft (2.1 m). The Park's three islands are experiencing active erosion, most notably at the southernmost island where the second iteration of Fort Mose and the study site was located. Management practices along the shoreline have established oyster mats to encourage the growth of the local oyster beds and counter soil erosion.

The Fort Mose II site is particularly vulnerable to storm-induced environmental changes. Archaeological features and components at this location are partially submerged along a riverbank and surrounding marshes that are notably unstable. Rising water levels, which introduce greater salinity fluctuations, impact the fragile equilibrium between saltwater and freshwater habitats, though the extent of threat these pose to the archaeological sites remains unclear. Once flourishing, the marsh's flora and fauna now face heightened risks of ecological imbalance and extinction. For Fort Mose II and Robinson Creek, the loss of native vegetation could significantly exacerbate erosion, potentially submerging the terrestrial context. While it was found, somewhat surprisingly, that the stratigraphy seems to be maintained as the terrestrial context is deflated into the creek bed (Figure 3), and that, less surprisingly, artifacts such as ceramics and glass can survive that transition, terrestrial

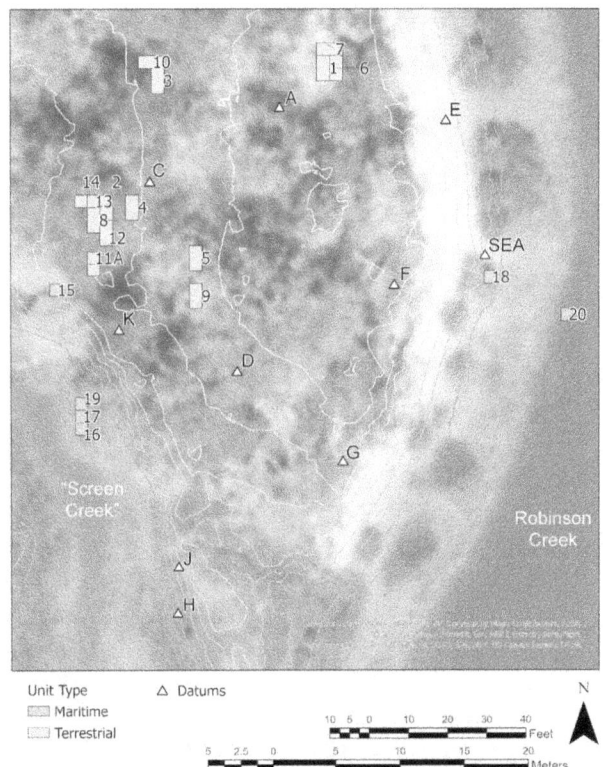

FIGURE 3. 2022 GIS site map of Fort Mose II, georeferenced onto aerial imagery with DEM, showing all terrestrial and underwater excavation units and most site datums. (Map by Airielle Cathers, 2023.)

archaeological features such as post molds are less likely to survive such erosion.

Throughout the excavations in 2021–2023, significant tidal shifts showed the extreme conditions the site was exposed to on a daily basis. As seen in Unit 11A (Figure 4), cracking and slumpage of the mud south of the unit exemplified the impact of erosion along the shoreline bluff of a small, unnamed, non-navigable creek known informally to researchers as "Screen Creek." Due to this constant erosion into the creek, this unit was shored up with multiple sandbags at the end of the field seasons to prevent, or at least slow, further action. Continued archaeological investigations of this significant site's terrestrial and maritime components have been deemed critically important by LAMP, Flagler College, University of Florida, and University of Texas project archaeologists before they are further erased by future erosion (Meide et al. 2023). It should also be noted that unauthorized visitor use of the site has shown to be the main anthropogenic threat. Still, frequent use and visitation by archaeologists and park rangers have assisted in the reduction of this factor.

Geospatial Analysis

While the field investigations led to a significantly better understanding of the erosional impact on the archaeological deposits, both on land and underwater, specific damage attributed to Hurricane Irma through archaeological inspection could not be determined. Subsequent geospatial analysis and LiDAR survey contributed to understanding how Hurricane Irma and other named storms impacted the site and its environs. This survey used digital elevation maps (DEMs) derived from LiDAR surveys to make such assessments. The data used were collected from 2010 to 2022, emphasizing the time frame immediately before and after the most recent major storms, Hurricane Irma and its predecessor Hurricane Matthew, passed over the St. Augustine region before the start of HIrmaDAMS.

The geospatial analysis for Fort Mose II showed significant change, with almost 60% of its marshland lost after Hurricane Matthew. In comparison, Hurricane Irma saw a substantial increase in flood levels, with an 8% overall increase in the St. Augustine region, most

FIGURE 4. Plan view of Unit 11A at the start of Level 3. Due to the slope, only the northeastern half of the unit has been excavated, i.e., the southeastern half of the unit is at an elevation equal to or lower than 30 cmbg. (Photo by Chuck Meide, courtesy of Lighthouse Archaeological Maritime Protgram 2021.)

notably along the Matanzas River. This is unsurprising, given the history of the site. Flagler-era dredging operations reduced the farmlands surrounding the site into wetlands, increasing erosion by creating a creek (Screen Creek) that now cuts through the site, compounding the risk faced by this site.

Conclusion

The findings from Fort Mose II and Tolomato Bar Anchorage showcase both the resilience and fragility of archaeological sites in the face of relentless natural forces. The research undertaken on these sites as part of HIrmaDAMS provided valuable insights into the effects of climate change on the preservation of maritime heritage. However, this is only scratching the surface of what can be learned about how these two sites are affected by the threats of climate, storms, and erosion. The path forward for continued research will require a multidisciplinary approach that incorporates methodologies from biology, geology, geography, and other academic fields. Doing so will allow for a more comprehensive understanding of the patterns and trends of environmentally induced impacts on cultural resources and will inform the development of more effective conservation measures. This ensures that future generations will still be able to connect with the rich tapestry of human history on our shores and beneath the waves.

References

BEESON, KENNETH H.
2006 *Fromajadas and Indigo: The Minorcan Colony in Florida*. The History Press, Cheltenham, UK.

BROOKS, HAROLD K.
1981 *Physiographic Divisions of Florida*. Cooperative Extension Service, Institute of Food and Agricultural Sciences, University of Florida, Gainesville.

CANGIALOSI, JOHN P., ANDREW S. LATTO, AND ROBBIE BERG
2018 National Hurricane Center Tropical Cyclone Report: Hurricane Irma. National Hurricane Center, National Oceanic and Atmospheric Administration (NOAA), Washington, DC.

CATHERS, AIRIELLE R.
2019 The Effects of Major Hurricane Events on Shipwreck Site Vulnerability in the Florida Keys. Master's thesis, Department of Environmental Science and Policy, University of Miami, Miami, FL.

2020 Hurricane Impact Modeling for Shipwreck Site Formation in the North Florida Keys and its Application to Resource Management. In *ACUA Underwater Archaeology Proceedings 2020*, Victor Mastone and David Ball, editors, pp. 33-42. Advisory Council on Underwater Archaeology.

EMMONS, MARY F.
2018 How Hurricane Irma Radically Shifted South Florida. Scuba Diving.com. <https://www.scubadiving.com/how-hurricane-irma-radically-shifted-south-florida-wrecks>. Accessed 17 May 2024.

FLORIDA DEPARTMENT OF ENVIRONMENTAL PROTECTION (FL DEP)
2024 Guana Tolomato Matanzas National Estuarine Research Reserve Management Plan, Florida Department of Environmental Protection, Tallahassee, FL. <https://floridadep.gov/sites/default/files/GTM-Management-Plan.pdf>. Accessed 17 May 2024.

GEARHART, ROBERT II, DOUG JONES, AMY BORGENS, SARA LAURENCE, TODD DEMUNA, AND JULIA SHIPP
2012 Impacts of Recent Hurricane Activity on Historic Shipwrecks in the Gulf of Mexico Outer Continental Shelf. OCS Study BOEMRE 2011-003. U.S. Dept. of the Interior, Bureau of Ocean Energy Management, Regulation, and Enforcement, New Orleans, LA. <https://www.boem.gov/sites/default/files/boem-newsroom/Technical-Announcements/2011/Tech-2011-003.pdf>. Accessed 17 May 2024.

LANDERS, JANE
1990 Gracia Real de Santa Teresa de Mose: A Free Black Town in Spanish Colonial Florida. *The American Historical Review* 95(1):9–30.

LIM, YOUNG-KWON, SIEGFRIED D. SCHUBERT, ROBIN KOVACH, ANDREA M. MOLOD, AND STEVEN PAWSON
2018 The Roles of Climate Change and Climate Variability in the 2017 Atlantic Hurricane Season. *Scientific Reports* 8, 16172. <https://doi.org/10.1038/s41598-018-34343-5>. Accessed 17 May 2024.

MEIDE, CHUCK, AIRIELLE CATHERS, NICHOLAS C. BUDSBERG, DOROTHY ROWLAND, CHRISTOPHER MCCARRON, THOMAS MACAVOY, LEAH TAVASI, AND HEATHER JEANS
2023 Final Report for the First Coast Maritime Archaeology Project (FCMAP) 2022-2022: Hurricane Irma Damage Assessment and Mitigation Strategy (HIrmaDAMS). Report to the State of Florida, Tallahassee, from the Lighthouse Archaeological Maritime Program, St. Augustine Lighthouse & Maritime Museum, St. Augustine, FL.

MEIDE, CHUCK, ALLYSON ROPP, P. BRENDAN BURKE, OLIVIA MCDANIEL, SAMUEL P. TURNER AND JACOB D. SHIDNER
2021   First Coast Maritime Archaeology Project 2014-2015: Report on Archaeological Investigations. LAMP Research Reports No. 5. Lighthouse Archaeological Maritime Program, St. Augustine Lighthouse & Maritime Museum, St. Augustine, FL.

MELILLO, JERRY M., TERESE RICHMOND, AND GARY W. YOHE (EDITORS)
2014   *Climate Change Impacts in the United States: The Third National Climate Assessment.* U.S. Global Change Research Program, Washington, DC. <https://www.globalchange.gov/our-work/third-national-climate-assessment>. Accessed 17 May 2024.

NOAA GEOPHYSICAL FLUID DYNAMICS LABORATORY (NOAA GFDL)
2019   Global Warming and Hurricanes: An Overview of Current Research Results. National Oceanic and Atmospheric Administration, Geophysical Fluid Dynamics Laboratory, Princeton, NJ. <https://www.gfdl.noaa.gov/global-warming-and-hurricanes/>. Accessed 17 May 2024.

NOAA NATIONAL CENTERS FOR ENVIRONMENTAL INFORMATION (NOAA NCEI)
2018   Costliest U.S. Tropical Cyclones Tables Updated. National Oceanic and Atmospheric Administration, National Centers for Environmental Information, National Hurricane Center, Miami, FL. <https://www.nhc.noaa.gov/news/UpdatedCostliest.pdf>. Accessed 17 May 2024.

NOAA NATIONAL ENVIRONMENTAL SATELLITE DATA AND INFORMATION SERVICE (NOAA NESDIS)
2018   One Year After Hurricane Irma: How Data Helped Track the Storm. National Oceanic and Atmospheric Administration, National Environmental Satellite Data and Information Service, Silver Spring, MD. <https://www.nesdis.noaa.gov/content/one-year-after-hurricane-irma-how-data-helped-track-storm>. Accessed 17 May 2024.

SCHAFER, DANIEL L.
2000   Governor James Grant's Villa: A British East Florida Indigo Plantation. *El Escribano: The St. Augustine Journal of History 37.*

SCOTT, THOMAS
1993   *Geologic Map of St. Johns County.* Florida Geological Survey Open File Map Series No. 68. Florida Geological Survey, Tallahassee.

U.S. DEPARTMENT OF AGRICULTURE (USDA)
2006   Official Series Description - Pellicer. United States Department of Agriculture, Soil Conservation Service, Washington, DC. <https://soilseries.sc.egov.usda.gov/OSD_Docs/P/PELLICER.html>. Accessed 17 May 2024.

U.S. GEOLOGICAL SERVICE (USGS)
2018   Hurricane Irma - Forecast and Documentation of Coastal Change. United States Geological Service, Reston, VA. <https://www.usgs.gov/centers/spcmsc/science/hurricane-irma-forecast-and-documentation-coastal-change>. Accessed 17 May 2024.

WHITE, WILLIAM A.
1970   *The Geomorphology of the Florida Peninsula (FGS: Bulletin 51).* Published for Bureau of Geology, Division of Interior Resources, Florida Department of Natural Resources by Designers Press, Orlando, FL.

• • • • • • • • • • • • • • • •

Airielle R. Cathers
Lighthouse Archaeological Maritime Program (LAMP)
St. Augustine Lighthouse & Maritime Museum
81 Lighthouse Avenue
St Augustine, Florida 32080

Bryce A. Peacher
Department of Anthropology
University of Central Florida
4000 Central Florida Boulevard,
Howard Phillips Hall, Room 309
Orlando, Florida 32816

Revisiting the Little Talbot Island Shipwreck (8DU3157), a 19th-Century Beached Shipwreck in Duval County, Northeast Florida

Chuck Meide

The Little Talbot Island Shipwreck, located on the beach in Little Talbot Island State Park in northeast Florida, was initially investigated and reported by state archaeologists in 1987. When first encountered, the site consisted of a section of hull measuring 16.13 meters (52.92 feet) by 5.25 meters (17.22 feet) from a composite-built ship. Since that time, the position and integrity of this hull section has been significantly impacted by successive storms. Accounts from rangers indicate it has been periodically buried and re-exposed, and has moved as much as three miles down the beach. After Hurricane Dorian in 2019, LAMP archaeologists visited the site to assess its current condition. LAMP returned in 2022 for more thorough documentation after Hurricanes Ian and Nicole. This article presents an overview of this shipwreck, with an emphasis on how it has changed over the years, particularly after the aforementioned storms.

El naufragio de la isla Little Talbot, ubicado en la playa del Parque Estatal Little Talbot Island, fue inicialmente investigado y reportado por arqueólogos estatales en 1987. Cuando se encontró por primera vez, el sitio consistía en una sección de casco que medía 16,13 metros (52,92 pies) por 5,25. metros (17,22 pies) desde un barco compuesto. Desde entonces, la posición e integridad de esta sección del casco se ha visto significativamente afectada por sucesivas tormentas. Los relatos de los guardabosques indican que ha sido enterrado y vuelto a exponer periódicamente, y que se ha movido hasta tres millas playa abajo. Después del huracán Dorian en 2019, los arqueólogos de LAMP visitaron el sitio para evaluar su estado actual. LAMP regresó en 2022 para obtener una documentación más exhaustiva después de los huracanes Ian y Nicole. Este artículo presenta una descripción general de este naufragio tal como ha cambiado a lo largo de los años, con énfasis en cómo se vio afectada su integridad después de cada tormenta mencionada anteriormente.

L'épave de Little Talbot Island, située sur la plage du parc d'État de Little Talbot Island, a été initialement étudiée et signalée par des archéologues de l'État en 1987. Lors de la visite initiale, le site consistait en une section de coque mesurant 16,13 mètres (52,92 pied) sur 5,25 mètres (17,22 pied) d'un navire composite. Depuis lors, la position et l'intégrité de cette section de coque ont été considérablement affectées par des tempêtes successives. Les récits des gardes-parcs indiquent qu'il a été périodiquement enterré et réexposé, et qu'il s'est déplacé jusqu'à trois miles sur la plage. Après l'ouragan Dorian en 2019, les archéologues du LAMP ont visité le site pour évaluer son état actuel. LAMP est revenu en 2022 pour une documentation plus approfondie après les ouragans Ian et Nicole. Cet article présente un aperçu de cette épave telle qu'elle a changé au fil des ans, en mettant l'accent sur la façon dont son intégrité a été affectée après chaque tempête susmentionnée.

Introduction

Little Talbot Island is located just north of the mouth of the St. Johns River and is one of the few remaining undeveloped barrier islands in northeast Florida. The entire island, with 8.05 kilometers (km) [5.0 miles [mi.]) of white sand beaches and rolling surf, comprises Little Talbot Island State Park. This area of the coast is highly dynamic and faces increasingly powerful storm action due to climate change. Erosion and accretion are so consequential in this area of the Atlantic coast that Little Talbot is currently larger than its neighbor to the north, incongruously named Big Talbot Island.

This high-energy coast with its powerful hurricanes has also had consequential impacts on a beached 19th-century shipwreck that was first investigated by Bureau of Archaeological Research (BAR) archaeologists in May 1987. Periodic monitoring by park rangers over the last 37 years has documented the repeated burial and exposure of the wreck, along with its loss of integrity and movement by some 3.0 mi .(4.83 km) southwards down the beach. The hull reappeared at the south end of the park after Hurricane Dorian, which struck on 4 September 2019. Archaeologists from the Lighthouse Archaeological Maritime Program (LAMP) and the Florida Public Archaeology Network (FPAN) visited the site eight days later for a one-day assessment, confirming that the extent, condition, and position of the wreck had changed considerably since the 1987 investigation.

LAMP visited the wreck again over five days in 2022 as part of the grant-funded Hurricane Irma Damage Assessment and Mitigation Strategy (HIrmaDAMS) project. This included a one-day site visit on 4 October to assess the condition of the wreck five days after Hurricane Ian, and a more thorough four-day assessment starting 19 days after Hurricane Nicole. On 29 and 30 November and 1 and 9 December, LAMP archaeologists and volunteers investigated the wreck, which had broken into two separate pieces. Labeled A and B, they were excavated and recorded through drone and hand-held photography and photogrammetry. A complete list of scantlings (hull member dimensions) was recorded, a total of 36 wood samples were collected, and 24 timber tags were applied to timbers that were thought to be potentially prone to disarticulation.

Initial Investigation, May 1987

In May 1987, a shipwreck in the park was reported to BAR archaeologists. A team directed by the late State Underwater Archaeologist Roger C. Smith traveled to the site for a two-day investigation on 25–26 May, producing a detailed site plan, photographic documentation and photomosaic, and a report published in the Florida Anthropologist (Haiduven and Smith 1987).

When initially found, the wreckage was located at the northern portion of the park at the foot of a large dune, submerged and exposed with the tides. The wreckage measured 16.13 meters (m) (52.92 feet [ft.]) by 5.25 m (17.22 ft.) with the interior facing up (Haiduven and Smith 1987:339–340). The wrecked vessel had been composite built, meaning that it had iron members in addition to wooden timbers comprising its hull (Figure 1). Five large iron knee riders were still present bolted to the hull, along with a sixth rider and two iron knees lying loose on the site. This use of iron framing elements in a wooden hull marked the transition between wooden and iron shipbuilding, and dates the vessel to the early to mid-19th century or later (Meide et al. 2001:117–119; Stammers 2001; Meide et al. 2021:139–148). Other hull members were wood and included ceiling planking, frames, and outer hull planking, while wooden treenails along with both copper alloy and iron fasteners were used to articulate the timbers. BAR researchers concluded that the ship likely dated to between 1820 and 1920, and that this surviving section of hull had been positioned on the port side of the vessel towards the bow (Haiduven and Smith 1987:345–348, Figure 8).

FIGURE 1. Two views of the Little Talbot Island Wreck taken in May 1987 during the initial investigation, showing the iron knee riders that were intact and attached to the hull. Also visible (at left in top image, in foreground in bottom image) is the diagonal wooden truss, another structural element bolted to the frames through the ceiling planking. (Photo courtesy the Florida Master Site File (FLMSF), Division of Historical Resources, State of Florida, 1987.)

The shipwreck had three particularly distinctive or unique hull construction features. The first of these are the aforementioned iron framing components. Iron knee riders, which have been seen on many other 19th-century shipwrecks, did not become widespread until after the first few decades of the 19th century, with a series of British patents for iron framing components granted in 1813, 1839, and 1841, and Lloyd's insurance classifications mandating iron riders in 1839 (MacGregor 1988:141–142; Stone 1993:30; Roth 2018:106–107; Meide et al. 2021:139–148).

The second distinctive feature was the 17.78 centimeters (cm) (7.0 inches [in.] square diagonal wooden truss starting low in the bow and running upwards and aft (Haiduvan and Smith 1987:339, 342, 346). Diagonal truss systems in wooden ships were developed in the early 19th century and, like iron knee riders, they were designed to strengthen and stiffen the hull to prevent hogging, which was especially problematic in longer vessels (hogging was the tendency for a vessel to droop at the bow and stern ends where the hull was least buoyant). This innovation is largely credited to Robert Seppings (1814, 1818), a British Royal Navy surveyor, who experimented with bracing systems for naval vessels as early as 1800–1805. They are relatively rare in the archaeological record.

The third unique feature was a salient beveling at the heels of the forwardmost frames. These frames were angled slightly forward and therefore represent cant frames, and their lower ends or heels were beveled to fit into and accommodate the curvature of the bow (Haiduvan and Smith 1987:338–341). This kind of frame beveling is also relatively rarely seen on shipwrecks. Several intact outer hull plank hooding ends survived in this area as well, additional evidence corroborating the interpretation of this piece of hull being from the forwardmost portion of the bow.

The 1987 researchers collected an unknown number of wood samples that were identified at the Rockport Apprenticeship. These samples suggested that treenails were made of locust, ceiling and frames of yellow pine, and outer planking of cypress (Haiduven and Smith 1987:342).

Post-Hurricane Dorian Assessment, September 2019

On 12 September 2019, with the cooperation of State Park personnel, three LAMP archaeologists along with a LAMP volunteer and an FPAN archaeologist visited the newly uncovered wreck (Meide et al. 2023:99–100, 170–176). They found that the hull remains had changed considerably since 1987, a fact well-known to park staff. Researchers encountered a section of hull measuring 6.73 m by 4.5 m (22.08 ft. by 14.76 ft.) lying unburied south of the South Beach Pavilion and southernmost parking lot, at the start of the supratidal portion of the beach, just before beach sand meets the vegetative zone. Park staff asserted that this was the same wreckage that had originally been located more than 4.83 km (3.0 mi.) to the north, having made its way south with ensuing storms since 1987.

While this was still a sizable section of articulated hull, it represented only a small portion of a significantly larger hull remnant that had presumably become disarticulated and lost. Only 17 frames were extant, compared to 61 noted in 1987. The hull had lost about 9.4 m (31.7 ft.) of length and 0.75 m (2.46 ft.) of width since 1987. The wreckage was also flipped upside down in relation to its orientation 32 years prior, so that its outboard or exterior surface was now facing up. In addition to the articulated timbers, two loose planks were present that were associated with the wreck, but whose original position was uncertain. There was no evidence of the iron knee riders that had been observed in 1987, though the remnants of one or more of these could have been hidden from view on the underside (inboard surface) of the wreckage.

The articulated hull was recorded by traditional means (baseline and offsets) and through photogrammetry. Figure 2 is a hull plan generated from the photogrammetric model. All individual hull members were numbered using the letter prefix F for frame, C for ceiling plank, and OH for hull plank. These same hull member designations assigned in 2019 were used again in 2022, as seen in the scantlings list (Table 1). Data collected in 2019 were not sufficient to confirm beyond a reasonable doubt that this wreckage was indeed part of the larger wreck originally documented in 1987.

Post-Hurricane Ian Assessment, October 2022

On 4 October 2022, only five days after Hurricane Ian raked the Florida coast, one LAMP archaeologist visited the park to relocate the wreck and assess any impacts from the storm (Meide et al. 2023:172, 177–179). While the hull remnant was exposed, more of it was buried than had been when last seen in 2019. Parts of two hull planks were missing, including a large portion (around 3.42 m [11.22 ft.] long) of OH6 and almost all of OH2. The ceiling planking previously recorded (C1–C5) was not visible but presumed intact and buried. No excavation was carried out at that time, and the partially obscured hull remains were recorded with photogrammetry. Subsequent comparisons of photographs taken at this time with those taken in 2019 indicated that, other than the missing portions of planking, the storm had not moved the hull remains or altered their position in any way.

Post-Hurricane Nicole Assessment, November–December 2022

The most substantial investigation of the site thus far occurred over four days in November and December 2022, after Hurricane Nicole (Meide et al. 2023:177,

Outer Hull Planks

Hull Timber	Width in.	Width cm	Thickness in.	Thickness cm	Surviving Length ft.	Surviving Length m	Comments
OH1	6 ½	16.5	3 1/8	8	11.35	3.46	Missing in 2022; measurements from 2019. Plank is narrower at its forward end, making it the narrowest.
OH2	6 ¼	15.87	2 ¾	6.98	4.23	1.29	Mostly gone by Nov 22. Surviving length was 4.35 m in 2019.
OH3 fd	7	17.78	2 ¾	6.98	12.27	3.74	Forward end. Both planks together are 4.83 m long.
OH3 aft	7 ¾	19.68	2 ¾	6.98	3.52	1.07	Aft end; shorter of two planks butted in same strake.
OH4	6 ½	16.61	2 ¾	6.98	20.44	6.23	Longest surviving hull plank
OH5	7 ¼	18.41	3	7.62	16.96	5.17	Butt survives at south end, only butt other than OH3.
OH6	8 ½	21.59	2 ¾	6.98	9.09	2.77	Significant amount was lost by Oct 22; was 5.12 m long in 2019.
OH7	8 ¾	22.22	2 ½	6.35	12.66	3.86	Butt end to the south.

Ceiling Planks

Hull Timber	Width in.	Width cm	Thickness in.	Thickness cm	Surviving Length ft.	Surviving Length cm	Comments
C1	6 ¼	16	3.15	8	13.58	4.14	All width and thickness measurements listed here were recorded in 2019, when the planks were less deteriorated. Surviving lengths could not be discerned in 2019 so those measurements were taken in 2022 after Section B with all the ceiling planking broke free from the rest of the wreck.
C2	4 ½	11.5	3.15	8	5.09	1.55	
C3	6	15	3.15	8	17.26	5.26	
C4	6	15	3.15	8	8.33	2.54	
C5	6	15	3.35	8.5	14.01	4.27	
C6	5 ½	14	2	5	2.49	0.76	

Frames

Hull Timber	Sided in.	Sided cm	Molded in.	Molded cm	Surviving Length ft.	Surviving Length m	Comments
F1	8	20.32	6 ¾	17.14	7.71	2.35	Intact frame member with both head and heel; measured at the join with F1, or above C1. Iron rider runs under this frame and F2.
F2	9	22.86	6	15.24	7.94	2.42	Almost intact member with surviving head; scantlings were measured below C6. Iron rider runs under this frame, angled to extend under F1 also.
F3	9 5/8	24.5	7 ¾	19.5	8.5	2.59	Missing in Nov 2022; 2019 measurements listed
F4	9 / 9 ½	22.86 / 24	4 ¾ / 7 ½	12.06 / 19	3.77 / 12.09	1.15 / 3.69	Upper member missing in Nov 2022. The 2019 total length indicates missing member was 8.32 ft./2.54 m long. Extant timber measured at lower end.
F5	8 ½	21.59	5 ¼	13.33	8.14	2.48	Head at upper end. Measured at lower end.
F6	8 ¾ / 9 ½	22.22 / 24	5 ¼ / 7 7/8	13.33 / 20	3.84 / 12.2	1.17 / 3.72	2019 scantlings were from now-missing upper member, which is calculated to have been 8.36 ft./2.55m long. 2022 measurements from lower end.
F7	8 ½	21.59	4 ½ / 7 ¾	11.43 / 19.5	8.27	2.52	2019 molded measurement was significantly different than what was recorded in 2022 so both are included. 2022 measurements taken from lower end.
F8	8 ¾ / 9 ½	22.22 / 24	5 / 7 7/8	12.7 / 20	4.36 / 12.93	1.33 / 3.94	Upper member missing in Nov 22, but measured in 2019. Length of missing member 2.61m/8.57 ft. Extant member measured at head (upper end).
F9	9 ½	24	7 ¾	19.5	8.91	2.72	Missing by Nov 22; 2019 measurements listed.
F10	9 ½	24	7 7/8	20	13.01	3.97	Missing by Nov 2022; 2019 measurements listed. May have been two members butted under planking.
F11	7 ½	19.05	6 ¼	15.87	8.69	2.65	Displaced but still in wreck. Iron bolt head 20cm in from lower end, with transverse treenails 9cm to above and 16cm below. Scantlings taken at east end.
F12	5 ¾	14.6	6 ¼	15.87	7.74	2.36	First (aftmost) cant frame); beveled heel
F13	6 ½	16.51	4 ¼	10.79	11.29	3.44	Cant frame; measured at center of frame; beveled heel.
F14	6	15.24	5	12.7	8.46	2.58	Cant frame with surviving head; iron fastener at lower end; scantlings taken at center of frame; beveled heel.

Frames							
Hull Timber	Sided		Molded		Surviving Length		Comments
	in.	cm	in.	cm	ft.	m	
F15	6 ½	16.51	4 ¾	12.06	13.94	4.25	Cant frame; deteriorated at both ends. Probably two members butted together under the hull planking. Scantlings recorded at center of frame. Beveled heel.
F16	6 ¾	17.14	5	12.7	10.56	3.22	Cant frame; measured at lower end. Beveled heel.
F17	6 ¼	15.87	7 ¼	18.41	7.78	2.37	Forwardmost cant frame; both ends deteriorated; scantlings recorded at center; beveled heel
Iron Knee Rider							
Knee Rider	4	10.16	1 9/16	4	5.41	1.65	Lower end of rider broken off under F2 about 1.06 m below the heel of F1. Yellow metal bolt through rider, C6, and F2 (adjacent to heel of F1) has head 13/16 in. (2.06 cm) and shank ¾ in. (1.91 cm) diameter
Treenails							
FS No.	Max. Diam		Min. Diam		Ave. Diam		Comments
	in.	mm	in.	mm	in.	mm	
22LT-11	1.36	34.42	1.3	33.13	1.33	33.78	Outboard portion of treenail from F13 at OH6
22LT-18	1.17	29.72	1.09	27.78	1.13	28.75	Outboard end of treenail in F7 at OH2; no wedge
22LT-20	1.09	27.64	1.05	26.71	1.07	27.18	Outboard end of treenail from F8 at OH2
22LT-22	1.1	27.86	1.02	25.94	1.06	26.90	Treenail from F15 at OH8; poor condition
22LT-36	1.36	34.53	1.28	32.41	1.32	33.47	Complete treenail from Timber E (disarticulated frame). Upper dimensions from wedged end; lower from non-wedged end.
	1.26	32.07	1.18	29.93	1.22	31.00	

TABLE 1. Scantlings table for the Little Talbot Island Shipwreck, as recorded in 2019 and 2022.

Notes: Most measurements were recorded in November-December 2022 but the numbers in italics were recorded in September 2019. If hull members were missing or seemed more deteriorated by November 2022 then their 2019 measurements are listed here. If a significant difference was noted between the 2019 and 2022 measurements both are included; otherwise the 2019 measurements of timbers still extant in November 2022 are omitted unless they were taken from one frame member and the 2022 measurements were taken from another member in the same frame. In some cases (probably F4, F6, F8, and F10 measured in 2019, and F15 measured in 2022) the overall length measurements for frames may have included two frame members butted together, with the butt join hidden by hull planking. When one frame member from a pair was found to be missing in 2022, its length has been calculated by subtracting the length of the remaining member from the 2019 overall length measurement; this is noted in Comments. All treenails listed were collected and measured in the laboratory with calipers.

believed that two treenails per frame were stronger, while also recognizing that if either planks or frame timbers were too narrow, using two treenails could risk splitting the wood. As this surviving hull section features outer planking that tends to narrow higher up and framing that narrows towards the bow, the shipwrights followed a particular pattern of positioning treenails, described in detail by Meide et al. (2023:189). An additional copper-alloy bolt was placed at each butt end below the waterline. Evidence of hull maintenance, including both replanking and the refitting of sprung planks, was also inferred from treenail placement, suggesting this ship had a relatively long working life.

Rows of sheathing tack holes, many with tack remnants, indicated the hull was originally coppered with 0.36 by 1.22 m (14.00 in. by 4 .00 ft.) sheets, a standard British size (Staniforth 1984:28). Tack holes, and the transition from iron to copper-alloy bolts, allowed for an estimate of the original waterline, somewhere between OH1 and OH2. Tack holes also indicated that extant planks had never been re-sheathed.

Tracking Wreck Movement and Change, 1987–2023

A decades-long record of site monitoring for a beached shipwreck is rare. A paper trail has been preserved in the Florida Master Site File (FMSF) for this site (8DU3157), which includes Cultural Site Visitation Reports completed by park personnel, along with written and emailed correspondence between park managers and state archaeologists, and dozens of photographs of the shipwreck taken over the decades. LAMP researchers meticulously analyzed the FLMSF records, many of which have redundant and out-of-order pages, to reconstruct how the Little Talbot Wreck has changed over

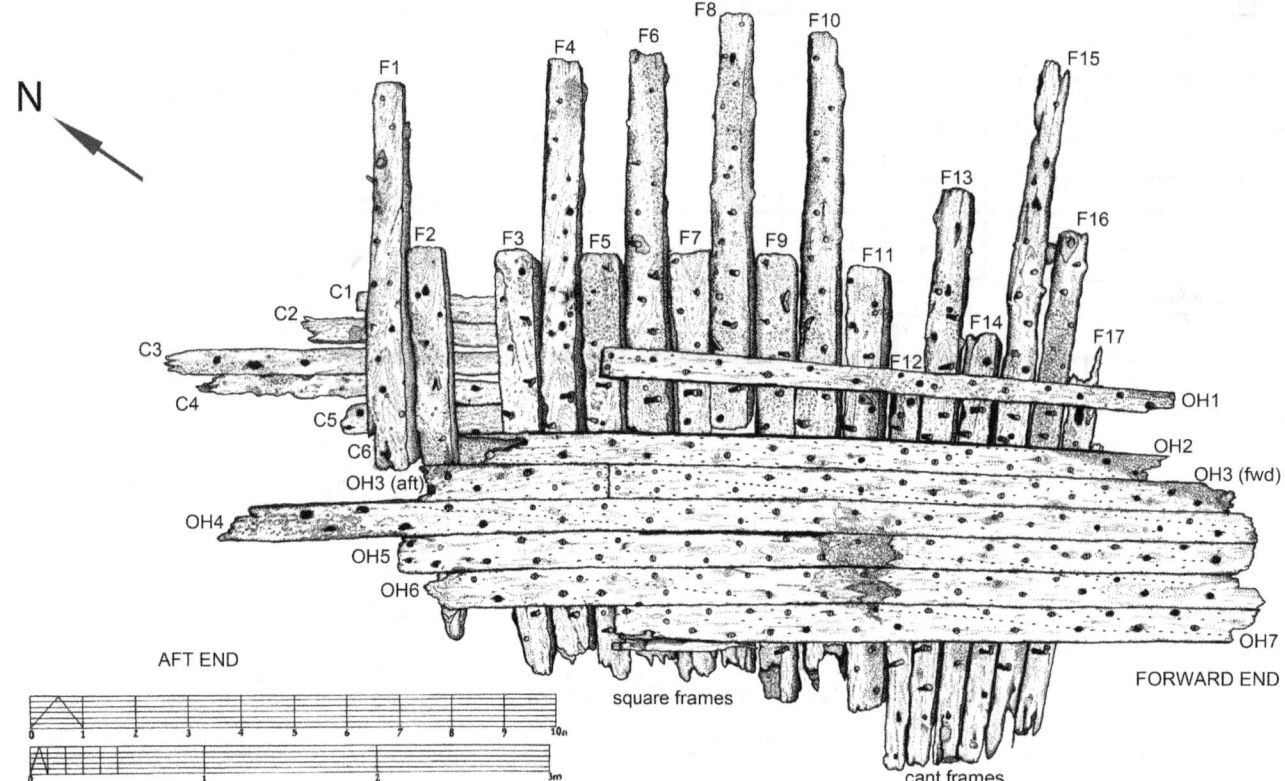

FIGURE 2. Hull plan of the Little Talbot Island Shipwreck as seen on 12 September 2019, eight days after Hurricane Dorian. Vessel bow would have been towards the right side of the drawing. (Illustration by Nicholas C. Budsberg, derived from a photogrammetric model generated by Emily Jane Murray of FPAN; courtesy of LAMP and the St. Augustine Lighthouse & Maritime Museum, 2019.)

180–204). The hurricane had moved the hull and torn it into two separate pieces. The larger piece, designated Section A, had been moved about 12.78 m (41.9 ft.) higher up the beach to the start of the vegetated zone. It had rotated about 129° counterclockwise, coming to rest with a large stump of driftwood wedged between its timbers, partially dislodging a frame. This hull remnant was the same, or rather part of the same, as that inspected in October 2022 and September 2019.

Section B, initially believed to be a newly encountered section of hull, was later confirmed to have been articulated with Section A as recently as the month before, indicating that it had broken free during Hurricane Nicole. Section B was mostly buried and in roughly the same location where the hull had been pre-Nicole. When excavated, Section B was found to consist of two articulated frame members (F1 and F2) along with the surviving remnants of ceiling planks C1–C6. These were heavily degraded, so while their current dimensions were recorded, the figures measured in 2019 are closer to their original scantlings and thus are listed in Table 1.

Researchers also noticed an iron framing member preserved beneath Section B. This is the last remaining segment of an iron knee rider still attached to the hull (of five attached and a sixth loose in 1987). Only 1.65 m (5.4 ft.) of the rider remains, bolted firmly to F1 and F2 with copper-alloy bolts, which is the primary reason the ceiling planking remained articulated with these two frames. The rider segment runs at a slight angle in relation to the frames, so that it runs under (on the inboard surface of) the frames and ceiling planks. This was the first of the three distinctive hull features noted in 1987 that was also observed in 2022, supporting the hypothesis that the wreckage observed in 2019–2022 was the same documented in 1987.

Not only was the hull ripped into two separate sections, but a number of additional timbers were disarticulated and missing. Frames F3, F9, and F10 were totally missing, while F4–F8 were all missing their upper members. F11 remained in the hull but was wrenched out of place with the upper end abaft its original position. Hull plank OH1 was completely missing, though the remnants of OH2 and OH6 that had survived

Hurricane Ian remained in place. Researchers therefore estimated that the wreck has lost a single hull plank and nine individual frame members, in addition to the two frame members and six ceiling planks articulated together as Section B. Scattered in the vicinity of Sections A and B were two broken pieces of a plank and one of the disarticulated frame members, but the others remain missing. The overall size of Section A after Nicole was 6.22 m by 4.24 m (20.41 ft. by 13.91 ft.), about 50 cm (19.7 in.) smaller in both longitudinal and top-to-bottom directions. Both hull sections were recorded by photogrammetry and, along with the disarticulated timbers, were positioned with GPS.

Timber Tagging

Researchers deployed 24 tags to known hull members, 16 on Section A and 8 on Section B (Meide et al. 2023:203–204). One of the HIrmaDAMS project objectives was to implement a timber tagging program at this shipwreck as a mitigation case study, the first time this system has been used on state lands in Florida. The Shipwreck Tagging Archaeological Management Program (STAMP) was developed through FPAN at the University of West Florida to use citizen scientists and crowdsourcing to mitigate the loss of information from ongoing deterioration of beached shipwreck sites (Burkhard 2023). The system entails the use of plexiglass tags with pre-printed quick response (QR) codes to allow the public to track disarticulated timbers easily with their personal mobile phones. These contacts are then uploaded to a database for use by managers to track the current location of stray timbers. At the time of this writing, several of these tagged timbers have been scanned and tracked by visitors to the park.

Wood Sampling and Analysis

Researchers also collected wood samples for species identification. A total of 37 numbered samples were collected from Sections A and B and the loose frame, some of which had more than one specimen (such as a treenail with a wedge, or a frame piece with a plug in a knot hole). A total of 45 samples were tested by paleoethnobotanist Lee Newsom (Meide et al. 2023:202–203, Appendix 2).

The results were quite unexpected in that all 45 specimens proved to be larch, also known as tamarack or hackmatack. Tree ring morphology strongly suggests eastern larch (*Larix laricina*) as opposed to western larch (*Larix occidentalis*). This makes sense for a ship built on the upper Atlantic seaboard, given eastern larch's range across the northeastern United States (U.S.) and Canada. In this region, larch was a prized wood for shipbuilding, and wood harvested from the root/stem junction of mature trees was especially prized to make "hackmatack knees." This part of the tree, like live oak in the southeastern U.S., featured natural curves and crooks which made curved or "compass" timbers, particularly useful for shipwrights. The boles of the tree tend to grow straight and upright, allowing for planking like that used on this ship for ceiling and outer planking.

Hull Analysis

This shipwreck represents a portion of the hull of a composite-built sailing vessel constructed in the mid to late 19th century, from the starboard side of the bow end and partially below the waterline (Meide et al. 2023:186–194). Figure 2 depicts the hull recorded in 2019, when it was most intact in recent years, while Table 1 lists scantlings and fastener diameters; both can be referred to in conjunction with the discussion below.

Frames were spaced very closely together, typically about an inch apart, and were joined transversely with iron fasteners. The frames in all but two cases were wider in the sided dimension than the molded. A distinctive change in the framing pattern is apparent between Frames F1–F11 (aft) and Frames F12–F17 (forward). The former series of frames are wider, tend to be spaced slightly apart along their entire lengths, and are perpendicular to the longitudinal run of the ship (thus "square frames"). Frames F12–F17, on the other hand, are noticeably narrower, have little if any space between them at their heels or lower ends, are beveled at their heels, and are angled slightly away from the preceding frames. These six are therefore cant frames, angled to form the bow of the vessel. The narrow cant frames included the only two examples of frames with molded dimensions greater than sided.

Hull planks were thicker than ceiling, and planks in the same strake were butted together. Butt joins in the outer planking were separated from joins directly above or below that point of the hull by three additional strakes of planking, whose joins were staggered farther aft. The surviving hooding ends visible in 1987 have since deteriorated.

Hull planking was fastened to the frames primarily with wedged treenails; researchers in 1987 reported they were wedged at both ends. Wedges were angled perpendicular to the length of the hull planking. In most cases one treenail, but sometimes two, was used to fasten the hull plank at each frame. It seems the shipwrights

Date	Observer	Description
25-26 May 1987	State (BAR) archaeologists, park staff, and volunteers led by Roger C. Smith	Original site assessment and investigation; 16.13 x 5.25 m (52.9 x 17.2 ft.) hull partially buried in the intertidal zone, inboard side up. Excavated and thoroughly documented and photographed (Haiduven and Smith 1987; many photos in FLMSF). Six iron knee riders and two iron knees on hull. No GPS position of wreck recorded but the red triangle in Figure 3 shows its approximated position.
20-Jul-03	Rick N. Argo, Park Services Specialist	Only portions of two upright iron knee riders were exposed; remainder of hull fully buried. Photograph in the FLMSF.
Oct-03	Rick N. Argo	Portions of three iron knee riders visible, not photographed.
Jul-04	Rick N. Argo	Hull and riders completely buried, no photographs taken.
Sep-04	Rick N. Argo	Significant amount of the hull was exposed after erosion from Hurricane Jeanne (26 September). Upper and lower extents of two iron knee riders were proud of the wooden remains; lower part of third rider was not visible. Photograph in FLMSF.
Oct-04	Rick N. Argo	After 32 days, much of the wreck was buried again; many frame ends still exposed along with significant portions of two iron knee riders. Photograph in FLMSF.
Apr-05	Rick N. Argo	Site completely buried except for upper extents and small portion of lower extents of iron knee riders. Photograph in FLMSF.
Sep-05	Rick N. Argo	Unknown portion of wooden timbers exposed, presumably with the two iron knee riders. No photographs taken.
Mar-06	Rick N. Argo	Hull mostly buried with a few timber ends visible. The southern of the last two iron knee riders has collapsed with its remnants partially exposed. Remaining knee rider intact with its upper and lower extend proud of the sand. These 2003-2006 accounts suggest the hull has remained in the same approximate location since first recorded in 1987 (Red triangle in Figure 3).
20-May-07	Tara Meeks, Park Service Specialist (Talbot Islands State Parks)	After an inspection following Subtropical Storm Andrea (10-12 May), it was documented for the first time that the shipwreck hull had moved a significant distance, now fully exposed some 3.306 km (2.05 mi.) to the south "on the southern end of Little Talbot Island Beach" at 30.44449°N, -81.40895° W (yellow dot in Figure 3). The remaining intact knee rider was detached and lost during the storm, though the distinctive diagonal truss remained in place. Eight photos taken and in FLMSF (Meide et al. 2023:figure 100). Note: the 8 June 2007 site file update incorrectly states the wreck moved "several hundred feet south" when it actually moved much further.
18-Oct-08	Mike Simmons, Environmental Specialist (Talbot Islands State Park), and Eric Steffey, presumably also park staff	Partially exposed portion of an iron knee or rider was "near the old site location toward the north end of Little Talbot Island's beach" at 30.469972°N, 81.411972° W (orange dot in Figure 3). It is not known if this piece was attached to any buried timbers or not. This could be an isolated remnant displaced from the original location further north. This site was described as "North Location," as opposed to the "South Location" where the main hull component came to rest the previous May. One photo taken (FLMSF). This spot was visited the following year but no cultural material was observed.
6-Feb-09	Mike Simmons	After the "South Location" was visited it was reported that the hull had shifted to 30.444444°N, -81.409139° W (yellow dots in Figure 3), a very slight change of position. The hull had rotated but was still positioned with its inboard surface upwards. Much of the hull was buried but significant portions of frames, planks, and what appears to be the diagonal truss were exposed. It was noted the hull was "broken into at least 3 visible pieces" though the nature of the separate components was not clear from description or photos. Twenty photographs taken but only seven were found in FLMSF.
after 7 Oct 2016, or possibly after 10 Sep 2017	Kimberly Warneka Porter, police officer and beachgoer	A local police officer visiting the beach after either Hurricane Matthew or Irma photographed a hull that is clearly the same that would next be seen after Hurricane Dorian in 2019. There is no way to confirm the exact location of the wreck as this informal site visit did not use GPS, but from photographs it appears to be at the southern end of the beach, within view of the inlet, and is probably therefore somewhat close to its 2019 position. Almost fully exposed below the high tide mark, oriented roughly east-west. Thirteen photographs posted on a Jacksonville blog (Gilmore 2018).
12-Sep-19	LAMP and FPAN (Chuck Meide, Austin Burkhard, Allyson Ropp, Diamond Dumas, Emily Jane Murray)	A 6.73 x 4.5 m (22.08 x 14.76 ft.) section of ship's hull was found fully exposed on the beach by Hurricane Dorian, some 1.7 km (1.06 mi.) further south than the previously reported position of the wreck (green dot in Figure 3). It was asserted by park staff that this was a fragment of the same hull. It was lying with its outboard side facing up. Thoroughly recorded, including with photogrammetry.
4-Oct-22	LAMP (Dorothy Rowland)	Just over three years later, after Hurricane Ian, this section of hull remained in the same position and orientation (green dot in Figure 3). It was partially buried but at least several planks were no longer extant. It was quickly recorded with photogrammetry.
29-30 Nov, 1 Dec, and 9 Dec 2022	LAMP (Chuck Meide, Airielle Cathers, Chris McCarron, Andrew Thomson, Eric Wilson, Ken Adams, et al.)	After Hurricane Nicole, it was found that the hull had moved around 13 m (42.7 ft.) higher up the beach, and rotated 129°. It had lost a number of previously articulated timbers, included a new component of multiple timbers found mostly buried at the Sep 2019/Oct 2022 location; this was designated Section B, with the previously known piece named Section A. Section B was excavated and subsequently reburied; both pieces were thoroughly recorded, and analysis proved that Section B was formerly part of Section A.
7-Jun-23	LAMP (Dorothy Rowland and LAMP field school students)	The site was visited after the close of HIrmaDAMS fieldwork. Section A was mostly buried and did not seem to have moved. Section B was heavily impacted, with all components except for F1 and the iron knee rider missing. Several tagged pieces of ceiling were observed at the southern end of the island amid the rip rap.

TABLE 2. Documented instances of observation of the Little Talbot Island Shipwreck, summarizing changes of location, exposure, and integrity, 1987–2023.

FIGURE 3. Map showing all reported locations for the Little Talbot Island Wreck between 1987 and 2022. The initial 1987 location pre-dated GPS technology and has been estimated from positioning reported in the FLMSF; all other locations based on GPS readings. (Image by Airielle Cathers, courtesy of LAMP and the St. Augustine Lighthouse & Maritime Museum, 2022.)

time. This analysis, with details related to changes in location, exposure, and integrity, is summarized in Table 2. In addition, Figure 3 is a map showing all reported positions of the Little Talbot Wreck.

The discovery of the wreck was made before the advent of GPS technology, so its 1987 position in Figure 3 is estimated from its location marked by hand on a map in the original site file. After the initial investigation, no mention of the wreck was made for 16 years, during which it was likely buried. After this hiatus, Park Services Specialist Rick Argo visited the site at least eight times between July 2003 and March 2006. He reported to Smith various conditions and levels of burial or exposure at each of his visits, but makes no note of the wreckage moving, so the wreck is assumed to have stayed in approximately the same place for 19 years after its discovery.

By July 2003, two of the wreck's four intact knee riders had collapsed. For a time, only the uppermost portions of the surviving riders were exposed above the sand, though the wreck was completely reburied the following year. Hurricane Jeanne exposed most of the hull again in September 2004, and afterwards the wreck slowly became reburied so that only the two riders were visible in April 2005. That September, its timbers were exposed again, and by March 2006 only one intact knee rider remained upright.

The wreck was impacted dramatically by Subtropical Storm Andrea on 10–12 May 2007, which moved it 3.306 km (2.05 mi.) down the beach. The final knee rider was broken, leaving only a partial, low-profile remnant attached to the hull (presumably the same piece observed in 2022), along with the wooden truss. These distinctive features confirm that the hull observed in 2007 is the same as that documented in 1987–2006.

The site was next visited by park staff in October 2008, after Hurricane Hanna. A loose iron knee component was sighted near the wreck's original location, referred to as the "Northern Location" (Figure 3). Four months later in February 2009 the two locations were visited again, probably after a nor'easter. The wreck at the "Southern Location" had shifted slightly, moving 18.86 m (61.88 ft). The diagonal truss remains visible in photographs taken that day.

At this point, there was another lapse in documented site visits, with no further mention of the wreck in the FLMSF until Hurricane Dorian in 2019. There was, however, an intervening mention of the shipwreck published in a local blog, which noted "[i]n 2017, Hurricane Matthew re-exposed these ruins to air and light" (Gilmore 2018). Gilmore mistakenly dated the 2016 Hurricane Matthew to 2017, so it is possible he meant Hurricane Irma of that year. Regardless, the photographs he posted, taken by Kimberly Porter, are valuable for assessing the condition of the wreck before it was next seen by archaeologists. At that time, the hull was situated with the outboard surface upwards, as it was in 2019, suggesting the previously documented hull had moved farther south and had flipped over. It was clearly the same hull that LAMP would document in 2019, though it was more complete: it featured three cant frames forward of F17 that were later missing, at least two additional frame members abaft F1, and the frame member between F2 and F3 that was later missing. Thirteen strakes of hull planking were extant in the 2016/2017 photographs, compared to the seven remaining in 2019. The additional strakes were situated above OH1, extending up to the ends of F2 and F11, allowing researchers analyzing these photographs to pinpoint the uppermost extent of copper sheathing tack holes and therefore the vessel's waterline. The planking ran considerably farther aft at this time, by perhaps 3 m (9.8 ft).

After the close of HIrmaDAMS in June 2023, a final visit was made to the site during the LAMP field school. The site had been further impacted, losing one frame (F2) and the ceiling planking from Section B. Several STAMP-tagged planks were noted some distance away, amid the riprap at the island's southern end.

One Wreck or Two?

A fundamental question beset researchers during the 2019–2022 investigations: was this one wreck or two? Some researchers felt the assertion that the 2019 hull was the same as the 1987 hull should be met with skepticism until evidence could prove it so. With this alternate hypothesis, the 2019 hull could be from an entirely different shipwreck, and the 1987 hull might still lie preserved and buried, perhaps near its original location.

A review of the FLMSF, as presented above, made clear that the wreck first observed in 1987 had definitely moved 3.3 km (2.05 mi.) south along the beach by 2009. While therefore plausible that the wreck could have moved another 1.824 km (1.13 mi.) in the ensuing decade, but could this be confirmed?

Comparing the 2019–2022 and 1987 hulls was challenging, since the 2019–2022 hull was lying outboard surface up, preventing a direct comparison with the inboard surface recorded in 1987. There were also some recording inconsistencies; for example, sided and molded dimensions for frames were not reported in 1987. But some scantlings, such as hull plank thickness, were virtually identical on the 1987 and 2019–2022 wrecks, while others were close or in the same range. All in all, scantling comparisons could not rule out that the two hulls were the same. The types and dimensions of fasteners and the iron rider also supported the hypothesis that these hulls were the same.

The strongest argument against the hulls being the same was the wood analysis reported in 1987, which, with results of locust, yellow pine, and cypress, was completely at odds with Newsom's results of 45 samples of tamarack. There are many unknown factors with the 1987 analysis: how many samples were collected and how reliable was the analyst? It is certain that a paleoethnobotanist was not employed to scrutinize thin sections microscopically, which is the standard practice now. The shipwright identifying the 1987 samples observed them directly to make his determination, and while researchers deemed this less reliable than microscopic analysis, they were also reluctant to reject it out of hand.

Further analysis of the photogrammetric models, however, convinced researchers that the two hulls were one and the same. This analysis confirmed that the three distinct features on the 1987 hull were also present on the 2019–2022 hull. The beveling at the cant frame heels had escaped notice in 2019 and 2022, but was readily apparent in the photomodels. In addition, individual cant frames recorded in 1987 and 2019–2022 could be corresponded by their sizes, shapes, and positions: F12 clearly matched 1987's Frame 52, for example, as F17 matched Frame 57.

Evidence was also observed indicating the presence of the large, diagonal wooden truss observed in 1987. A close inspection of the 2019 photomodel identified several substantial fasteners on the outer hull aligned at roughly 50° to 55°, all in addition to the standard planking treenails, which appear to represent the truss that was once on the inboard surface of the hull.

The final evidence was the position of the last remaining knee rider remnant still attached to the hull. Analysis of photographs in the FLMSF confirmed that the 1987 hull had lost all of its attached riders by 2007 except for a remnant of the forwardmost. The horizontal distance from the forwardmost square frame (Frame 51) back to the first iron knee rider, measured on the 1987 hull plan, was roughly the same (within about 5 cm [1.9 in.]) as that measured on the 2019 photomodel (from F11 back to F2 at the rider). These measurements confirm that the distance between the start of the cant framing and the first knee rider was essentially identical on both the 1987 hull and the 2019 hull. Figure 4 shows the relationship between the two hull plans by reversing (mirror-imaging) the 2019 hull plan and scaling it down to match the 1987 hull plan, and superimposing the two. This demonstrates how the cant frames and knee riders match on the two hulls, and also provides a graphic image of how much of the 1987 hull has been lost over the prior 32 years.

Conclusion

Given the evidence presented here, the wreck documented in 2022 is clearly the same as that originally

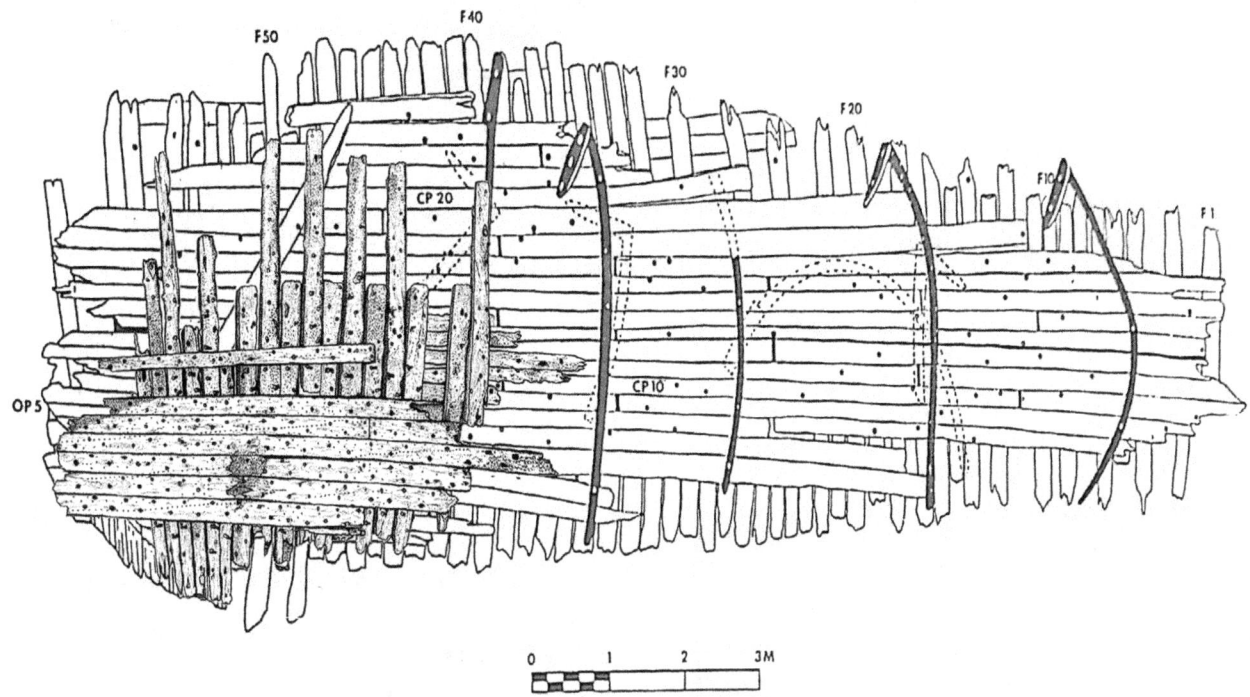

FIGURE 4. Superimposed comparison of Little Talbot Island Shipwreck hull as recorded in 1987 and in 2019, showing the alignment of frames and the forwardmost iron knee rider, along with the significant loss of integrity the wreck has suffered during the intervening 32 years. The 2019 hull plan was flipped horizontally (mirror-imaged) since it represents the outboard surface rather than the inboard surface depicted on the 1987 plan, and then scaled to fit. (Image by Chuck Meide, courtesy of LAMP and the St. Augustine Lighthouse & Maritime Museum, 2019.)

investigated in 1987, and it is truly unique among beached shipwrecks in that it has been monitored by archaeologists and resource managers for over 35 years, allowing for long-term documentation of movement and change over time in relation to particular storm events. Despite the loss of so many hull members over the decades, this wreck still has much to tell us. With the level of recording it has recently undergone, and the STAMP tags affixed to many of its timbers, it has the potential to continue to provide information on beached shipwreck site formation processes in the face of climate change, sea level rise, and increased storm activity for well into the future.

Acknowledgements

The HIrmaDAMS project was sponsored in part by the State of Florida's Division of Historical Resources, with funds from the National Park Service's Emergency Supplemental Historic Preservation Fund. Thanks also to Little Talbot Island State Park, FPAN, Lee Newsom, and the entire Lighthouse/LAMP team, including our new executive director Amy Craft Klassen.

The late Dr. Roger C. Smith was never far from my mind while working on this shipwreck. When as an FSU graduate student I first reached out to Roger for his participation in a ship construction workshop, he gave me a copy of his and Haiduven's publication, so I have long associated him with this site. I hope our work honors his legacy.

References

BURKHARD, AUSTIN
2023   STAMP: A Method to Document, Monitor, and Manage Beached Shipwreck Sites with Citizen Science. In *Citizen Science in Maritime Archaeology: The Power of Public Engagement*, Della A. Scott-Ireton, Jennifer E. Jones, and Jason T. Raupp, editors, pp. 197-215. University Press of Florida, Gainesville.

GILMORE, TIM
2018 Little Talbot Island Shipwreck. Jax Psycho Geo, Jacksonville, FL. 13 July. <https://jaxpsychogeo.com/north/little-talbot-island-shipwreck/>. Accessed 21 May 2024.

HAIDUVEN, RICHARD, AND ROGER C. SMITH
1987 Survey of Ship's Wreckage (8DU3157) at Little Talbot Island Park, Duval County, Florida. *The Florida Anthropologist* 40(4):336–347.

MACGREGOR, DAVID R.
1988 Fast Sailing Ships: Their Design and Construction, 1775–1875. Conway Maritime Press, London, UK.

MEIDE, CHUCK, JAMES A. MCCLEAN, AND EDWARD WISER
2001 Dog Island Shipwreck Survey 1999: Report of Historical and Archaeological Investigations. Underwater Archaeology Research Report No. 4. Florida State University, Program in Underwater Archaeology, Tallahassee.

MEIDE, CHUCK, ALLYSON ROPP, P. BRENDAN BURKE, OLIVIA MCDANIEL, SAMUEL P. TURNER, AND JACOB D. SHIDNER
2021 First Coast Maritime Archaeology Project 2014-2015: Report on Archaeological Investigations. LAMP Research Reports No. 5. Lighthouse Archaeological Maritime Program, St. Augustine Lighthouse & Maritime Museum, St. Augustine, FL.

MEIDE, CHUCK, AIRIELLE R. CATHERS, NICHOLAS BUDSBERG, DOROTHY ROWLAND, CHRISTOPHER MCCARRON, THOMAS MACAVOY, LEAH TAVASI, AND HEATHER JEANS
2023 Final Report for the First Coast Maritime Archaeology Project 2020–2022: Hurricane Irma Damage Assessment and Mitigation Strategy (HIrmaDAMS). Lighthouse Archaeological Maritime Program, St. Augustine Lighthouse & Maritime Museum, St. Augustine, FL.

ROTH, MADELINE J.
2018 Discovered Repeatedly: Archaeological Documentation and Site Restoration of Pacific Reef Wreck (BISC-29, 8DA11953). Master's thesis, East Carolina University, Greenville, North Carolina.

SEPPINGS, ROBERT
1814 On a New Principle of Constructing His Majesty's Ships of War. Read 10 March 1814. Philosophical Transactions of the Royal Society of London 104:285–302.

1818 On the Great Strength Given to Ships of War by the Application of Diagonal Braces. Read 27 November 1817. *Philosophical Transactions of the Royal Society of London* 108:1–8.

STAMMERS, MICHAEL K.
2001 Iron Knees in Wooden Vessels: An Attempt at a Typology. *International Journal of Nautical Archaeology* 30(1):115–121.

STANIFORTH, MARK
1984 The Introduction and Use of Copper Sheathing: A History. B*ulletin of the Australian Institute for Maritime Archaeology* 9(1&2):21–48.

STONE, DAVID LEIGH
1993 *The Wreck Diver's Guide to Sailing Ship Artifacts of the 19th Century*. Underwater Archaeological Society of British Columbia, Vancouver, British Columbia, Canada.

• • • • • • • • • • • • • • • •

Chuck Meide
Lighthouse Archaeological Maritime Program (LAMP)
St. Augustine Lighthouse & Maritime Museum
81 Lighthouse Avenue
St. Augustine, Florida 32080

Effective Management of Recreational Diving on Archaeological and Historical Shipwreck Sites in the Red Sea: Sadana Island

Alicia Johnson

Each year, the SCUBA industry creates a billion-dollar industry and numerous job opportunities, many of which are in developing countries. Egypt's Red Sea, renowned for its abundant and historical shipwrecks, annually attracts thousands of divers. While diving historical shipwrecks is often a highlight for divers, high numbers of visitors place underwater cultural heritage sites at greater risk of degradation. When managed effectively, historic shipwrecks can be intellectually, culturally, and financially enriching. Seemingly, the lack of oversight, regulation, and education of divers places these underwater cultural heritage sites at risk for illegal salvage, looting, destruction of archaeological integrity, and increased decomposition of the wreck sites. Using the 18th-century Ottoman merchant ship wrecked off Sadana Island as a case study, effective project management plans can be suggested by the evaluation of traits, conditions, and circumstances of an at-risk underwater cultural heritage site in Egypt's Red Sea.

Cada año, el buceo genera una industria de mil millones de dólares y numerosas oportunidades laborales; muchos de los cuales están en países en vías de desarrollo. El Mar Rojo de Egipto, famoso por sus abundantes e históricos naufragios, atrae anualmente a miles de buceadores. Si bien el buceo en naufragios históricos suele ser un atractivo para los buzos, un gran número de visitantes coloca los sitios con patrimonio cultural subacuático en mayor riesgo de degradación. Cuando los sitios históricos se gestionan eficazmente, pueden resultar enriquecedores, intelectual, cultural y financieramente. Al parecer, la falta de supervisión, regulación y educación de los buzos pone a estos sitios en riesgo de saqueo, destrucción del contexto arqueológico. Se pueden diseñar e implementar planes eficaces de gestión de proyectos mediante la evaluación de diferentes características, condiciones y circunstancias de dos sitios con naufragios que son patrimonio cultural subacuático en riesgo en el Mar Rojo: el naufragio romano en el arrecife Fury Shoals y el barco mercante otomano del siglo XVIII en la isla de Sadana.

Chaque année, l'industrie de la plongée sous-marine crée une industrie d'un milliard de dollars et de nombreuses opportunités d'emploi, dont beaucoup se trouvent dans des pays en développement. La mer Rouge égyptienne, réputée pour ses épaves abondantes et historiques, attire chaque année des milliers de plongeurs. Bien que la plongée dans des épaves historiques soit souvent un fait saillant pour les plongeurs, un grand nombre de visiteurs expose un site du patrimoine culturel subaquatique à un risque accru de dégradation. Lorsqu'elles sont gérées efficacement, les épaves historiques peuvent être enrichissantes intellectuellement, culturellement et financièrement. Apparemment, le manque de surveillance, de réglementation et d'éducation des plongeurs met ces sites du patrimoine culturel subaquatique en danger contre le sauvetage illégal, le pillage, la destruction de l'intégrité archéologique et la décomposition accrue des sites d'épaves. Des plans de gestion de projet efficaces peuvent être conçus et mis en œuvre en évaluant les différents traits, conditions et circonstances de deux sites d'épaves du patrimoine culturel submergé à risque de la mer Rouge : l'épave romaine de Fury Shoals et le navire marchand ottoman du XVIIIe siècle de l'île de Sadana.

Introduction

Since Cousteau's introduction of the Aqualung in the 1950s, the evolution of recreational scuba diving has created a lucrative "Blue Economy" and a community centered around dive travel (Than 2010; World Bank 2017; Henderson 2019; Brown et al. 2020). Several of the globe's premiere underwater cultural heritage (UCH) diving sites, such as Egypt's *Thistlegorm* and Micronesia's Chuuk Lagoon, attract many divers to the wrecks and surrounding sites (Jeffery 2004; Schofield 2019; Brown et al. 2020). Prior to the advent of recreational diving, impenetrable depths, largely inaccessible to humans, fostered in situ preservation for many UCH sites. Recreational scuba diving has since enabled access and increased risk to sites that previously were, to some extent, naturally protected (Edney 2016; Wright 2016; Gregory et al. 2022; Velentza 2022). Egypt's extensive maritime trade offers opportunities to explore and preserve diverse heritage sites from various cultures; the Red Sea holds numerous historic shipwrecks and extraordinary marine biodiversity (Shaalan 2005).

Known for its warm water temperatures, high salinity levels, and rough currents, the Red Sea's environmental conditions add additional obstacles in the survival of historic shipwrecks (Edwards and Ormond 1987; Sheppard et al. 1992; Gladstone et al. 1996; Blue 2011). As non-renewable resources, efforts are needed to document, evaluate, and determine effective preservation solutions to protect Egypt's shipwrecks (Secci 2011). If managed effectively, these UCH sites can be scientifically, culturally, and economically enriching for the public (Manders 2011; Maarleveld et al. 2013; Edney 2016). Comparing images taken in 2013 and 2022 of *Carnatic*, a 19th-century shipwreck and popular dive site, reveals visible degradation to the site (Figure 1). The visible change in coral health as well as the loss of the ship's stanchions exemplify the need to protect Red Sea UCH sites and to evaluate the environmental and human factors worsening their decay (Wright 2016).

As recreational diving increases, the question arises of how UCH sites, specifically archaeological and historical shipwrecks, can be identified, protected, preserved, and promoted to ensure their sustainability, availability, and cultural benefit to the public (Lemmin-Woolfrey 2023).

For this study, recommendations to develop management plans for recreational divers are created by evaluating the at-risk UCH wreck site of the 18th-century Ottoman merchant ship at Sadana Island (Ward 2001; Blue et al. 2012). The selected study is presented with its background, threats, and recommendations for improved management. Finally, the article closes with a discussion that puts the case study of the Red Sea in the context of the larger problem of UCH management and recreational diving.

Objectives

UNESCO's recommendation for both terrestrial and underwater cultural heritage sites which are not facing immediate threats is in situ preservation (Maarleveld et al. 2013). In situ preservation can offer both long- or short-term solutions for the management of UCH sites, providing an immediate and cost-effective method to mitigate ongoing environmental degradation and to preserve organic matter. Manders (2008:31) argues that while in situ approaches are useful for preservation purposes, the approach has the potential to diminish the recreational diver's experience. Researchers such as Edney (2016) and Mckinnon (2015) reiterate the importance of considering diver personalities, ethnicities, habits, and education to better understand and rectify issues caused by divers, such as graffiti, moving artifacts, looting, or damaging the wreck itself. Employing multi-disciplinary approaches such as photogrammetric surveys, site observation, and in situ preservation strategies at specific at-risk locations can provide a more cohesive management style for a site that is popular among divers. Given that the Sadana Island Wreck has experienced significant looting, in situ preservation methods—such as covering the wreck with sediment, installing protective cages like those used in Croatia (Rossi 2014; Dorušić and Čvrljak 2019), or enhancing diver education—could

The Carnatic, sank in 1869 on Sha`b Abu Nuhas reef

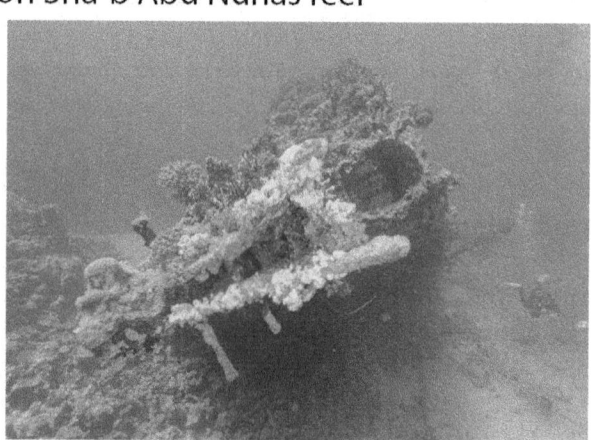

photos by:
Simon Brown (left)
Alicia Johnson (rght)

2013   2022

FIGURE 1. Side-by-side photo comparison of *Carnatic* in 2013 and 2022. (Photo by Simon Brown, 2013 left, and author, 2022 right.)

help mitigate the ongoing risk of looting, and considers funding for future excavations could be limited.

This study evaluates a UCH case study to highlight recreational diving risks that could impede the long-term preservation of underwater archaeological sites in the greater Red Sea region. Recommendations for safeguarding these sites are proposed without compromising the income-generating recreational diving prominent in Egypt's Red Sea. The aim is to offer a model for managing at-risk UCH sites while considering the financial interests of developing touristic economies.

Research Methodology

This research involved extensive analysis of recommended guidelines for underwater cultural heritage management, textual analysis of relevant research, publication of accessible digital media, outreach and working with the diving community, and fieldwork activities in Egypt as part of the Wrecks at Risk project (Manders 2011; Edney 2016; Brown and Henderson 2024). The study is supplemented by the researcher's active engagement with Red Sea diving facilities and community, encompassing numerous dives throughout the Red Sea and social science via interviews with dive tourists and professionals. The researcher engaged in community activities within the Egyptian greater community to establish ties with the community to improve understanding of the diverse traditional practices, desires, and perspectives of the Egyptian community. This process enabled the researcher to gain insights from the local and international dive community and evaluate methods which could be applied in the management of UCH in Egypt's Red Sea.

Demonstrated in previous research, diver impact can be monitored and managed by enacting preservation efforts, developing outreach initiatives, investigating diver behaviors, and conducting regular site surveys (Edney 2006; Lucrezi et al. 2019). Due to the nature of human interaction with UCH sites in the Red Sea, the researcher considers public outreach with the dive community, a primary stakeholder of UCH, to be an essential component to the realization of sustainable cultural heritage management (CHM) plans for historic shipwrecks.

By evaluating the demographic of divers, their behaviors, and their skill levels, the researcher aims to better understand the risks divers pose to each site and the steps needed to create management plans to mitigate diver impact, protect a site's archaeological integrity, and ensure accessibility for the public to enjoy. Communication with the dive community for updates on the status of sites, the researcher's observations of diver behavior, and regular dives on various sites to inspect damage to other shipwrecks in the area over the duration of three years shaped the assertions in this paper.

The researcher worked closely with local dive shop Mirage Divers (a well-known and established Bedouin-owned dive shop in operation since 2007) and various live-aboard safaris to engage with the dive community about their knowledge of UCH and to access various dive sites. Continued outreach with the dive community is integral to establish site management and to raise awareness on the procedures divers and local guides can take to report, preserve, and enjoy UCH. In addition to outreach with the local dive community, the researcher used social media channels to disseminate photographs, blogs, videos, and information media to gauge public interest and to educate the public about the benefits, risks, and methods to preserve and enjoy UCH.

Management plans and data for UCH are limited in Egypt. Recommendations presented in this article were conceptualized by the aforementioned methods and comparative examination of UCH management efforts carried out on comparable UCH sites (Anderson et al. 2006; Viduka 2011). Other sites, studies, and practices of management approaches include the Scapa Flow wrecks, the Parco Sommerso di Baiae, World War I (WWI) and World War II (WWII) sites such as Gallipoli Peninsula National Historical Park, SS *Burdigala*, HMS *Britannic* in the Mediterranean, and the "Ghost fleet of Truk Lagoon" in Micronesia (Edney 2006, 2016; Secci 2011; Stefanile 2014; Argyropoulos and Stratigea 2019). By evaluating previous approaches, obstacles, and successes of UCH management plans, this study seeks to compile suggestions to develop CHM plans for historic shipwreck sites of the Red Sea (Anderson et al. 2006; Maarleveld et al. 2013; Argyropoulos and Stratigea 2019).

The Sadana Island Wreck

As shipwrecks are a historical asset, each site offers archaeologists and divers an idiosyncratic opportunity to revisit the maritime culture and practices of various time periods and civilizations. Whereas some eras have more extensive documentation, such as Mediterranean Roman trade, the understanding of trade between early modern Asia and the Middle East remains shallow and restricted to terrestrial evidence (Ward 2001; Blue et al.

2012; Pedersen 2014). Thus, the discovery of the Sadana Island shipwreck, dating to A.D. 1765, is an opportunity to deepen the understanding of the Ottoman trade and its people (Figure 2).

North of Safaga, the Sadana Island Wreck stands in contrast to the more modern wrecks in the Red Sea. Unlike Arab, European, and Mediterranean merchant vessels, the Sadana Island Wreck is non-Arab, non-European, and non-Mediterranean (Raban 1971; Ward 2001). Alongside the wreck off Sharm-el-Sheikh and the recently discovered Umm Lujj Wreck in Saudi Arabia, the Sadana Island Wreck is one of the few Ottoman wrecks that have endured (Raban 1971; Ward 2001; El-Akkad 2022). As a unique site of an underexplored era, the Sadana Island Wreck can offer unknown information regarding Red Sea trade during the Ottoman Period. Research by Barendse (2000), Panzac (1992), and Pearson (1988:458, 1994:152) advocates for the archaeological importance of the Sadana Island Wreck. According to Ward and Baram (2006:136), the significance of the Sadana Island Wreck in the Red Sea can be understood in the context of global economic markets, particularly the acquisition of highly desired products such as coffee and Chinese porcelain. They emphasize that while studies often concentrate on European interactions in the international trade of Asia or the Islamic world, it is equally important to recognize and study trade within the Middle Eastern region.

Whereas European and Asian trade has been studied to a greater extent, less is known about the 18th-century Ottoman history of trade. As current knowledge of the early modern Asian and Middle Eastern trade is in a developmental phase, the Qing dynasty porcelain found on the Sadana Island Wreck adds perspective to the cultural understanding between South Asian manufacturers and Islamic consumers (Ward and Baram 2006). The site's porcelain predominantly showcases geometric and floral designs, suggesting the manufacturers were aware of Islamic religious and cultural prohibitions against depicting living creatures. This awareness led Qing artisans to create desired designs suitable for foreign markets (Ward 2001; Braun 2005).

The merchant vessel's proximity to the shore can be explained by the ship traveling a common trade route, possibly Jeddah to Suez, and taking shelter at night in the bay when it sank (Ward 2001). The Ottoman era merchant ship is 50 meters (m) in length and was first reported to authorities by a local sports diver in 1994; the site spans an impressive 800 square meter (m^2) area, ranging from 27–45 m of depth (Blue et al. 2012). From 1995–1998, excavation took place under the management of the Institute of Nautical Archaeology (INA) and Supreme Council for Antiquities (SCA) (Ward and Baram 2006). Although the ship differs in design from contemporary vessels, the contents of its cargo resemble the wreck at Sharm el-Sheikh, which also included coffee, spices, pottery, and textiles (Raban 1971; Ward 2001). Much of the site's organic cargo has since disintegrated and more durable items, such as porcelain, have been looted by sports divers.

Threats to the Site

Teeming reefs and historic shipwrecks, mere meters off the shore, are alluring to sports divers and make Egypt one of the world's top countries to dive (Hawkins et al. 1992). Considering the close-knit relations within the diving community, worthwhile dive sites are often shared among friends, leading previously unknown places to become popular quickly. In recent years, social media and geo-tagging has fostered over-tourism to remote sites and the ensuing degradation of previously well-preserved sites (Siegel et al. 2023). Additionally, sites with artifacts, like the Sadana Island Wreck, become even more desirable, as obtaining a piece of porcelain or a jug from a famous wreck is seen as a diving achievement (Khalil 2020).

Whereas some wrecks have environmental protections afforded by great depths or distance from shore, the Sadana Island Wreck is in shallow waters, close to shore, and surrounded by Hurghada's bustling tourism. The Sadana Island site faces looting and additional risks due to its accessibility and lack of oversight (Ward 1998; Blue et al. 2012). During the sinking, the crew were likely able to swim ashore and salvage a portion of the foundering ship's cargo. The ship's resting place enabled it to become a popular modern diving site in the 1990s and 2000s. As of 2024, the site is closed to the public due to the pervasive looting and its proximity to a nearby military base.

Looted antiquities and other ill-gotten trophies are often perceived as a token of achievement, and their collection can be a goal for some divers; such behavior can be seen on multiple wrecks all over the world (Dwyer 2017). The Sadana Island Wreck has suffered significant damage and diminished archaeological integrity due to sport divers looting the site (Haldane [Ward] 1996; Haldane 1998; Ward 1998; Khalil 2020). Khalil's (2020:1) Sadana Island Wreck report states a "local boat captain [was in possession of] a ceramic jar from the wreck given to him by a tourist." Based on the suspected

FIGURE 2. Map of Sadana Island shipwreck site. (Image by Mohamed Salama, 2020.)

number of looted items, recorded diver behavior exhibited on the wreck, and the attitude divers demonstrate towards artifacts, one could argue members of the diving community perceive artifacts as personal trophies rather than as cultural heritage.

The site's accessibility and capacity for planned surveys is limited by unpredictable weather conditions and strong currents present with tidal change. The natural inlet creates a wind tunnel and on windy days the surface water is tumultuous. While more experienced divers might be able to treasure hunt in rough seas, excavations and surveys are difficult to manage in unpredictable weather conditions. In addition to weather conditions, the site extends into deeper water and requires archaeologists with technical diving qualifications to carry out deeper and higher-risk projects. As noted in Khalil's (2020:1) report, the Sadana Island Wreck needs further excavation:

> *It was realized that the seabed at the depth of 50 m still contains archaeological remains beneath the soft sediments...and the site required further and more thorough investigation by a larger team, using a bigger boat and excavation equipment. Also, the exposed artefacts [should] be excavated.*

Due to the exposed nature of the remaining portions of the hull, Dr. Emad Khalil, an active leader of past Sadana Island Wreck projects, suggested further excavation to safeguard artifacts that remain at risk of looting. Additional projects on the site would assist in the continued study and preservation of the site. As of 2024, the site is less accessible due to the presence of the Egyptian military in the surrounding area.

In Egypt, like numerous other developing countries, excavations are often dependent upon obtaining the necessary permits and permissions. Since Egypt's 2011 Revolution, permit approval for excavations has plummeted and permits for potential excavation projects, often involving international participation, are frequently revoked. While avenues exist for the Supreme Council of Antiquities to legally process permits, the greater government system is wary of the perceived security threat archaeological missions might induce (Meskell 2000; Marchant 2011). Nonetheless, more than 300 archaeological missions have been enacted in recent years and an uptick of tourism, combined with the opening of the Grand Egyptian Museum, encourages increased cooperation between maritime archaeologists and the government (Raafat 2023). As the Sadana Island Wreck has been excavated with students from various universities, further excavations can offer burgeoning maritime archaeologists training and will develop internal capacity (Maarleveld et al. 2013; Demesticha et al. 2019; MacKintosh 2019). The Sadana Island Wreck has suffered severe looting, and while further excavations would enhance the preservation of the site, the greatest risk to the site continues to be treasure-hunting behaviors by recreational divers. The site's recent closure to the public has slowed looting, but the site remains largely at risk of significant destruction of archaeological integrity.

Recommendations for UCH Management

A substantial hurdle in the undertaking of maritime archaeological projects is the funding available. Limited resources for funding in Egypt are an obstacle in addition to the involved community's awareness of available resources (Demesticha et al. 2019). Increased government spending and additional foreign support would benefit UCH efforts in the area and help to ensure that sites such as the Sadana Island Wreck are evaluated and documented on a periodic basis.

As the site needs further excavation, additional in situ preservation would be beneficial until the funds can be allocated for a full excavation (Manders 2012; Maarleveld et al. 2013). The extent of looting on the site indicates the remaining artifacts are at risk of being looted or damaged; excavation of the remaining artifacts and replica replacements could be a possibility (Stefanile 2014; BBC 2020). As of 2023, the pending opening of the Grand Egyptian Museum offers a potential opportunity to locally house, preserve, and display artifacts to the public.

Although the site is partially accessible to divers, little information is available for anyone who does visit the area. Without information to explain the historical context of the site, people are limited in their ability to connect with UCH. For the public to see the value of investing funds to protect and preserve UCH, research shows the public needs to be educated about a site's location, history, and its benefit to the community (Whitehead and Finney 2003; Edney 2016; Demesticha et al. 2019; Shaikhon 2021). If site fees are collected, guests feel more justified in their willingness to pay if they see, or are aware of, ongoing preservation work at the site (Walpole et al. 2001; Lucrezi et al. 2019). Familiarizing the public with management and preservation procedures would be beneficial in increasing the public's receptiveness and willingness to fund efforts or pay site/entrance fees.

Preservation efforts could be funded by the recreational divers, who are open to paying a fee to access a protected and preserved site (Orams 1998; Davis and Tisdell 1999; Barker and Roberts 2004; Lucrezi et al. 2019). Research shows that divers are willing to pay an entrance fee or park fee for sites which have visible upkeep (Walpole et al. 2001; Whitehead and Finney 2003). If the site were reopened and publicized, the revenue created could fund preservation initiatives and effectively engage the public. The Sadana Island Wreck is already known to many local divers and visible preservation efforts would be well received by the community.

Despite Egypt's internationally renowned diving, little information on the wreck, how to visit the site, or its historical significance is available to the greater public. Academic writing is visible through a basic Google search, but the sole video about the site has a mere 500 views (Khalil 2020). While literature is available for skilled English readers, little content and information are available to reach the broader Egyptian- and Arabic-speaking public. The Sadana Island Wreck has had enough research in the past that a collaborative blog with a diving organization could expand the public's awareness and interest in the site and its preservation. Eye-catching, simple, and easily consumed information tends to capture the average reader's attention and has better retention than academic papers, which are often inaccessible due to paywalls. An outreach video concept could showcase the site while using narration or text to explain the damage caused by looting and the procedures to follow if a diver discovers a UCH site or witnesses its destruction.

Proactively involving the local dive community with ongoing projects, news/updates, surveys, clean-up projects, and informative seminars would be beneficial to the preservation of the Sadana Island Wreck and other UCH sites. Given the significant looting by sport divers, researchers should discuss the ramifications it causes to the site and educate the diving community. Promoting public support for and knowledge about the Sadana Island Wreck will enable visitors to be more satisfied with their experience, leading to reduced looting and increased opportunities for preservation efforts and projects.

Given the great success of Franck Goddio's 2006 "Egypt's Sunken Treasures" traveling exhibit, organizing a similar exhibit featuring the Sadana Island Wreck finds and site photographs for display at various museums in Egypt and internationally seems promising. The excavated cargo is largely stored in Alexandria, where it is inaccessible to the public, and the highlights of the excavation are on display at the Hurghada Museum. As the site has suffered the most damage by looting, it can be best preserved with outreach to the dive community to change divers' perceptions of artifacts and UCH (Edney 2006, 2016). Other methods, such as using social media to showcase and introduce the site to the public, exhibiting the found artifacts, and conducting regular surveys will increase the public's appreciation of their heritage. Public recognition and support will lead to increased preservation efforts to ensure the Sadana Island Wreck is no longer at risk.

Conclusion

Part of the broader eastern Mediterranean region, maritime archaeology in Egypt is a young discipline that has progressed in the past 15 years (Demesticha et al. 2019). Concerted efforts have been made in Egypt regarding underwater projects (e.g., Pharos Lighthouse), international collaborations (e.g., Honor Frost Foundation, Centre d'Etudes Alexandrine), and increased funding opportunities for students of maritime archaeology enrolled in Centre of Maritime Archaeology and Underwater Cultural Heritage (CMAUCH). In 2022, CMAUCH was awarded a UNESCO Heritage Chair, recognizing its expertise and contribution to the preservation and study of UCH (UNESCO 2021). Nonetheless, challenges such as limited funding, training, and the scarcity of related industries need to be addressed to ensure sustainable development and wider public appreciation of Egypt's maritime cultural heritage (Demesticha et al. 2019).

Community science and local training offers an avenue for low-cost initiatives yielding a high reward. Increasing capacity within the local maritime archaeology community and involving the dive community, the primary point of contact for site visitors, is crucial for developing public relations and changing attitudes about the cultural and historical significance of UCH sites. The potential of involving the community with surveys and other noninvasive community science will help to change divers' perceptions of the site and will offer verified information on the harmful effects of looting. Diver attitudes are highly indicative of the treatment exhibited on a site, and constructive collaboration with the public would be helpful in preventing and reporting future looting (Edney 2006, 2016). Documenting UCH sites via photogrammetry can create a detailed digital record and allow for comparison of the site's condition with regular surveys. The 3D model of the site could be hosted on a website (e.g., Sketchfab) and will increase accessibility for the public and researchers.

The dive community of the Red Sea is proactive towards personal preservation methods; as such, efforts to involve the community would be well-received. If local dive professionals are trained in surveying methods, they could help in maintaining and coordinating affordable documentation and active citizen science (Anderson et al. 2006; Edwards et al. 2016; Garcia et al. 2018; Argyropoulos and Stratigea 2019; Wiseman et al. 2021; Viduka 2022). As UCH stakeholders, divers take pride in a site for which they feel responsible, and a managed site partnered with local community involvement will enable more care of the site (Dodds 2012; Wongthong and Harvey 2014). Moreover, organizing public seminars or events to educate dive guides about the site's history and the significance of preventing looting would aid in the site's preservation (Figure 3).

UCH funding is quite limited in the region and a suggested proposal to excavate, document, and create promoted and managed wreck trails, like the Panhandle Shipwreck Trail in Florida, would be a wise investment (Smith 2014). As divers are active on social media, the creation of a digital application providing information on each wreck Red Sea wreck site has the potential to be a popular and useful tool for the dive community and increase awareness while instilling positive diver behavior. When sites are managed effectively, they can bring in additional revenue and visitors to the area (Richards 2018; Henderson 2019). Running social media campaigns partnered with appropriate channels would raise awareness of UCH sites and offer an inexpensive method to generate public interest and incentivize funding for research projects (Henderson 2019).

As seen in the Sadana Island Wreck case study, the Red Sea's UCH sites are at risk due to pollution, climate change, lack of oversight, legal regulation, diver behavior,

FIGURE 3. Recent damage done to the port cleat of *Thistlegorm* caused by insufficient mooring access. (Photo by author, 2023.)

and practices harmful for historic wrecks (Edney 2016; Wright 2016; Gregory et al. 2022; Velentza 2022). Active threats to preservation efforts include looting, destruction of archaeological integrity, over tourism, and increased decomposition to the shipwreck and its contents (Haldane [Ward] 1996; Campbell 2013; McKinnon 2015; Edney 2016; Khedr and Salama 2018). As a non-renewable resource, it is economically and culturally beneficial to ensure that UCH sites, such as the Sadana Island Wreck, are protected with appropri-

FIGURE 4. Numerous recreational divers exploring the wreck of *Numidia* in the Red Sea. A popular site for dive safari boats, the scuba industry is a strong component of Egypt's tourism sector. (Photo by author, 2023.)

ate site management plans to maximize public engagement and preserve the sites (Secci 2011; Maarleveld et al. 2013) (Figure 4).

Acknowledgements

I would like to express my deep appreciation to all those who have contributed to my research in the Red Sea. I am particularly grateful to my supportive and patient supervisor, Emad Khalil, and to my family, friends, and mentors: Simon Brown, Jon Henderson, Ian Rojas, Bryce Pigeon, Arturo Rey da Silva, Ayman Taher, Ziad Morsi, Lucy Blue, and the responsible members within the Red Sea diving community. I am also indebted to Mirage Divers for their invaluable assistance with diver outreach. Finally, I wish to extend a special thank you to the Honor Frost Foundation, Egypt's Camber of Diving and Water Sports, Scuba Schools International, DiveAssure, and the ACUA for their unwavering support of my early career in maritime archaeology. Without their support, this work would not have been possible.

References

ANDERSON, ROSS, CASSANDRA PHILIPPOU, AND PETER HARVEY
2006   Innovative Approaches in Underwater Cultural Heritage Management. *Maritime Archaeology: Australian Approaches*:136–150.

ARGYROPOULOS, VASILIKE, AND ANASTASIA STRATIGEA
2019   Sustainable Management of Underwater Cultural Heritage: The Route from Discovery Engagement - Open Issues in the Mediterranean. *Heritage* 2(2):1588–1613.

BARENDSE, R. J.
2000   Trade and State in the Arabian Seas: A Survey from the Fifteenth to the Eighteenth Century. *Journal of World History* 11:173–225.

BRITISH BROADCASTING CORPORATION (BBC)
2020   A Roman City at the Bottom of the Sea. British Broadcasting Corporation. https://www.bbc.com/reel/video/p093gtp2/a-roman-city-at-the-bottom-of-the-sea.

BARKER, NOLA H. L., AND CALLUM M. ROBERTS
2004   Scuba Diver Behaviour and the Management of Diving Impacts on Coral Reefs. *Biological Conservation* 120(4):481–489.

BLUE, LUCY
2011   Red Sea. In *Oxford Handbook of Maritime Archaeology*, Alexis Catsambis, Ben Ford, and Donny Hamilton, editors, pp. 495–512. Oxford University Press, Oxford, UK.

BLUE, LUCY, J. D. HILL, AND THOMAS ROSS
2012   New Light on the Nature of Indo-Roman Trade: Roman Period Shipwrecks in the Northern Red Sea. In *Navigated Spaces, Connected Places: Proceedings of Red Sea Project V held at the University of Exeter September 2010*, Dionisius A. Aqius, John B. Cooper, and Athena Trakadas, editors, pp. 91–100. Archaeopress, Oxford, UK.

Braun, Kathy
2005 A Cargo of Islamic Ceramics from the Eighteenth-Century Sadana Island Shipwreck in the Red Sea: Form and Function of Qulal and Other Shapes. Master's thesis, Department of Anthropology, Florida State University, Tallahassee.

Brown, Simon, and Jon C. Henderson
2024 Recording the SS Thistlegorm: Rapid Multi-Image Underwater Photogrammetric Survey of a Large Second World War Wreck. *Journal of Marine Science and Engineering* 12(2):280.

Brown, Simon, Jon C. Henderson, Alex Mustard, and Mike Postons
2020 *Diving the Thistlegorm: The Ultimate Guide to a World War II Shipwreck.* Dived Up, Bournemouth, UK.

Campbell, Peter B.
2013 The Illicit Antiquities Trade as a Transnational Criminal Network: Characterizing and Anticipating Trafficking of Cultural Heritage. *International Journal of Cultural Property* 20(2):113–153.

Davis, Derrin, and C. A. Tisdell
1999 Tourist Levies and Willingness to Pay for a Whale Shark Experience. *Tourism Economics* 5(2):161–174.

Demesticha, Stella, Lucy Semaann, and Ziad Morsy
2019 Capacity Building in Maritime Archaeology: The Case of the Eastern Mediterranean (Cyprus, Lebanon, and Egypt). *Journal of Maritime Archaeology* 14:369–389.

Dodds, Rachel
2012 Sustainable Tourism: A Hope or a Necessity? The Case of Tofino, British Columbia, Canada. Journal of Sustainable Development 5(5).

Dorušić, Vedran, and Matko Čvrljak
2019 Technological Protection of an Underwater Archeological Site; a Newly Discovered Roman Shipwreck from the 1st Century BC, on the Island of Pag, Croatia. In *International Conference in Management of Accessible Underwater, Cultural and Natural Heritage Sites: "Dive in Blue Growth,"* pp. 16–18. Athens, Greece.

Dwyer, Dialynn
2017 The Lures and Dangers of Diving to the *Andrea Doria*. Boston.com. <https://www.boston.com/news/local-news/2017/08/02/the-lures-and-dangers-of-diving-to-the-andrea-doria/>. Accessed 17 May 2024.

Edney, Joanne
2006 Impacts of Recreational Scuba Diving on Shipwrecks in Australia and the Pacific. *Journal of the Humanities and Social Sciences* 3440:201–233.

2016 A Framework for Managing Diver Impacts on Historic Shipwrecks. *Journal of Maritime Archaeology* 11:271–297.

Edwards, Alasdair, and Rupert Ormond
1987 Red Sea Fishes. In *Red Sea*, Alasdair J. Edwards and Stephen M. Head, editors, pp. 251–287. Elsevier Ltd, Amsterdam, Netherlands. <https://doi.org/10.1016/B978-0-08-028873-4.50018-9>. Accessed 17 May 2024.

Edwards, Kevin, Nicolas Bigourdan, Ian McCann, and Cooper Darren
2016 3DMAPPR: A Community-Based Underwater Archaeological Photogrammetry Program in Perth, Western Australia. *Journal of the Australasian Institute for Maritime Archaeology* 40:1–16.

El-Akkad, Ferra
2022 Shipwrecks in the Red Sea: Heritage Gems Deserve to be Saved. Al-Ahram Weekly - Ahram Online. <https://english.ahram.org.eg/News/478956.aspx>. Accessed 17 May 2024.

Garcia, Ana Catarina, and João Pedro Barreiros
2018 Are Underwater Archaeological Parks Good for Fishes? Symbiotic Relation between Cultural Heritage Preservation and Marine Conservation in the Azores. *Regional Studies in Marine Science* 21. Elsevier B.V.:57–66. https://doi.org/10.1016/j.rsma.2017.10.003.

Gladstone, William, Captain Roy Facey, and Khaled Hariri
2006 State of the Marine Environment Report for the Red Sea and the Gulf of Aden, 2006. Report to Regional Organization for the Conservation of the Environment of the Red Sea and Gulf of Aden, Jeddah, Saudi Arabia.

Gregory, David, Tom Dawson, Dolores Elkin, Hans Van Tilburg, Chris Underwood, Vicki Richards, Andrew Viduka, Kieran Westley, Jeneva Wright, and Jørgen Hollesen
2022 Of Time and Tide: The Complex Impacts of Climate Change on Coastal and Underwater Cultural Heritage. *Antiquity* 96(390):1396–1411.

Haldane [Ward], Cheryl
1996 Sadana Island Shipwreck, Egypt: Preliminary Report. *International Journal of Nautical Archaeology* 25(2):83–94.

Haldane, Douglas
1998 The Logistics of the Sadana Island Shipwreck Excavation. *INA Quarterly* 25(3):6.

Hawkins, Julie P., and Callum M. Roberts
1993 Effects of Recreational Scuba Diving on Coral Reefs: Trampling on Reef-Flat Communities. *Biological Conservation* 66(3):255.

HENDERSON, JON
2019 Oceans without History? Marine Cultural Heritage and the Sustainable Development Agenda. *Sustainability* 11(18):5080.

JEFFERY, BILL
2004 World War II Underwater Cultural Heritage Sites in Truk Lagoon: Considering a Case for World Heritage Listing. *International Journal of Nautical Archaeology* 33:106–121.

KHALIL, EMAD
2020 Sadana Island Shipwreck Revisited, CMAUCH-2018–2020. Honor Frost Foundation, London, UK. <https://honorfrostfoundation.org/grants-awarded/research-grants/egypt/cmauch/sadana-island-shipwreck/>. Accessed 17 May 2024.

KHEDR, MOHAMED, AND MOHAMED SALAMA
2018 Sadana Island Shipwreck Revisited. General Union of Arab Archaeologists 21. <https://www.researchgate.net/publication/375030167_Sadana_Islands_Shipwreck_Revisited>. Accessed 24 January 2023.

LEMMIN-WOOLFREY, ULRIKE
2023 How Underwater and Deep-Sea Tourism Became so Popular. <https://www.bbc.com/travel/article/20230620-how-underwater-and-deep-sea-tourism-became-so-popular>. Accessed January 22, 2024

LUCREZI, SERENA, MARTINA MILANESE, CARLO CERRANO, AND MARCO PALMA
2019 The Influence of Scuba Diving Experience on Divers' Perceptions, and its Implications for Managing Diving Destinations. PLoS ONE 14. <https://doi.org/10.1371/journal.pone.0219306>. Accessed 17 May 2024.

MAARLEVELD, THIJIS, ULRIKE GUÉRIN, AND BARBARA EGGER (EDITORS)
2013 Manual for Activities Directed at Underwater Cultural Heritage: Guidelines to the Annex of the UNESCO 2001 Convention. UNESCO, Paris, France.

MACKINTOSH, ROBERT
2019 Capacity in Maritime Archaeology: A Framework for Analysis. *Journal of Maritime Archaeology* 14:391–408.

2008 In Situ Preservation: "The Preferred Option." *Museum International* 60(4):31–41.

MANDERS, MARTIJN R.
2012 UNIT 3 Management of Underwater Cultural Heritage. UNESCO, Thailand. <https://www.academia.edu/23401008/Unit_3_Management_of_Underwater_Cultural_Heritage>. Accessed 17 May 2023.

MANDERS, MARTIJN R. (EDITOR)
2011 Guidelines for Protection of Submerged Wooden Cultural Heritage. WreckProtect.org. <https://english.cultureelerfgoed.nl/publications/publications/2019/01/01/wreckprotect-guidelines>. Accessed 17 May 2024.

MARCHANT, JO
2011 Archaeology Meets Politics: Spring Comes to Ancient Egypt. *Nature* 479:464–467.

MCKINNON, JENNIFER F.
2015 Memorialization, Graffiti and Artifact Movement: A Case Study of Cultural Impacts on WWII Underwater Cultural Heritage in the Commonwealth of the Northern Mariana Islands. *Journal of Maritime Archaeology* 10:11–27.

MESKELL, LYNN
2000 The Practice and Politics of Archaeology in Egypt. *Annals of the New York Academy of Sciences* 925(1):146–169.

ORAMS, MARK
1998 *Marine Tourism: Development, Impacts and Management*. Routlege, London, UK.

PANZAC, DANIEL
1992 International and Domestic Maritime Trade in the Ottoman Empire during the 18th Century. *International Journal of Middle East Studies* 24:189–206.

PEARSON, MICHAEL
1988 Brokers in Western Indian Port Cities: Their Role in Servicing Foreign Merchants Author. *Modern Asia Studies* 22:455–472.

1994 *Pious Passengers: The Hajj in Earlier Times*. Sterling Publishing, New Delhi, India.

PEDERSEN, RALPH K.
2014 Shipwreck Archaeology in the Red Sea and the Potential of Exploration along the East African Littoral. Paper presented at the Exploring China's Ancient Links to Africa Conference, Addis Ababa, Ethiopia. <https://www.ancientportsantiques.com/wp-content/uploads/Documents/PLACES/RedSea/BlackAssarca&Jeddah-Pedersen2014.pdf>. Accessed 17 May 2024.

RAAFAT, SHAIMAA
2023 Egypt Aims to Attract 30 million tourists in 2028: Tourism Minister. Daily News Egypt 22 March. Giza, Egypt. <https://www.dailynewsegypt.com/2023/03/22/egypt-aims-to-attract-30-million-tourists-in-2028-tourism-minister/>. Accessed 31 March 2023.

RABAN, AVNER
1971 The Shipwreck off Sharm El Sheikh. *Archaeology* 24:146–155.

Richards, Greg
2018 Cultural Tourism: A Review of Recent Research and Trends. *Journal of Hospitality and Tourism Management* 36:12–21.

Rossi, I. R.
2014 Experience in Current Management of Underwater Cultural Heritage in Croatia; the Case of the Protective Cages. *Archaeologia Maritima Mediterranea* 11:45–62.

Schofield, Danielle
2019 A Brief History of the SS *Thistlegorm*. PADI Blog, 5 April. <https://blog.padi.com/a-brief-history-of-the-ss-thistlegorm/>. Accessed 17 May 2024.

Secci, Massimiliano
2011 Protection Versus Public Access: Two Concepts Compared within the Italian Underwater Cultural Heritage Management System. *Journal of Maritime Archaeology* 6:113–128.

Shaalan, Ihab Mohamed
2005 Sustainable Tourism Development in the Red Sea of Egypt Threats and Opportunities. *Journal of Cleaner Production* 13(2):83–87.

Shaikhon, Ahmed Motawea Hussein
2021 Managing Underwater Heritage in Egypt. *International Journal of Multidisciplinary Studies in Architecture and Cultural Heritage* 4(1):58–74.

Sheppard, Charles, Andrew Price, and Callum Robert
1992 *Marine Ecology of the Arabian Region: Patterns and Processes in Extreme Tropical Environments.* Academic Press, London. UK.

Siegel, Lauren A., Iis Tussyadiah, and Caroline Scarles
2023 Exploring Behaviors of Social Media-induced Tourists and the Use of Behavioral Interventions as Salient Destination Response Strategy. *Journal of Destination Marketing and Management* 27:100765.

Smith, Lindsay S.
2014 The Florida Panhandle Shipwreck Trail: Promoting Heritage Tourism in the Digital Age. In B*etween the Devil and the Deep: Meeting Challenges in the Public Interpretation of Maritime Cultural Heritage*, Della A. Scott-Ireton, editor, pp. 109–118. Springer, New York, NY.

Stefanile, Michele
2014 Underwater Cultural Heritage, Tourism and Diving Centers: The Case of Pozzuoli and Baiae (Italy). In *Proceedings of the V International Congress of Underwater Archeology (IKUWA V)*, pp. 213–224. Ministerio de Educación, Cultura y Deporte, Cartagena, Columbia.

Than, Ker
2010 Jacques Cousteau Centennial: What He Did, Why He Matters. National Geographic.com. <https://www.nationalgeographic.com/adventure/article/100611-jacques-cousteau-100th-anniversary-birthday-legacy-google>. Accessed 17 May 2024.

United Nations Educational, Scientific and Cultural Organization (UNESCO)
2021 UNESCO Chair on Underwater Cultural Heritage established at Alexandria University, Egypt | Articles. UNESCO. < https://www.unesco.org/en/articles/unesco-chair-underwater-cultural-heritage-established-alexandria-university-egypt>. Accessed 22 January 2022.

Velentza, Katerina
2022 Maritime Archaeological Research, Sustainability, and Climate Resilience. *European Journal of Archaeology* (November):1–19.

Viduka, Andrew
2011 Managing Underwater Cultural Heritage: A Case Study of SS *Yongala*. *Historic Environment* 23(2):12–18.

2022 A Maritime Archaeological Conservation Citizen Science Programme for Individual Benefit and Good Public Outcomes: GIRT Scientific Divers. *Journal of Community Archaeology and Heritage* 9(2):71–87.

Walpole, Matthew J., Harold J. Goodwin, and Kari G. R. Ward
2001 Pricing Policy for Tourism in Protected Areas: Lessons from Komodo National Park, Indonesia. *Conservation Biology* 15(1):218–227.

Ward [Haldane], Cheryl
1998 Sadana Island Shipwreck: Final Season. *INA Quarterly* 24:3–6.

2001 The Sadana Island Shipwreck: An Eighteenth-Century AD Merchantman off the Red Sea Coast of Egypt. *World Archaeology* 32(3):368–382.

Ward, Cheryl [Haldane], and Uzi Baram
2006 Global Markets, Local Practice: Ottoman-period Clay Pipes and Smoking Paraphernalia from the Red Sea Shipwreck at Sadana Island, Egypt. *International Journal of Historical Archaeology* 10:135–158.

Whitehead, John C., and Suzanne S. Finney
2003 Willingness to Pay for Submerged Maritime Cultural Resources. *Journal of Cultural Economics* 27:231–240.

Wiseman, Chelsea, Michael O'Leary, Jorg Hacker, Francis Stankiewicz, John McCarthy, Emma Beckett, Jerem Leach, Paul Baggaley, Charles Collins, Sean Ulm, Jo McDonald, and Jonathan Benjamin
2021   A Multi-Scalar Approach to Marine Survey and Underwater Archaeological Site Prospection in Murujuga, Western Australia. *Quaternary International* 584 (September 2020):152–170.

Wongthong, Panwad and Nick Harvey
2014   Integrated Coastal Management and Sustainable Tourism: A Case Study of the Reef-based SCUBA Dive Industry from Thailand. *Ocean and Coastal Management* 95:138–146.

World Bank
2017   *The Potential of the Blue Economy*. World Bank, Washington, DC.

Wright, Jeneva
2016   Maritime Archaeology and Climate Change: An Invitation. *Journal of Maritime Archaeology* 11(3):255–270.

. . . .

Alicia Johnson
2130 Via Esplanade
Punta Gorda, Florida 33950

Public Engagement within Icelandic Maritime Archaeology: Addressing Challenges in the Management of Submerged Sites

Alexandra Tyas

This article discusses the current state of maritime archaeology within Iceland and highlights challenges in the field which need to be overcome in order to improve the management of sites. The management and monitoring of submerged sites in particular in Iceland is severely deficient due to a number of factors, and elsewhere professionals are increasingly turning towards community engagement methods to overcome some of these issues. This article therefore evaluates the possibilities for community engagement in Icelandic maritime archaeology. It also evaluates the understanding of the varying methods and terminology related to community engagement techniques, and if these are understood within the Icelandic archaeology profession. Surveys and interviews form the basis for recommendations for increased engagement with maritime archaeology and the management of submerged sites.

Este artículo tiene como objetivo discutir el estado actual de la arqueología marítima en Islandia y destaca los desafíos dentro del campo que deben superarse para mejorar la gestión de los sitios. La gestión y el seguimiento de los sitios sumergidos, en particular en Islandia, son muy deficientes debido a una serie de factores, y en otros lugares los profesionales recurren cada vez más a métodos de participación comunitaria para superar algunos de estos problemas. Por lo tanto, este artículo evalúa las posibilidades de participación comunitaria en la arqueología marítima dentro de Islandia. También evalúa la comprensión de los distintos métodos y terminología relacionados con las técnicas de participación comunitaria, y si esto se entiende dentro de la profesión arqueológica islandesa. Un estudio piloto de arqueología marítima comunitaria, así como encuestas y entrevistas con arqueólogos, buzos deportivos y administradores del patrimonio, forman la base de las recomendaciones hechas en este documento para futuras mejoras tanto en la participación como en la gestión de sitios sumergidos.

Cet article vise à discuter de l'état actuel de l'archéologie maritime en Islande et met en évidence les défis à relever dans ce domaine afin d'améliorer la gestion des sites. La gestion et le suivi des sites submergés, en particulier en Islande, sont gravement déficients en raison d'un certain nombre de facteurs, et ailleurs, les professionnels se tournent de plus en plus vers des méthodes d'engagement communautaire pour surmonter certains de ces problèmes rencontrés. Cet article évalue donc les possibilités d'engagement communautaire dans l'archéologie maritime en Islande. Il évalue également la compréhension des différentes méthodes et terminologies liées aux techniques d'engagement communautaire, et si cela est compris au sein de la profession d'archéologue islandais. Une étude pilote communautaire d'archéologie maritime, ainsi que des enquêtes et des entretiens avec des archéologues, des plongeurs sportifs et des gestionnaires du patrimoine, constituent la base des recommandations formulées dans ce document pour améliorer l'engagement et la gestion des sites submergés.

Introduction

Ongoing research hypothesizes that involving communities in archaeology could lead to enhanced heritage management. When the public participates they become integrated into the heritage cycle, where a site's value is directly tied to the enjoyment and understanding it offers (Thurley 2005). In theory, this concept is straightforward: if the public enjoys visiting a site, they are more likely to advocate for its preservation. However, in practice, numerous challenges must be addressed before the public can be fully embraced in Icelandic archaeology. This article delves into some of the challenges encountered during doctoral research on public engagement in maritime archaeology in Iceland (Figure 1). It provides a comprehensive overview, discussing the initial concept, challenges faced, and subsequent new approach. The questions this research seeks to answer relate to why community and volunteer contributions to archaeology currently are lacking in Iceland, and whether engagement methods could be used to highlight the importance of maritime archaeology in the future.

FIGURE 1: Map showing locations of surveyed or excavated sites in Iceland: Site 1 - Melckmeyt (Einarsson 1993; McCarthy and Martin 2019); Site 2 - Kolkuós (unpublished); Site 3 - Sample of whaling stations in the Westfjords (Edvardsson and Egilsson 2011; Helgason et al. 2019); Site 4 - *Phønix* (Edvardsson and Egilsson 2015); 5 - Unidentified wreck in lake Þingvallavatn (Thingvellir National Park 2023). (Image by author, 2023.)

Background

Iceland, a small nation located in the northern Atlantic Ocean, was established in the 9th century by Norse settlers. Its subarctic climate and frequent natural disasters often wreaked havoc on the Icelandic farming society, occasionally leading to significant population declines (Bjornsson 2006; Edvardsson 2022). Consequently, survival necessitated a pivot towards the exploitation of marine resources. This reliance has continued over time, with fishing still being a cornerstone of the Icelandic economy (Sigfusson et al. 2013). The permanent dependence on the sea is evidenced by centuries of human activity along Iceland's coastlines. Isotopic studies conducted at sites dating to the settlement period (A.D. 870 to 930) show the importance of marine resources, where even in inland locales traces of marine foods in the diet are evident (Price and Gestsdóttir 2006; McGovern et al. 2007). Ironically, very little maritime archaeological research is conducted in a country whose maritime history is the basis for its habitation and settlement. The emphasis within the field is primarily placed on terrestrial sites dating from the settlement or Viking eras, spanning from A.D. 870 to the mid-11th century.

The practice of archaeology in Iceland dates back to the late 19th century, coinciding with the enactment of the first laws aimed at safeguarding cultural heritage sites. The inaugural underwater excavation in Iceland occurred in 1993 (surveying a Dutch merchant ship wrecked in 1659), and subsequent sporadic underwater and coastal surveys have unveiled significant potential for further research owing to higher levels of preservation than previously assumed (Einarsson 1993; Edvardsson and Egilsson 2011, 2015; Elliott 2018; Helgason et al. 2019; McCarthy and Martin 2019; Thingvellir National Park 2023) (Figures 2 and 3). Despite a gradual increase in maritime archaeology projects since this first excavation in 1993, the discipline remains comparatively marginalized when compared with its terrestrial counterpart. This is further evidenced by the possibility to include most references (both published surveys and media reports) to underwater excavations or exploratory surveys within the one citation bracket above, also shown in Figure 1. More work has, however, been completed on coastal maritime sites around the country due to their increased accessibility.

FIGURE 2: Whale ear bone located at a 19th-century Norwegian whaling station in the Westfjords. Remains of bones can be seen covering the sea floor as evidence of whale processing. (Image by author, May 2023.)

Challenges in Icelandic Maritime Archaeology

Iceland faces many challenges in improving the management of its maritime heritage sites, particularly those underwater, a situation shared by many nations. First, underwater archaeology in Iceland is still within its very early phase, and based on the author's experience at conferences, in interviews, and with research, it would be fair to suggest Iceland is around 20 years behind other Western countries. To provide some context for this estimation, between 1990 and 2019, of over 1,000 archaeological research license applications, only 8 concerned underwater sites (Minjastofnun Íslands n.d.; Tyas 2023). The legal framework safeguarding underwater sites underwent its most recent update in 2012, and only then described underwater heritage as a distinct category (Lög um menningarminjar nr. 80/2012). Second, it is also important to note here that Iceland has yet to ratify the 2001 UNESCO Convention on the Protection of the Underwater Cultural Heritage, due to potential conflicts with the 1982 Convention on the Law of the Sea. The ratification could impact fishing rights and access, posing a challenge to one of Iceland's primary exports. Although the convention aims to preserve underwater cultural heritage its scope extends to regulating activities

FIGURE 3: Remains of the three-masted transport ship *Ína* used by Norwegian whalers. (Image by author, April 2024.)

at sea that might impact archaeological sites, which therefore includes fishing zones (Dromgoole 2013). During an interview with a staff member of Iceland's Ministry of Culture, it was suggested the country is unlikely to reconsider convention ratification in the foreseeable future. Talks and discussions regarding the ratification failed to even make it to the point of official documentation (Rúnar Leifsson 2023, pers. comm.).

Another challenge the country faces regarding improvement of its submerged heritage management is the lack of professionals within the field. Currently in Iceland there are two active underwater archaeologists (three if we were to include the author, who is still in their education phase). This leads to struggles, or perhaps more appropriately, non-existence, of site monitoring due to most research being limited to the archaeologists' own individual fields of interest. The Cultural Heritage Agency of Iceland has not assigned this task and does not have an internal employee currently certified to undertake this. Therefore, all known sites in Iceland, including those under a further protection level, are not monitored, and most have not had an initial survey undertaken upon their discovery.

Archaeology education in Iceland is exclusively available at the University of Iceland in Reykjavík. Maritime archaeology has been offered in this program only twice: once in the Spring semester of 2024 and, prior to that, a decade ago for a single semester. Consequently, specializing in maritime studies necessitates seeking education elsewhere, outside of Iceland. This presents additional challenges as it requires convincing any individuals studying abroad to consider returning to Iceland, where they may need to take on the role of pioneering the further development of underwater archaeology--far from an easy task.

Initial Research to Shifting Approach

With the challenges and history of Icelandic maritime archaeology highlighted above, this research began with the idea of engaging the country's sport diving community in monitoring underwater sites. A questionnaire distributed among the Iceland sport diving community regarding their willingness to participate revealed overwhelmingly positive responses (Tyas 2023). The pilot study of the diving community commenced with training sessions encompassing heritage awareness seminars, collaborative meetings, practical survey training, and a dive to survey a shipwreck with only vague location information. These sessions were well-attended, with community members expressing eagerness to learn and participate. However, the study encountered several barriers, leading to its pause for reassessment. First, communication with the Icelandic Cultural Heritage Agency proved challenging, hindering the recognition of and further collaboration with trained volunteers. Second, despite opportunities to benefit from the Nautical Archaeology Society's international training program, registration was required from a local institution, prompting concerns regarding exclusivity and causing administrative hurdles. These barriers together raised concerns about the sustainability of community involvement in maritime archaeology beyond the pilot study. To address these issues, improvements in engagement infrastructure and research into the attitudes of professionals towards public outreach are needed before the study's continuation. The pilot study only highlighted the rarity of community engagement practices in maritime archaeology, and the need for further research for its future development and best practice methodology.

Therefore, the research shifted away from the pilot study to address broader concerns within the whole archaeological profession in Iceland. Instead of evaluating the pilot study to formulate a method for further community work with submerged sites, the emphasis is now towards conducting qualitative research to highlight potential future directions in community engagement. Thus, the research has evolved to now be an examination of the whole archaeological approach towards community engagement in the country.

This shift in approach has also necessitated an alteration in the methodology of the whole research project, which is connected to a doctoral degree. It included further interviews with professionals in the field to gather opinions on the involvement of the public with their work, and also led to the ongoing development of a new survey aimed at understanding the Icelandic public's perceptions of heritage. The survey has the purposes of gathering the overall opinions of public involvement within the heritage sector, understanding the public ranking of values related to heritage sites, and identifying current knowledge of heritage site management.

Initial results from interviews and surveys aimed at professionals highlighted some further considerations to the research. First, it became clear that due to the overall lack of community engagement in archaeology, as well as in other professions, the Icelandic language does not yet have the development to differentiate between the terms associated with public engagement. Definitions of what community engagement actually means, as compared with those definitions set out in literature (Marshall 2002; Moser et al. 2002; Atalay 2012; Little 2012; Agbe-Davies 2014; McDavid 2014), were identified by 30% of participants.

Findings from both surveys and interviews underscored a widespread recognition of the significance and importance of public involvement in archaeology. Upon delving deeper into the extent to which the public or community should be engaged, the results revealed some reluctance among professionals to relinquish control to avocationals. Initial thoughts from these results suggest that the level of understanding of engagement with the public remains strongly within the top-down approach, with much work to be done to raise awareness and understanding of the potential benefits of engaging the public in a more inclusive way.

New Approaches

The research focus shifted to address the broader concerns raised during the initial pilot study, with the aim of tackling these issues more effectively. Primarily, there is a focus on maintaining ongoing engagement with the diving community to ensure their continued confidence and participation in future endeavours. Previous case studies have highlighted that successful community involvement hinges on the value of the information produced, coupled with feedback to participants about their contributions (Dawson et al. 2020). As such, I suggest that short-term projects may be less enticing for volunteers who are willing to dedicate their time to becoming trained and effective project members, and care needs to be taken to ensure original pilot study participants know their work was appreciated.

Following analysis of interviews and surveys, it also became clear that the perception of engagement from the professional standpoint needs to change as well. One identified approach was to introduce public archaeology as a course at the University of Iceland, for current second- and third-year archaeology students. The course ran in the Spring semester of 2024, and a pre- and post-course evaluation of the students' knowledge and opinions of public engagement showed how much they learned even within a short time period. In the pre-evaluation, when asked about their understanding of public archaeology, responses received included "presentations to the public on our work," "archaeology for the public about the public," and "archaeology where the public is allowed to be involved somehow." The same question was asked in the post-evaluation, and responses included: "now I understand that public archaeology is more than just presenting results and methods to people. It's also about working with and FOR them," "[…] we have to be more willing to open the doors to archaeology to the public so the field can grow and become better," and "archaeologists can't work without the public." In the post-evaluation, students were also asked if any aspects of the course could be enhanced; the majority of responses suggested that public archaeology should be introduced within the first year of study, prior to students undertaking their first excavation. The rationale provided was that, during this excavation, students were frequently approached by members of the public. Having received no prior instruction on public engagement, they viewed these interactions as an annoyance rather than as opportunities for learning and development. The outcomes of these pre- and post-evaluations were likely the best-case scenario in terms of results and show that with education, knowledge sharing, and in-depth discussions on the various aspects of engagement, it is possible to change views and opinions of future professionals.

The next steps in the research process will be to approach archaeologists already working in the field, and to offer a workshop and discussion based on engagement of the public. Interviews will continue, and the developing survey on heritage perceptions will be shared with the wider public.

Conclusion

Iceland holds significant promise for the advancement of both maritime archaeology and community engagement in the future. However, there are challenges to overcome in order to ensure that community engagement is both meaningful for participants and sustainable over the long term. Interviews and surveys have revealed a general lack of knowledge about various forms of engagement activities, underscored by the absence of corresponding terminology within the Icelandic language. These findings indicate that diverse engagement techniques are not currently widespread, with public outreach events being the primary avenue for public involvement in archaeology. While previous research has shown community interest in participating in projects, the focus must now shift to professionals in the field to foster attitude changes, explore activity options, and raise awareness of the benefits of engagement for heritage management. This has already been proven to be successful through the pre- and post-evaluations of students undergoing the first ever course in public archaeology in the country. The current state of community archaeology in Iceland is lacking, and the issues highlighted in this article require attention to establish a more robust foundation for engagement in the future. Through advocating for increased community involvement and promoting maritime archaeology, I hope that, some day, public and community engagement with Iceland's heritage will become the norm.

References

Agbe-Davies, Anna S.
2014   Community Engagement in Archaeology. In *Encyclopedia of Global Archaeology*, Claire Smith, editor, pp. 1599–1607. Springer, New York, NY.

Atalay, Sonya
2012   *Community-Based Archaeology: Research With, By, and for Indigenous and Local Communities.* University of California Press, Berkeley.

Björnsson, Lýður
2006   18. Öldin. In *Saga Íslands VIII, Sigurður Líndal and Magnús Lyngdal*, editors, pp. 1–289. Bókmenntafélag, Reykjavík, Iceland.

Dawson, Tom, Joanna Hambly, Alice Kelley, William Lees, and Sarah Miller
2020   Coastal Heritage, Global Climate Change, Public Engagement, and Citizen Science. *Proceedings of the National Academy of Sciences* 117(15):8280–8286.

Dromgoole, Sarah
2013   *Underwater Cultural Heritage and International Law.* Cambridge University Press, Cambridge, UK.

Edvardsson, Ragnar
2022   Marine Resources, Submerged Heritage and Local Communities in the Subarctic Sea. In *Routledge Handbook of Seascapes*, Gloria Pungetti, editor, pp. 98–111. Routledge, Oxfordshire, UK.

Edvardsson, Ragnar, and Arnar Þór Egilsson
2011   Archaeological Assessment of Selected Submerged Sites in Vestfirðir. *Archaeologia Islandica* 9:9–28.

2015   Phønix: A Preliminary Report on the 19th-Century Danish Steamer Wrecked on the Snæfellsnes Peninsula, Iceland. *International Journal of Nautical Archaeology* 44(1):196–202.

Einarsson, Bjarni F.
1993   Mjaltastúlkan Í Gígnum. *Yearbook of the Icelandic Archaeological Society.* <http://timarit.is/view_page_init.jsp?pageId=2057702>. Accessed 3 June 2024.

Elliott, Alexander
2018   Iceland's oldest shipwreck researched. RÚV: The Icelandic National Broadcasting Service, Reykjavík. 11 December. <https://www.ruv.is/frett/icelands-oldest-shipwreck-researched>. Accessed 27 March 2024.

Helgason, Gylfi, Alexandra Tyas, and Ragnar Edvardsson
2019   Fornleifarannsókn á 19. Aldar Hvalveiðistöðvum á Vestfjörðum. *Árbók: Hins Íslenzka Fornleifafélags* 108:55–85.

Little, Barbara
2012   Public Benefits of Public Archaeology. In *The Oxford Handbook of Public Archaeology, Robin Skeates*, Carol McDavid, and John Carman, editors, pp. 395–413. Oxford University Press, Oxford, UK.

Marshall, Yvonne
2002   What Is Community Archaeology? *World Archaeology* 34(2):211–219.

McCarthy, John, and Kevin Martin
2019   Virtual Reality for Maritime Archaeology in 2.5D: A Virtual Dive on a Flute Wreck of 1659 in Iceland. In *23rd International Conference in Information Visualization - Part II, Adelaide, Australia*, pp. 104–109.

McDavid, Carol
2014   Community Archaeology. In *Encyclopedia of Global Archaeology*, Claire Smith, editor, pp. 1591–1599. Springer, New York, NY.

McGovern, Thomas H., Orri Vésteinsson, Adolf Fridriksson, Mike Church, Ian Lawson, Ian A. Simpson, Arni Einarsson, Andy Dugmore, Gordon Cook, Sophia Perdikaris, Kevin J. Edwards, Amanda M. Thomson, W. Paul Adderley, Anthony Newton, Gavin Lucas, Ragnar Edvardsson, Oscar Aldred, and Elaine Dunbar
2007.   Landscapes of Settlement in Northern Iceland: Historical Ecology of Human Impact and Climate Fluctuation on the Millennial Scale. *American Anthropologist* 109(1):27–51.

Minjastofnun Íslands
n.d.   Fornleifauppgröftur. Minjastofnun Íslands, Reykjavík, Iceland. <https://www.minjastofnun.is/is/fornleifar/fornleifauppgroftur>. Accessed 3 June 2024.

Moser, Stephanie, Darren Glazier, James E. Phillips, Lamya Nasser el Nemr, Mohammed Saleh Mousa, Rascha Nasr Aiesh, Susan Richardson, Andrew Conner, and Michael Seymour
2002   Transforming Archaeology through Practice: Strategies for Collaborative Archaeology and the Community Archaeology Project at Quseir, Egypt. *World Archaeology* 34(2):220–248.

Price, T. Douglas, and Hildur Gestsdóttir
2006 The First Settlers of Iceland: An Isotopic Approach to Colonisation. *Antiquity* 80(307):130–144.

Sigfusson, Thor, Ragnar Arnason, and Karyn Morrissey
2013 The Economic Importance of the Icelandic Fisheries Cluster - Understanding the Role of Fisheries in a Small Economy. *Marine Policy* 39(May):154–161.

Thingvellir National Park
2023 Archaeological Research Continues. Thingvellir National Park, Iceland. 24 August. <https://www.thingvellir.is/en/education/news/general-news/archaeology_august_2/>. Accessed 3 June 2024.

Thurley, Simon
2005 Into the Future: Our Strategy for 2005–2010. *Conservation Bulletin* 49:26–27.

Tyas, Alexandra
2023 Underwater Archaeology in Iceland: Past Work, Current Management and Future Possibilities in Community Engagement. *International Journal of Nautical Archaeology* 52(1):195–204.

. . . .

Alexandra Tyas
University of Iceland, School of Humanities
Aðalbygging
102 Reykjavík
Iceland

ACUA Award Winners for 2024

George Fischer Student Travel Award

The George R. Fischer Student Travel Award provides support in the sum of $1,000 (USD) for international students currently studying maritime archaeology to attend and present a paper at the annual Society for Historical and Underwater Archaeology conference. George Fischer, a founding member of the ACUA, long supported and advocated for student participation in the annual conference not only for the experience and to foster an exchange of ideas, but also for the opportunity to meet other students and professionals outside of their home countries. This award, in honor of George, supports the professional development of students embarking on their nascent careers. This, in turn, furthers the overall mission of the ACUA to foster the growth and development of underwater and maritime archaeology throughout our watery world.

Two students were recognized at the 2024 Conference in Oakland, California: Iness Bernier, a Master's student in archaeology at the University of Nantes, France, presented a poster on *The Architectural Influence Of Ships Sailing The Red Sea Under The Ottoman Empire, The Contribution Of Underwater Archaeology*.

Leah Tavasi, a PhD student at the University of Oxford, England, presented a paper entitled, *Sales of Sail: The Production and Economy Behind Roman Sails*.

ACUA & RECON Offshore Diversity, Equity, and Inclusion Student Travel Award

The ACUA & RECON Offshore Diversity, Equity, and Inclusion Student Travel Award provides support in the amount of $1,000 (USD) to a student currently studying maritime archaeology or a related field who is presenting a paper or poster on an underwater or maritime archaeology topic at the annual Society for Historical and Underwater Archaeology conference. The goal of this travel award is to increase diversity, equity, and inclusion and to encourage student involvement at the meetings. Diversity is inclusive of race, ethnicity, gender, sexual orientation, abilities, and socioeconomic background.

Dante Petersen Stanley, a Master of Arts graduate student in the Maritime Program at East Carolina University received the 2024 award and presented a paper entitled *Archaeological Analysis of Japanese Visual Knowledge of Western Vessels Before 1853*.

FIGURE 2. Jennifer McKinnon (ACUA Chair), Dante Petersen Stanley (award winner), and Michael C. Krivor (RECON Offshore) at SHA 2024 award presentation.

FIGURE 1. Iness Bernier (award winner), Dr. Jennifer McKinnon (ACUA Chair), and Leah Tavasi (award winner) at SHA 2024 at award presentation.

ACUA Photo Competition Winners for 2024

If the old adage is true, "a picture is worth a thousand words," then the images created by archaeologists, historians, avocationals, and volunteers speak volumes about historical and underwater archaeology. Images can capture our imagination, take us to foreign lands, and show us faraway sites.

To honor our artistic colleagues, each year the ACUA sponsors a photo and video competition in conjunction with the annual Society for Historical Archaeology Conference on Historical and Underwater Archaeology. The competition is open to all SHA members and registered meeting attendees. The images are judged and displayed during the conference. Winners receive both a ribbon and the adulation of their peers.

Winning images from the 2024 photo competition are provided courtesy of the photographer and are presented below for all to enjoy. The winning video can be viewed on the ACUA YouTube channel available through the ACUA website (https://acuaonline.org/). Full color versions of the winning photographs are available on the ACUA website: (https://acuaonline.org/photo-contest/oakland-2024/).

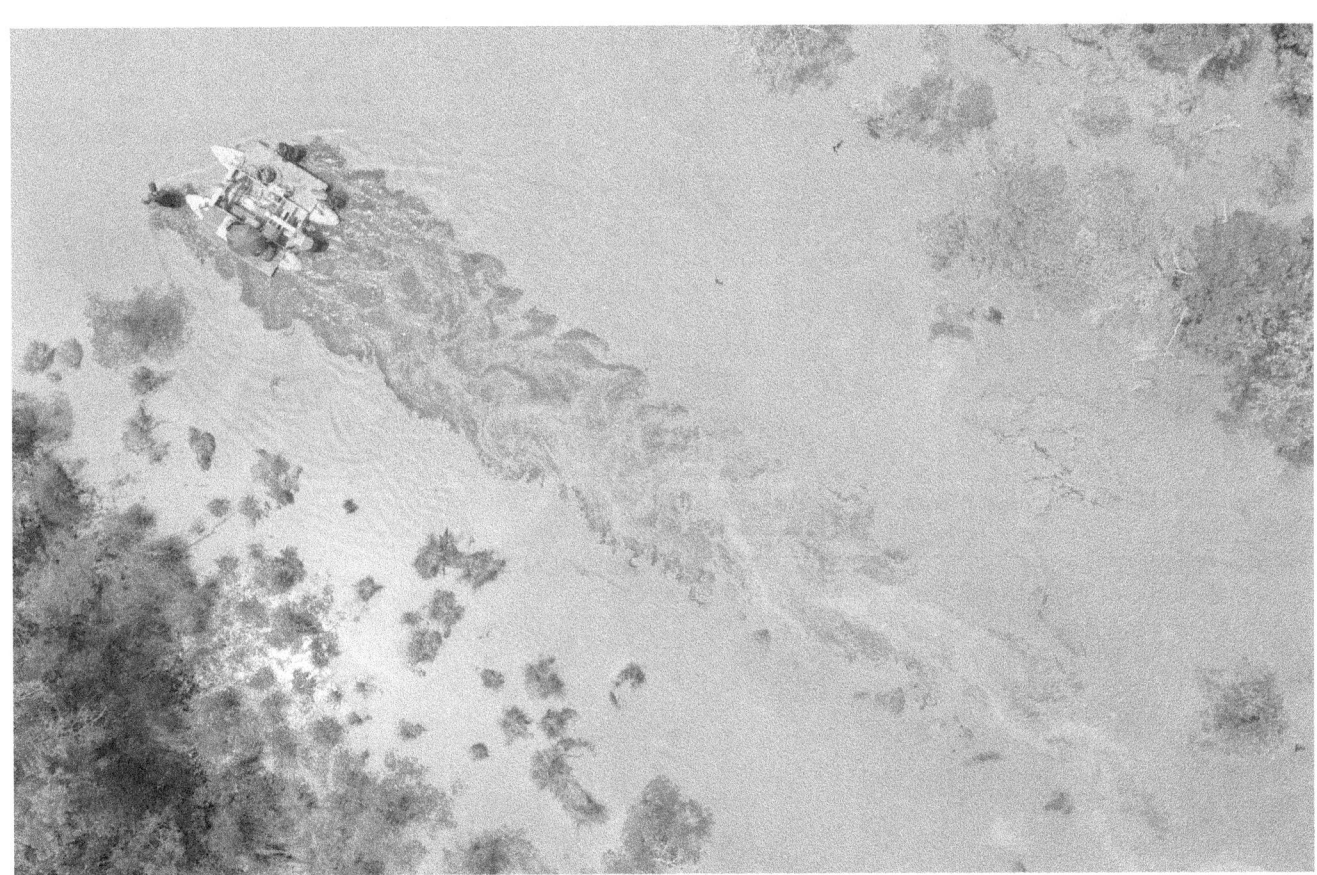

Category A: Color Archaeological Site

First & People's Choice: Anna Shackleford. Sub-bottom profiling for 1607 Greate Road
Second: Theirry Boyer. Big Tub Harbor wrecks, Tobermory
Third: Nicole Grinnan. Teamwork makes The Dreamwork

Category B: Color Archaeological Field Work in Progress

First & People's Choice: Chuck Durfor. Sword Just Recovered from 1617 well
Second: Brett Seymour. Pistol Recovery on HMS *Erebus*
Third: Daniel Fiore. Solar Survey

Category C: Color Archaeological Lab Work in Progress

First & People's Choice: Chuck Durfor. Zooarch analysis of Jamestown's starving time
Second: Jonathan Moore. Jonathan Puqiqnak cleaning aritacts from HMS *Erebus*
Third: Charles Beeker. Students mechanically cleaning submerged artifacts

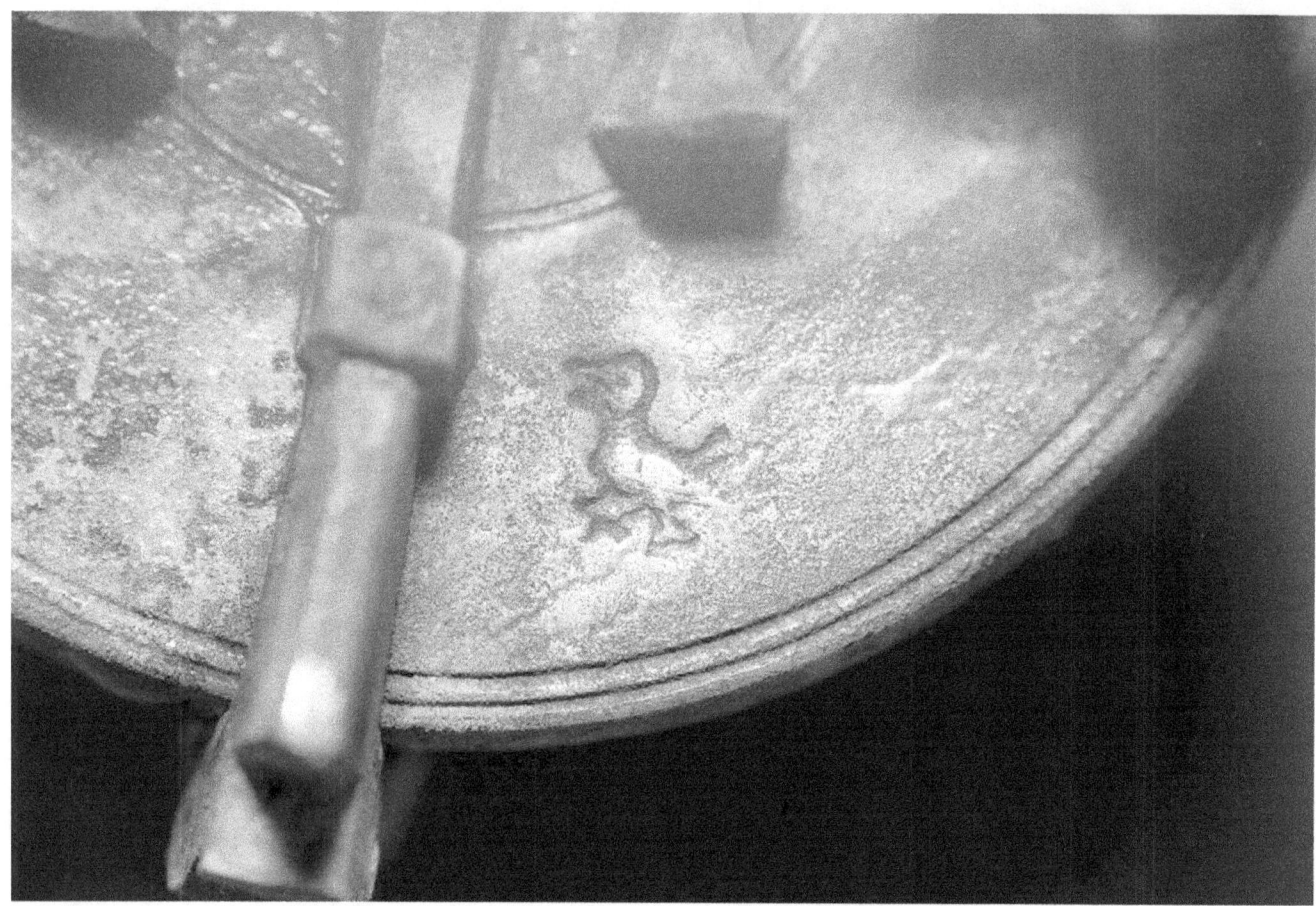

Category D: Color Artifact

First & People's Choice: William Doub. 16th c Nuremburg coppersmith makers mark
Second: Chuck Durfor and Janene Johnston. Wooden core and silver thread buttons
Third: Shawn Arnold. Rebirth

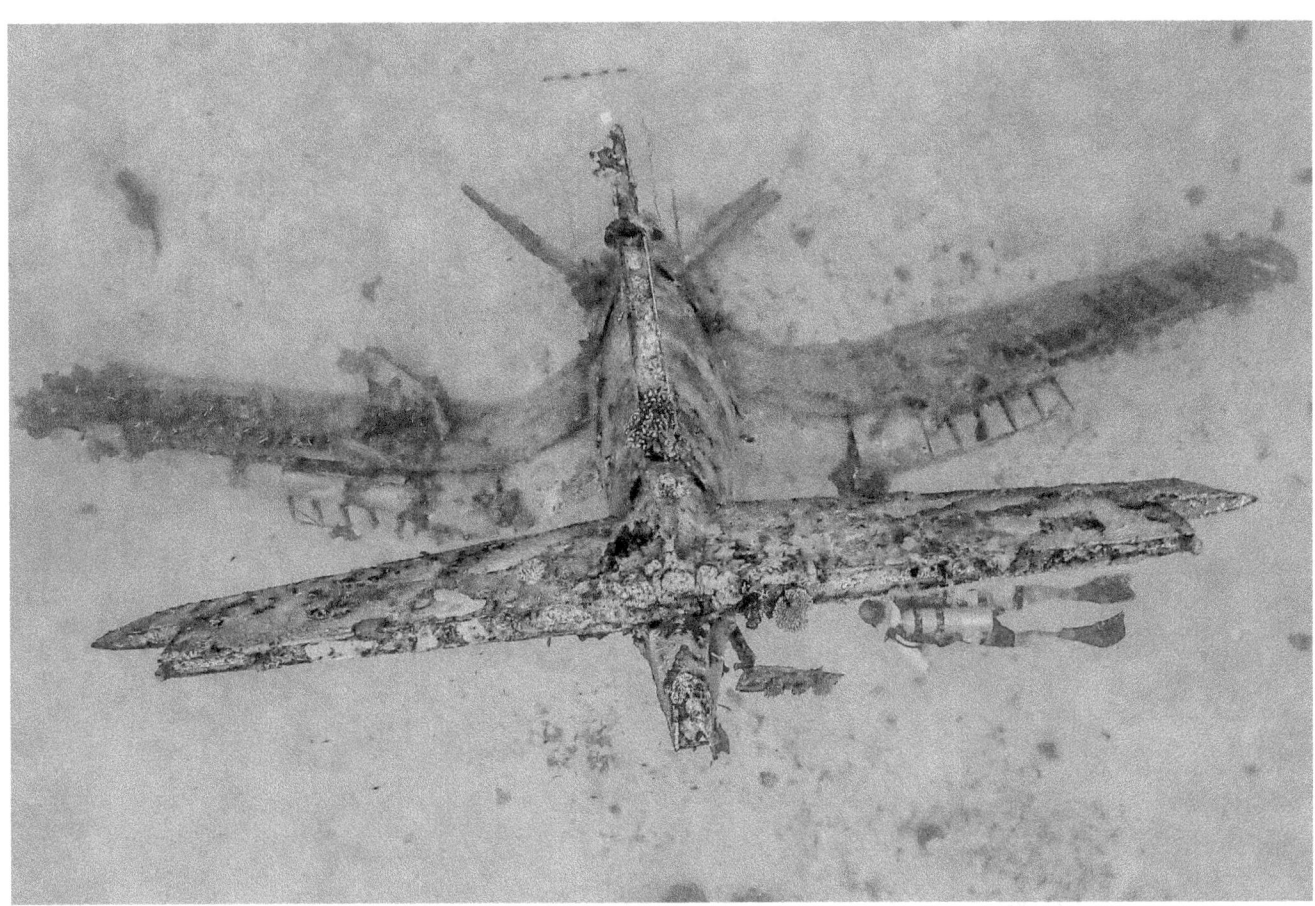

Category E: Black & White Image

First & People's Choice: Shawn Arnold. Nosedive
Second: Nicole Grinnan. A PB2Y Coronado wing at depth
Third: Chuck Durfor and Emma Derry. Faceted Finds

Category F: Color Archaeological Portrait

First & People's Choice: Natalie Reid. The joy of finding a bill
Second: Nicole Grinnan. Bria Brooks, Gaduate student at UWF
Third: Aimie Neron. Theirry Boyer ready to do underwater conservation

Category G: Diversity

First & People's Choice: Aimie Neron. ROV Dive Hole Digging: Parks Canada underwater archaeologists helping Gjoa Haven Inuit Guardians preparing the diving hole for the ROV on HMS **Erebus.**
Second: Shawn Arnold. BSEE Ecologist, Air Quality, and Water Quality experts assist in setting up a Mesotech scanning sonar for archaeological site verifications

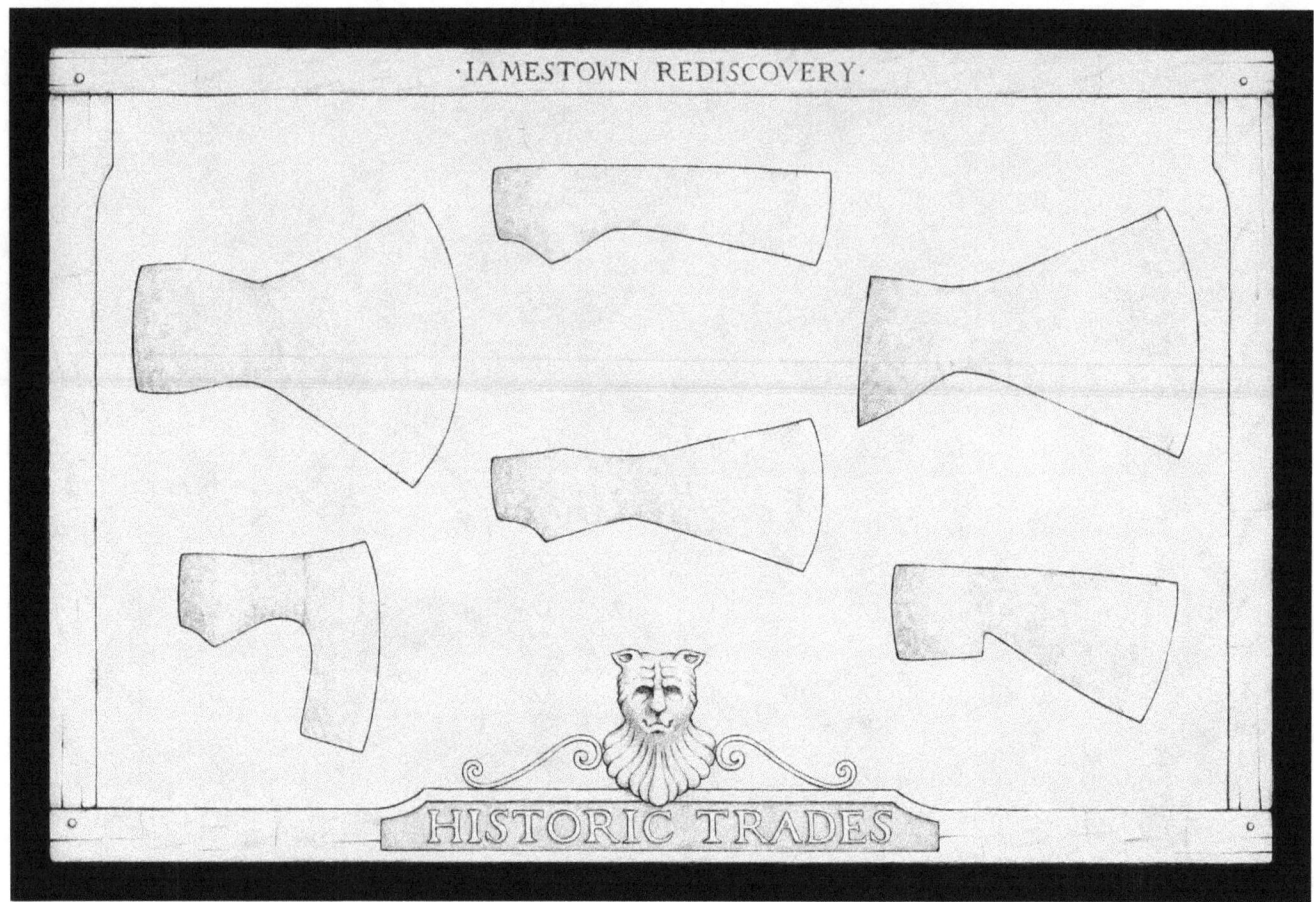

Category H: Artist's Perspective (Illustration)

First & People's Choice: Jesse Robertson. Jamestown's Axes drawn by historic tradesman
(Category did not receive enough submissions for 2nd or 3rd place awards.)

Category I: Archaeology in 3 Minutes Video

First & People's Choice: Alicia Johnson. hhistlegorm *Wrecks at Risk*
Second: Mike Thomin and Nicole Grinnan. Exploring Deepwater World War II Battlefields
Third: Wyatt Fritz. Punta Espada shipwreck investigations

Category I: Archaeology in 60 Seconds or Less Video

First & People's Choice: Mike Thomin and Nicole Grinnan. Florida Historic Cemetery Inventory
Second: Rachel Hines. 1896 Mardi Gras Badge

www.ingramcontent.com/pod-product-compliance
Lightning Source LLC
Chambersburg PA
CBHW081133170426
43197CB00017B/2846